THE CHURCH

THE CHURCH
Its unity in confession and history

by

G. Van Rongen

INHERITANCE PUBLICATIONS
NEERLANDIA, ALBERTA, CANADA
PELLA, IOWA, U.S.A.

Canadian Cataloguing in Publication Data
Van Rongen, G., 1918-
  The church

  Includes index.
  ISBN 0-921100-90-6

  1. Belgic Confession—History and criticism.
  2. Reformed Church—Creeds--History. 3. Reformed Church—History.
  I. Title.
  BX9429.B4V35 1998   238'.42492   C98-910575-X

Library of Congress Cataloging-in-Publication Data
Rongen, G. van
  The church : its unity in confession and history / G. van Rongen.
    p. cm.
  Includes index.
  ISBN 0-921100-90-6
    1. Church—Unity—History of doctrines.   2. Reformed Church—Doctrines
  —History.
  3. Belgic Confession. I. Title.
  BX9423.C43R66 1998
  238'.42—dc21
                                                              98-29001
                                                                   CIP

Cover Picture: *St. Maartenskerk, Zaltbommel, The Netherlands* by Cor De Kock

Published by Inheritance Publications
Box 154, Neerlandia, Alberta Canada T0G 1R0
Tel. & Fax (403) 674 3949
Web site: http://www.telusplanet.net/public/inhpubl/webip/ip.htm
E-Mail inhpubl@telusplanet.net

Published simultaneously in U.S.A. by Inheritance Publications Box 366, Pella,
Iowa 50219

Available in Australia from Inheritance Publications
Box 1122, Kelmscott, W.A. 6111 Tel. & Fax (09) 390 4940

Printed in Canada

Contents

Part 1
THE CHURCH
Articles 27 through 29 of the Belgic Confession of Faith
Introduction and Comments

ARTICLE 27

ARTICLE 28

ARTICLE 29

Part 2
Unity of Faith and Church Unity
in Historical Perspective

Part 3
The Liberation of the Forties

For my wife,
in our joint love
for the Lord Jesus Christ
and His Church.

PROLOGUE

It's a small world

The planet on which we live is becoming smaller and smaller. It seems as if it is no longer true that the East is far from the West. Distances are shrinking. At the same time, our world of interest is becoming larger and larger. What is happening on the other side of the globe can be watched as it happens.

In the field of church life, too, this process of shrinkage and expansion is going on. These modern times have brought us into contact with other churches which we had hardly ever heard of a few decades ago. After the war, our immigrant churches went through a period in which we settled into a new country and had to build up our church life from scratch. Now, however, we are able to have closer contact with our ecclesiastical environment and have discovered some of these churches.

This has raised the question: How are these other churches to be regarded? Must we, with a good conscience, leave them alone? Or, knowing that Christ wants His Church to be one, ought we to initiate dialogue with them? This is why our immigrant churches in various countries have been involved, sometimes for many years, in discussions with other churches.

Discussions within our churches

Meanwhile there are also discussions taking place within our churches. It is not always immediately clear whether or not we can acknowledge other churches as faithful churches of the Lord Jesus Christ. There is a difference of opinion among us not only about this issue, but also about the extent to which what we confess regarding the Church must be interpreted and applied.

This variety of opinion obliges us to undertake a thorough study of the Scriptures, first of all. It demands knowledge of what we, as churches, express in our confessional standards. Above all, it requires an awareness of our obligation to act in accordance with the will of our Saviour expressed in what is called His "high-priestly prayer" in John 17 — "that they all may be one," being sanctified in the truth of God's Word. We can act in this way only when we know what it means that we ourselves have been incorporated into the Church. If we ourselves are not aware of what being a member of the Church means, how can we be willing and able to call others to join us and, "with one accord, go to the temple of the LORD"?

The best we can do in such a situation is to read and study our confessional standards and try to learn some lessons from history. That is the aim of this book. For that reason, we shall pay particular attention, first of all, to what the Belgic Confession says about this important subject, focusing on Articles 27, 28, and 29, since they contain the Scriptural fundamentals. Then we shall listen to what Church history teaches us about unity of faith as something basic to Church unity. Finally, we shall see how Church unity was endangered but, by God's grace, also preserved in the events connected with the Liberation in the Dutch churches during the 1940s.

Part 1

THE CHURCH

Articles 27 through 29
of the Belgic Confession of Faith
Introduction and Comments

PREFACE

The focus of this study

The Belgic Confession of Faith is not the only subordinate standard of our churches which respectfully acknowledges the Church-gathering work of the Lord Jesus Christ. Lord's Day 21 of the Heidelberg Catechism and sections of the Canons of Dort (II.9 and V.9) do so, as well. Yet we must limit our commentary to the Belgic Confession. Articles 27 through 29 not only contain the Scriptural fundamentals regarding the doctrine of the Church, but at the same time they strongly emphasize the believers' duty to preserve and promote the unity of the Church.

It is my intention to take the readers with me in a line-by-line examination of the text of these articles. I am of the opinion that this study could be very beneficial to our church life, let alone to the discussions and contacts we have with others.

It is well known that these articles focus, in particular, upon the marks of the true Church as summarized in Article 29. But what about the context in which those marks are mentioned? What about the aim of the Belgic Confession of Faith in including those articles on the Church?

In Article 29 we are told how to distinguish the Church, that is to say, the Church which is defined in Article 27 and of which Article 28 urges us to maintain the unity. The consequence of a concentration on the marks of the true Church is that not everyone is sure how to deal with the catholicity of the Church. What must be done about the relation between the one holy catholic and apostolic Church and the local congregations or the confederation of churches?

I would not like to claim that this book will answer every possible question that could be raised in this respect, let alone do so to everyone's satisfaction. As for the latter, we realize that there can be a long time between sowing and reaping, and that is true of spiritual things, as well (Psalm 126).

Isolation

Another reason to study the contents of these articles is the advance made by today's "Evangelicalism." One of its characteristics is its "inter-denominationalism," which has led some of its leaders to deny the necessity of the Great Reformation. As Reformed confessors who wish to maintain our confession concerning the Church in Articles 27 through 29, we are thus isolated from much of the discussion taking place around us. A thorough knowledge of these articles may form an effective bastion against the influence of this movement. For that reason, special attention will be paid to what we call the fourth aim of the Belgic Confession of Faith.

The biblical basis

What the Church is can be learned only from what God has revealed about it, from Scripture! In this respect the proof texts play a prominent role. There are some difficulties with regard to these proof texts. As a rule we have followed Lepusculus Vallensis who, in his book on the Belgic Confession of Faith,[1] took them from the oldest Dutch edition, published in 1562. Sometimes, however, that version mentions only the chapters concerned and not the applicable verses, so the verse references are not always original. Besides, Vallensis also added a number of texts, printing them within brackets. The English version of this book, compiled by Rene Vermeulen,[2] deleted these brackets. We, however, have omitted the proof texts added by Vallensis.

Another problem is that it is not always clear whether some proof texts belong to the end of a certain article or to the opening sentence of the next article. Wherever necessary we have rendered an account of our choice.

Special attention will be given to the very first proof text in Article 27 which, as it were, dominates the scene.

We shall also pay some attention to other confessions and historic material, and in particular to the French Confession of 1559, which had a direct influence upon the Belgic Confession.

Different "layers"

We have spread the material over a number of "layers." The actual commentary on our Confession is printed in the larger type. Some additional comments or quotations from other documents will be found in the smaller type. The footnotes, in smaller type yet, contain references to the literature.

---

[1] Lepusculus Vallensis, *De Nederlandsche Geloofsbelijdenis in het licht der H. Schrift*, 2nd ed. (Zwolle: Stichting voor Gereformeerde Publicaties, 1952).

[2] Lepusculus Vallensis, *The Belgic Confession and its Biblical Basis*, trans. Rene Vermeulen (Neerlandia: Inheritance, 1993).

INTRODUCTION

1. The Church

Eleven or twelve?

How many articles does the Apostles' Creed contain?

This may seem like a strange question since this Creed is also known as "the twelve articles." Yet more than sixty years ago someone complained that many people limit the number of its articles to eleven.[3] To be sure, when they recite the Creed they say, no fewer than four times, "I believe": "I believe in God the Father . . . I believe in Jesus Christ . . . I believe in the Holy Spirit . . . I believe a holy catholic Church." In practice, however, they replace these two words once by "I can see" or "I cannot see." This happens as soon as they have arrived at the article that reads: "I believe a holy catholic Church, the communion of saints." Then they no longer take their starting-point in faith but in what they think they can see or cannot see. With regard to the contents of eleven articles they can solemnly say, "I believe," but not with regard to the article on the Church.

As Reformed people and churches, we insist on confessing our faith in no fewer than twelve articles. The Church is also the object and subject of faith. We can see the Church only with the eyes of faith, having been taught by the inspired Word of God what the Church actually is.

This perspective, then, is fundamental to all that you will read in this book. We are dealing with something that has been revealed to us in God's Word, and we are of the strong conviction that what we confess concerning the Church in Articles 27 through 29 of the Belgic Confession of Faith is in full accordance with and based on the Scriptures, and is therefore a further explanation of what we confess when we say with the Creed: "I believe a holy catholic Church."

Three or four?

Many of our readers may be surprised to hear that John Calvin was of the opinion that the Apostles' Creed could be divided into four parts.[4] We are

---

[3] K. Schilder in *De Reformatie* 12.21 (Feb. 19, 1932); reprinted in *De Kerk*, vol. 1 (Goes: Oosterbaan & Le Cointre, 1960) 150-155.

[4] The answer to the question "What follows?" in John Calvin's Geneva Catechism of 1541 reads, "The fourth part, where it is said that we believe a catholic Church" (Thomas F. Torrance, ed., *The School of Faith: The Catechisms of the Reformed Church*, trans. Thomas F. Torrance [London: James Clarke, 1959] 19.

familiar with a division into three parts. Our Heidelberg Catechism answers the question "How are these articles divided?" as follows: "Into three parts: the first is about God the Father and our creation; the second about God the Son and our redemption; the third about God the Holy Spirit and our sanctification."[5]

> Caspar Olevianus wrote this about Calvin, in apparent agreement with him: "As the Creed consists of four parts, the first related to God the Father, the second to the Son, the third to the Holy Spirit, and the fourth to the Church, so the author, in fulfilment of his task, divides his *Institutes* into four parts, corresponding with those of the Creed."[6]

The Belgic Confession of Faith summarizes the offices and works of the three Persons of the Trinity in their relationship to us, but it is not presenting a formal division of the Apostles' Creed when it deals with these offices and works in more detail.[7] Whether the Creed be divided into three parts or four, it should be clear that the Church plays a significant role in all that we believe and confess. In the Confession it takes no less than a sixth of the full text, spread over six articles (27-32).

The great significance of the Church may have led John Calvin and Caspar Olevianus to accept a fourfold division of the Apostles' Creed, but we do not follow them in this respect. We have subscribed wholeheartedly to the Three Forms of Unity, and thus adhere to a division into three parts. Nevertheless, together with these reformers, we gratefully and obediently acknowledge what God has revealed regarding the Church in His Word.

Scriptural basis

That our Confession is based on the Word of God is clearly proven by the many Scripture references added to its text. We shall refer to these proof texts with every sentence or pericope in the text of Articles 27 through 29 and, if it is necessary or useful, we shall discuss them briefly. They have been taken from the oldest Dutch text, published in 1562.

> Every now and then we shall also refer to the *Confessio Gallicana*, the French Confession, written for the most part by John Calvin and adopted by the Reformed Churches in France in 1559, and to the proof texts in some editions of the original French version of the Belgic Confession of Faith.

---

[5] Lord's Day 8, Q&A 24.

[6] Caspar Olevianus in an epitome of the *Institutes* in John Calvin, *Institutes of the Christian Religion* (Grand Rapids: Associated Publishers and Authors, [c.1973]) 5.

[7] Article 9: "The Father is called our Creator by His power; the Son is our Saviour and Redeemer by His blood; the Holy Spirit is our Sanctifier by His dwelling in our hearts."

In practice

It is important to read the text of the articles on the Church in the light of these proof texts. If we do not, we too could easily fall into the trap of reducing the number of articles in the Apostles' Creed from twelve to eleven.

We are living in the midst of an ecclesiastical world full of confusion. In such a climate, how are we to evaluate the many churches all around us, especially those churches which seem to be faithful to the gospel and which have been put in our path?

The danger is that we can be too simplistic in our approach and reason, more or less consciously, in this way: Given that our churches are true churches according to Article 29, how similar are these other churches to ours? In other words, the norm we apply is what we claim to see and our starting-point is experience.

For this reason, it is really necessary — and, in the present situation, more urgent than ever — to read our Confession in the light of the underlying Scriptures as they are presented in the many proof texts to which our Confession refers.

2. Historical Background

The essence and aim of the Confession

What is the Belgic Confession really? This seems to be a very simple question, easily answered. We could, for example, formulate the answer as follows: The Belgic Confession is a document officially adopted by our churches in which and by means of which we confess our faith. Now all of us, as Reformed people and churches, are aware of what we believe — even in some detail, since this Confession is quite long.

Such a statement is true. For our purpose, however, it is also too general. Therefore we should add another question: What is the aim of our Confession?

Here again, most of us would be able to give an answer. At school and elsewhere, we have heard about the intention of its author, Guido de Brès, and the Reformed in the Southern Netherlands. They wanted a copy to reach King Philip the Second of Spain who, as lord of the Low Countries, had supported the Roman Catholic inquisition in persecuting all those who had broken with the Church of Rome. The Reformed churches wanted to prove that they should no longer be identified with the rebellious Anabaptists, and that they had returned to the doctrine and church life of the ancient apostolic Church. Therefore the king should not act in such a way that he share the responsibility for their persecution!

Much more needs to be said, however. The aim of our Confession is so much broader and stronger that we can even speak of a fourfold aim! It is in this context that we are able to understand clearly the particular aim of the Belgic Confession in the articles which deal with the Church, Articles 27 through 29.

The origin of the Confession

In order to shed some clear light on these articles, we must first appreciate something of the background and origin of our Confession and get to know its main author. We must have some knowledge of the various places where he lived and worked, as well as of his influences. We must also know about other publications for which he was responsible.

His name, Guido de Brès, is familiar to most of us. His parents were faithful members of the Church of Rome, but he was not even 25 years old when he was converted to the Reformed faith. The reading of the Scriptures were instrumental in this conversion, as were books written by Martin Luther, Martin Bucer, John Calvin, and other reformers.

Soon after his conversion he had to flee to London. His stay in the Wallonian section of the congregation of Reformed refugees from 1547 to

1552 was very beneficial to him. It was a well-established congregation, and one characteristic of it was the institution of the "prophecy," a discussion of the sermons heard by the congregation. In the French-speaking section, the "prophecy" was particularly important in the training of some members for the ministry, among whom was de Brès. As a preacher, he must have benefited from this institution.

When he was able to return to the continent he settled at Ryssel, and there, in 1555, he wrote a booklet, *The Staff of the Christian Faith*,[8] in response to another booklet in which a Roman Catholic author tried to prove that his church was the continuation of the ancient Christian Church. De Brès demonstrated from Scripture and ancient writers that this was not so; on the contrary, the Reformed churches were the apostolic Church in continuation!

Four years later, he had to flee again, and as a result, while in Frankfurt, he met John à Lasco, who had been one of his teachers in London. Most likely he also met none other than John Calvin while he was there. In any case, soon after this he had some good contacts with Theodore Beza in Lausanne and with Calvin in Geneva.

His wanderings were not over even when he was able to return to his native country, for there he became a kind of "ambulant" minister of the congregations at Doornik, Valenciennes, and Ryssel. For safety reasons he lived under the name "Jerome" during this time.

Another booklet by de Brès

It was during those years that de Brès wrote another booklet. It was partly based on what he had published before in *The Staff of the Christian Faith*. It also revealed the clear influence of people like Beza and Calvin on him. This booklet subsequently became our Confession!

In the meantime, this publication was used as reading and teaching material among the members of the Reformed congregations in his area. It served as a kind of guideline for what could be called "post-profession study."

This simple material was badly needed, for church life was not yet firmly established and persecution still continued. Public church services were impossible. Since he was well aware of these circumstances, de Brès' ministerial activities consisted mainly of reading the Scriptures and explaining them, as well as being responsible for prayers at mealtime in the houses of some of the church members.

---

[8] *Le baston de la foye chrestienne* (1555).

The first aim

From all of this we may conclude that the first aim of the printing and publication of this booklet was the strengthening of faith, a great need in those days of hardship and persecution. We must not exclude the possibility that doubts may, at times, have surfaced in the hearts of some of those who had broken with the Church of Rome. Some of their own relatives and former friends could have put them under tremendous pressure!

In such a situation, it was very important that some material which clearly summarized the Scriptural doctrine over against that of the Church of Rome be readily available, material which would help these people stand firm and defend themselves against attacks and, further, would encourage them to win others for the Reformed faith. A clear exposition of what the Church of the Lord Jesus Christ really is and where it can be found would be very helpful in such a situation because it is every Christian's duty to maintain the unity of the true Church.

The second aim

As we mentioned before, it was easy to identify the Reformed with the Anabaptists, and this also had political ramifications. The Anabaptists did not acknowledge anyone as a Christian unless he or she was one of them, including the (mainly Roman Catholic) civil authorities. In various matters, they were so strict that there was a strong trend among them toward what we now call "polarization." When the ideas of a certain group were not accepted by others, the latter were cast out. Since this happened time and again, we can appreciate why in Article 29 our Confession makes mention of "all sects which are in the world today" which "claim for themselves the name of Church." There must have been innumerable schisms among the Anabaptists.

Meanwhile, the Reformed themselves were easily confused, especially those who had recently broken with the Church of Rome. Furthermore, it was imperative that they be strengthened in their faith in the face of the erroneous Anabaptist ideas. This is why the Confession clearly rejects these ideas, such as the Anabaptist view of the government, referred to at the end of Article 36.

The exposition of the Reformed doctrine in opposition to Anabaptist teaching reached its peak in Articles 27 through 29 where the Scriptural teachings on the Church were introduced. These articles clearly state (a) what the Church actually is, (b) that all those schisms are contrary to the will of God, and (c) where the true Church with the sound doctrine can be found. Here, too, these articles have a clear aim.

The third aim

From all of this we may conclude that what is today the Belgic Confession was intended to strengthen the faith of the Reformed and to fortify their defense against the doctrine and practice of both Roman Catholics and Anabaptists. This also plays a prominent role in what we could call its third aim: to act as an instrument to persuade the government that there was no justification for persecuting the Reformed.

This is why, in a correct and faithful edition of the Confession, we find the text of the letter which accompanied the copy that — as we all know — was thrown over the wall of the Doornik castle during the night of November 1, 1561, in the hope that it would be passed on to the governess, Margaret of Parma, King Philip's sister, and thus would finally reach the royal palace in Spain.

It may not be so well known that the parcel also included a letter addressed to the lower authorities, who, at that time, were not so hostile but rather were, more or less secretly, supporting the Reformed. One of them was William of Orange, the founder of the free state of the Netherlands.

That the governess was not won for the Reformed cause may be well known. When some people, following the example of what had happened in the city of Paris, had started singing the Genevan Psalms publicly — the so-called "chanteries" — the governess appointed some "commissionaries" who were instructed to intensify the persecutions. This happened in 1561 and led to the discovery of a tiny garden-house, de Brès's study room, where they found more than 200 copies of what is now the Belgic Confession, together with books written by Luther, Zwingli, Bucer, Calvin, and others.

De Brès himself had to flee again, once more ministering at several places. He travelled to Antwerp, where a large congregation had been established, and to Brussels, where he met William of Orange and discussed the possibility of a closer relationship between the Calvinists and the Martinists (named after Martin Luther), in order to obtain the support of the German princes and rulers for the Dutch resistance movement. His last commission was at Valenciennes, where he was taken captive on April 16, 1567, and hanged in the night of May 30.

Since this was a time of intensified persecution, we must conclude that the third aim de Brès had in mind with this booklet was not realized. As for what is confessed about the Church, the same must be said: The nature as well as the location of the Church, as the Lord Jesus Christ and His apostles had founded it, were clearly expounded in vain. In the meantime, however, the authorities were unable to find excuses for their evil actions!

The fourth aim

Taking all of this into account, we can state that this Confession was expected to bind the Reformed together in a firm unity of faith so that together they would be able to stand firm in faith during these difficult times. Its first aim, to strengthen the faith of the believers, was subordinate to this defensive purpose.

There was also a fourth aim, though. The Belgic Confession was meant to be used not only defensively but also offensively: others must be encouraged to join the Reformed, and therefore they were shown where they could find the (true) Church of the Lord Jesus Christ.

Before we deal with this very important aim, we shall bring together some historical material to confirm what we have learned thus far.

The involvement of others

We have already said that Guido de Brès was the author of the Belgic Confession of Faith. Other people, however, were also involved in compiling this document. Among them was Hadrianus Saravia, the minister at Antwerp and Brussels, who later on became professor at Leyden and Canterbury.

After it had been completed, the brotherhood at Ryssel, Doornik, and Valenciennes were asked for their opinion, as were Christophorus Fabritius at Antwerp, Cornelis Cooltuyn at Alkmaar, Enkhuizen, and Emden, Petrus Dathenus and Caspar VanderHeyden at Frankenthal in the Palatinate, and others. This may have had some impact on its text.

It is not strange, therefore, that the original title page — after the line which presents the name of the booklet, *Confession of Faith* (in the original Dutch translation: *Belydenisse des gheloofs*) — has the words: "Made with common agreement of the believers, scattered throughout the Netherlands, who desire to live in accordance with the purity of the holy gospel of our Lord Jesus Christ."[9]

The French language

There is another point which we should not forget: this Confession was originally written in French. We should remember that Guido de Brès, its main author, spoke French. At the very beginning of their first synod, meeting in secret at St. Germain, a suburb of Paris, the French Reformed churches decided that a confession of faith ought to be compiled. That confession was published in 1559, and it is no wonder that de Brès used it as an example in preparing his own.

---

[9] "Ghemaeckt met een ghemeyn accort door de gheloovige, die in de Nederlanden over al verstroyt zijn, de welcke na de suyverheyt des Heylighen Evangeliums ons Heeren Jesu Christi begheeren te leven."

He did not just copy it nor did he yield to the pressure put on him from Geneva and France simply to adopt the French Confession for the churches in the Netherlands. These churches had their own particular struggle against the Anabaptists, who were much stronger in their country than in France. Apart from this, there was also a political aspect: King Philip of Spain was not on friendly terms with France, and the adoption of a French document had the potential to damage the cause of the Reformed in the Netherlands.

But de Brès did made use of the French Confession — which, as mentioned before, was mainly the work of John Calvin. He fully agreed with its aim, expressed by the Synod of St. Germain, that the confession to be compiled and adopted by the churches would testify to the concord among the churches and keep strange opinions from creeping into their life.

> As a side note, it may also be of interest that it was more or less a matter of course that the Belgic Confession, in its original French version, was adopted by the Dutch churches. The French-speaking congregations were in the majority at that time, since today's Belgium was also included in the Netherlands. To this French majority we owe our name "Reformed," which is a translation of the French term *Reformée*. A Dutch translation of the Confession followed soon afterwards.

Even the great amount of agreement between the French and the Belgic Confessions may prove that the Reformed in the Netherlands wanted to express unity of faith with the French sister churches: they stood firm for the same cause of Christ, in their defense as well as in their offence.

The offensive character of the Catechism

This brings us to the offensive character of our Confession, its fourth aim. To see this, we return to its original title page.

After the title itself and the information about the common agreement of the believers, a text is quoted, a verse taken from 1 Peter 3: "always be ready to give a defense to everyone who asks you a reason for the hope that is in you." This epigram characterizes the document as a confession to be used in addressing those who are outside. It even challenges those who have adopted it as their personal confession to come out into the open with it. The fourth aim of the Belgic Confession is thus to attract others and convince them that as believers they must join the Reformed.

That this was the aim of the Confession is confirmed by the texts from the New Testament which accompany and support the letter to King Philip and which are placed, in the original editions, immediately after the title page and before the actual text of the Confession. They are introduced by the following line: "Some passages in the New Testament by means of which all believers are exhorted to confess their faith before men."

It would be useful if a second edition of the English translation of Lepusculus
Vallensis's book would include these texts, together with some more
introductory material.

We reprint these texts here so that everyone will be able to see what the
Belgic Confession is aiming at.

Matthew 10:32-33 is quoted first of all: "Therefore whoever confesses Me
before men, him I will also confess before My Father, Who is in heaven. But
whoever denies Me before men, him I will also deny before My Father Who
is in heaven."

The next text is Mark 8:38 and Luke 9:26: "For whoever is ashamed of Me
and My words in this adulterous and sinful generation, of him the Son of Man
also will be ashamed when He comes in the glory of His Father with the holy
angels."

Then 1 Peter 3:15 is repeated from the title page, followed by Romans
10:10, which reads, "For with the heart one believes unto righteousness, and
with the mouth confession is made unto salvation."

The list is completed by 2 Timothy 2:12: "If we deny Him, He also will
deny us."

It should be clear that these texts were not reprinted — certainly not
exclusively nor in the first place — to stimulate the perseverance of those who
had already broken with the Church of Rome and joined the Reformed by
warning them of what would happen if they became unfaithful. They were
intended, rather, to address those believers in particular who had not yet taken
the same step. Like people in today's situation, the "concerned" within a
church that has fallen into decay are being prompted by these texts to
recognize and respond to the call to step out and to be genuinely Reformed.

Here the Reformed took — and take — an offensive position. They were
— and are — trying to convince those who really believe in the Lord Jesus
Christ as their Saviour that they should not be ashamed before men — the
Roman Catholic clergy, their relatives, friends, and business relations. They
must have the courage to let them know that, contrary to the Church of Rome,
they acknowledge the Lord Jesus as the one only and perfect Saviour and the
"only universal Bishop," the Head of the Church.

The Nicodemites

Our Confession was written in a climate in which various efforts were
being made to attract others who were still outside, believers who were in
apostate churches and in particular in the Church of Rome, and to urge them
to act according to what Article 28 calls "the ordinance of God."

The reformers had to struggle not only against the Church of Rome and the
Anabaptists but also against the so-called "Nicodemites." These were people

who stayed within the Church of Rome, although in their hearts they agreed with the doctrine of the Reformed. They were named after Nicodemus who, according to the story of John 3, came to the Lord Jesus in the darkness of the night. Some of them met secretly at night in private houses. They knew quite well that the Church of Rome was packed with idolatry in the Mass, in Mary-olatry, in the invocation of saints, and in other ceremonies. Yet they still attended Mass, paid for indulgences, said their Hail Marys, and so forth.[10]

Among them were those who tried to hide their lack of courage behind some excuses. They claimed to be convinced that they must stay within "Babylon" in order to be able to lead that church to reformation. Others used the argument that no church is perfect and that in any church there are many difficult and even godless people, so that it made no sense to swap one imperfect church for another. "Not separation but reformation from the inside" was a slogan used already in those days. We may recognize the various excuses from our own day!

They even organized themselves into secret networks to do things like visiting imprisoned fellow-believers or giving financially assistance to those who, for the sake of their faith, had to flee their country. Such underground groups were active in France, Great Britain, and The Low Lands.[11]

Reformed disapproval of the Nicodemites

This attitude of accommodation — they still attended the papal mass! — was rejected by the Reformed leaders. One of these leaders was Marten Micron of the London congregation of Dutch refugees. In 1552 he wrote a treatise on the wrong motives of these groups of Nicodemites,[12] and we can understand why he wrote this booklet: these Nicodemites undermined the existence of the refugee churches.

Approximately a decade earlier, John Calvin wrote two tracts in which he strongly disapproved of the attitude of the Nicodemites and urged them to join the Reformed. In 1543 he published his first tract in which he shows how a man who knows the truth of the gospel has to behave himself when he is among the followers of the Pope.[13] The next year he wrote a second tract on the

---

[10] More about the Nicodemites may be found in my *Nicodemites, Past and Present*, The Reformed Guardian, new series (forthcoming).

[11] Andrew Pettegree, *Marian Protestantism: Six Studies*, St. Andrews Studies in Reformation History (Aldershot: Scolar Press, 1996).

[12] Marten Mikroen, *Een claer bewijs, van het recht-gebruyck des Nachtmaels Christi, ende wat men van de Misse houden sal* (1552) in *Bibliotheca Reformanda Neerlandica*, 1:560; L. Doekes, "De Reformatorische Onderscheiding van de Ware en Valse Kerk," *Lucerna: Gereformeerd Interfacultair Tijdschrift* 5.6 (Mar. 1965): 265f.

[13] Translation of the title by J. Faber in *Clarion* 28.17 (Aug. 25, 1979); the French title is *Petit traicté monstrant que c'est que doit faire un homme cognaissant la verité de l'evangile, quand il est entre les Papistes*. Professor Faber adds the following judgment: This tract was written "against cowards who in their hearts acknowledged the truth of the gospel. But under seemingly pious appeal to the examples of Naaman (2 Kings 5:18) and Nicodemus continued to partake of Romish idolatry."

same issue. It appeared under a somewhat ironic title, *Apology of John Calvin to Messieurs the Nicodemites* . . .[14] In a number of his letters he urged various prominent persons to join the Reformed or congratulated them after they had taken this step.[15]

> The Nicodemites were even the topic of the only letter John Calvin ever wrote to Martin Luther. It is dated January 21, 1545, and it may be interesting to know that this letter never reached Luther. A young messenger brought it to Philip Melanchthon, who had been asked to act as an intermediary, but Melanchthon did not have the courage to pass the letter on to Martin Luther since Luther was in a bad mood because the Swiss reformers disagreed with his view on Christ's presence in the Lord's Supper.
>
> Together with his letter, Calvin sent the translated text of the two treatises mentioned above with the request that Luther would let him know his opinion about their contents, especially since the Nicodemites considered Calvin to be too hard on them.[16]

The French Confession

It is therefore no wonder that the French Confession of 1559 contains an article which reads: "We believe that no one ought to seclude himself [from the Church] and be contented to be alone; but that all jointly should keep and maintain the union of the Church, and submit to the public teaching, and to the yoke of Jesus Christ" (Art. 26).[17]

This is the path by which some anti-Nicodemite lines entered into our Confession. As we can all see, what John Calvin set forth came, by way of the French Confession, to be adopted by de Brès in our Article 28.

Warning the Nicodemites against their wrong attitude and attracting them to the Reformed church was one of the main concerns of the Reformed. This concern also determined the role which our Confession — and Articles 28 and 29 in particular — was intended to play.[18]

---

[14] *Excuse de Jehan Calvin a messieurs les Nicodemites, sur la complainte qu'ils font de sa trop grand rigueur.*

[15] See Rudolf Schwarz, *Johannes Calvins Lebenswerk in seinen Briefen*, 3 vols. (Neukirchen: Neukirchener Verlag, 1961-62) and *Letters of John Calvin* (Edinburgh: Banner of Truth, 1980). In one of these letters Calvin stated that the Nicodemites "want to swim in between two waters" (Congratulatory letter of January 16, 1561, to the Queen of Navarre who had joined the Reformed).

[16] For the text of Calvin's letter to Martin Luther, see my *Nicodemites, Past and Present*.

[17] All quotations from confessions other than the Belgic and Westminster are from Arthur C. Cochrane, ed., *Reformed Confessions of the 16th Century* (London: SCM Press, 1966) unless otherwise noted. Some of the proof texts in the French Confession make a strong appeal to those who are still outside to join the congregation. Among them are Hebrews 10:25 — "Let us not give up meeting together, as some are in the habit of doing, but let us encourage one another, and all the more as you see the Day approaching" — as well as Ephesians 4. These proof texts can be found in the French version of Article 28 of our Confession and are also among the proof texts added to the oldest Dutch version of 1562.

[18] That the Reformed leaders were making significant efforts to encourage the Nicodemites to break with the Church of Rome and join the Reformed is also clear from an event which took place at the Synod of Emden in 1571. A church tabled the question whether it was "permissible to baptize a child of a papist who testifies that, in his opinion, the form of baptism as used in the Reformed churches was more pure

Our confession concerning the Church

It should be clear that this fourth aim of our Confession — to attract others — has been expressed in the articles on the Church in particular. They answer questions such as "What is the Church really?" "What is the duty of every believer for the preservation of the Church's unity?" and "Where can this Church be found?"

With the contents of these articles the Confession aims to attract others, showing them the way they must go and encouraging them by letting them know about the blessings they can expect to receive when they join the true Church of Christ.

The limitations of the articles

Before we deal further with the offensive character of Articles 27 through 29, we would like our readers to be well aware of one of the implications of this particular aim. The contents of the articles on the Church are determined by the Confession's aim and purpose and are therefore also limited in their focus. This means that much more could be said about the Church than appears in these articles.[19]

This is certainly true as a general statement, since what Scripture reveals about the Church has so many aspects that they cannot all be included in a Confession, which is supposed to be only a summary of the biblical doctrine. That is also true in particular: we should be well aware of the limitation in the focus of these articles which results from the peculiar aim of the Belgic Confession.

We can only be grateful for this limited focus. It has prevented de Brès and his co-authors from including too much theology in this document. By this we mean, for example, that our Confession does not present a series of distinctions. The only one we find here is the distinction between the true Church and the sects, including the false church.

This does not mean that any other distinction would be unconfessional or even unscriptural. It depends on the character of such a distinction and on the way in which it is used, interpreted, and applied.

---

than the one used in the papacy." Synod advised them to read a letter written by "the brethren from Geneva" in which some directions were given concerning how to deal with such cases. It also mentions that they had written to the Scottish churches on the same issue (F. L. Rutgers, *Acta van de Nederlandsche Synoden der zestiende eeuw*, 2nd ed. [Dordrecht: J. P. van den Tol, 1980] 93f.).

So the efforts to win the Nicodemites involved the Reformed churches of several countries. It is not surprising therefore that later on, at the provincial synod of Zealand in 1610, a decision was made to add to "the Prayer of Bucer and Calvin" the following sentence: "We also beseech Thee, gracious God, to bring back to Thyself in true penitence to all who depart from Thy truth, that we all with one accord may serve Thee in holiness and righteousness all the days of our life." (Part of this sentence can still be read in the "Public Confession of Sins and Prayer Before the Sermon" printed on page 645 of the *Book of Praise*).

[19] For example, unlike the Westminster Confession (XXV.2), the Belgic Confession does not make mention in Article 27 of the position which the children of believers have in the Church. For that, though, see Article 34.

An illustration

Think, for instance, of the different ways in which John Calvin and Abraham Kuyper present the distinction between the invisible Church and the visible Church.

Before we proceed further with this matter, I would like to emphasize that I am not in favour of reintroducing this distinction. There are too many problems with it. For one thing, this distinction is no longer interpreted and applied in the sense in which the reformers used it. It is true, however, that we cannot survey the whole Church of the Lord Jesus Christ. There is an invisible — or rather an unsurveyable — aspect of it: the Church is a worldwide body, extending through all ages, and many of its members are already with the Lord. There is also a visible aspect, although not in the strict sense of the word since we can really see the Church only with the eyes of faith. Besides, the distinction itself can easily lead to the idea that there are two different churches, and that being a member of "the visible Church" is of minor importance compared with belonging to "the invisible Church" (which some even call "the true Church"!). This is the bad fruit of interpreting and applying this distinction as Abraham Kuyper and others did.

We cannot, however, accuse John Calvin of having done this. In his *Institutes of the Christian Religion* he states that Scripture speaks about the Church in two different ways (*bifariam*). He writes: "When in the Creed we profess to believe the Church, reference is made not only to the visible Church of which we are now treating, but also to all the elect of God, including in the number even those who have departed this life" (IV.i.2).[20] In connection with the last part of this sentence, Calvin refers to 2 Timothy 2:19, where the apostle declares that God alone knows who are His, keeping them under His seal.[21]

He makes the same distinction later on when he says: "The judgment which ought to be formed concerning the visible Church which comes under our observation, must, I think, be sufficiently clear from what has been said. I have observed that the Scriptures speak of the Church in two ways. Sometimes when they speak of the Church they mean the Church as it really is before God. . . . Often, too, by the name of Church is designated the whole body of mankind scattered throughout the world, who profess to worship one God and Christ, who by baptism are initiated into the faith; by partaking of the Lord's Supper profess unity in true doctrine and charity, agree in holding the word of the Lord, and observe the ministry which Christ has appointed for the preaching of it. In this Church there is a very large mixture of hypocrites. . . . Hence, as it is necessary to believe the invisible Church, which is manifest to the eye of God only, so we are also enjoined to regard this Church which is so called with reference to man, and to cultivate its communion" (IV.i.7).[22]

---

[20] All citations from the *Institutes* are from John Calvin, *Institutes of the Christian Religion*, trans. Henry Beveridge, 2 vols. (1845; London: James Clarke, 1953).

[21] Remarkably 2 Timothy 2:10 is also one of the proof texts for the phrase "sanctified and sealed by the Holy Spirit" (Art. 27) in the original Dutch version of the Belgic Confession. It seems as if the Confession is more or less referring to this "unsurveyable" aspect of the Church: only God knows who are His.

[22] Several confessional documents emphasize the element of election: to the Church belong those whom God has chosen to everlasting life. This may explain their use of the visible-invisible distinction: the number of elect is invisible to us, but God sees them. Expositions along these lines can be found in Calvin's *Institutes*, in his Geneva Catechism of 1541, in Chapter XVI of the Scottish Confession (1560), in Article 4 of the Confession of the English Congregation at Geneva (1556), more or less clearly in Craig's Catechism (1581), which for some time was used in the Church of Scotland together with the Heidelberg Catechism, in the Westminster Confession of Faith (1647), and in Q&As 62-65 of the Larger

Can we say that these statements are unscriptural or unconfessional? Let me reply with the words of one of my teachers, Klaas Schilder: Legitimate objections can be made against this kind of distinction. "We do not believe an invisible Church, though we believe what is expressed by that name."[23] Today, as explained above, the same distinction is used and applied in a dangerous — indeed, an unscriptural and unconfessional — way. This is another reason not to use it.

Once again, we may be grateful that our own Confession does not make this distinction. We owe this benefit to the Confession's special aim, to attract other believers.

Another illustration

We can also be grateful that our Confession does not present another distinction, the distinction between pure and impure churches, or pure and less pure ones.

First of all, strictly speaking, there is no such thing as a pure church here on earth. We have noted John Calvin's reference to hypocrites within the Church, and the Belgic Confession agrees when it says, "We are not speaking here of the hypocrites, who are mixed in the Church along with the good and yet are not part of the Church, although they are outwardly in it" (Art. 29). Other Reformed confessions and writings share this emphasis,[24] following in the footsteps of

---

Catechism (1648). Ulrich Zwingli wrote something similar in his introduction to *Fidei Ratio*, addressing Emperor Charles V.

In the days of the Reformation, the visible-invisible distinction was used in opposition to the Church of Rome. A very clear example of this use may be found in Zwingli's letter to the king of France, which acted as an introduction to his *Fidei expositio* (1531). There he says: "We too believe that there is one holy catholic or universal Christian Church; but that this Church is either visible or invisible. The invisible is, according to Paul's doctrine, the Church which descends from heaven. [Zwingli should not have referred to Paul but to Revelation 21:2 — GvR] . . . The visible Church, however, is not the Pope together with the other bearers of the bishop's mitre, but those people anywhere in the world who confess Christ." Zwingli then goes on to explain that in the visible Church there are unbelievers and even hostile people. He is (wrongly) of the opinion that the civil government has the duty to remove those people from the Church.

In *De Reformatie* 24.44-45 (July 30, 1949; Aug. 6, 1949), reprinted in *De Kerk*, vol. 3 (Goes: Oosterbaan & Le Cointre, 1965) 315-321, Klaas Schilder wrote about this *bifariam*, proving that when Calvin uses the visible-invisible distinction, he has one single Church in mind.

[23] K. Schilder, *Christelijke Religie* (stencilled lecture notes on Art. 27 of the Belgic Confession of Faith).

[24] In his *Institutes*, John Calvin states that every church has imperfections, one church even more than the other (IV.i.12ff.). The Geneva Confession, another document from the hand of Calvin, says that "even if there be some imperfections and faults" in certain churches, we "rightly discern the Church of Jesus Christ wherever the gospel is purely and faithfully preached, heard, and kept, and the sacraments are properly administered" (Art. 18). The Scottish Confession even mentions the possibility that a church might not exhibit each of the three marks of the true Church and yet still be a manifestation of it (Chap. XVIII). The Second Helvetic Confession refers to the situation in the church at Corinth where there were "wranglings and dissensions," and to the churches of Galatia "in which the apostle found fault with many serious offences; yet he calls them holy churches of Christ" (Chap. XVII). Zacharias Ursinus, in his lectures on the Heidelberg Catechism, realized quite well that, whereas "the true foundation has always been preserved," some have built upon it "gold, and others straw" (Zacharias Ursinus, *Commentary on the Heidelberg Catechism*, trans. G. W. Williard [1852; Phillipsburg, NJ: Presbyterian and Reformed Publication Company, n.d.] 289).

No church is perfect. In his booklet *The Doctrine of the Church in Reformed/Presbyterian Contacts* (Kelmscott: Pro Ecclesia, 1991), C. Bouwman correctly says, "Within the 'camp' of the true churches there may well be variations of purity (as there was among the seven churches in Asia Minor)" (17). For the use of the term "pure," see footnote 26.

Augustine who stated that the Church is God's threshing floor: the chaff must be separated from the wheat.

We restrict ourselves here, however, to a mention of Antonius Walaeus, who was a member of the well-known (inter)national Synod of Dordrecht in 1618-19 and was one of the authors of the *Synopsis Purioris Theologiae*. In his treatise on the Church, he makes a clear distinction between the pure Church (another name for the true Church) and churches of various degrees of impurity, the false church being an extreme example of the latter.[25]

When some theologians later replaced the true-false distinction with the distinction between pure and less pure, this was calamitous.[26]

A third illustration

Brief reference can be made to a third illustration. It relates to the well-known words "pluriformity" and "ecumenical."

Whereas Abraham Kuyper — ignoring the true-false distinction — stated that, just as there is a great variety of colours in the spectrum, so there are many and various churches, all of which have been given part of the truth and which together form the church, one of my teachers, Dr. S. Greijdanus, taught us that there is pluriformity *within* the true Church.

As for the term "ecumenical," the word is widely (mis)used in the circles of the World Council of Churches, but, in the context of a commemoration of the Liberation of the 1940s, Dr. N. H. Gootjes of the Theological College in Hamilton stated that, in the title of the Deed of Liberation or Return, the term "Return" is used in the sense of returning to the community of the ecumenical Church.[27] This emphasizes our duty as "liberated" churches to take our place within that ecumenical Church so that we do not isolate ourselves but rather seek contact and unity with others.

The Confession's special aim

In order to do justice to others — even to other confessional standards — we must be conscious of the special aim with which the Belgic Confession

---

[25] This distinction runs parallel to the distinction made in Article 29 of our Confession between the true Church on the one hand and the sects, together with the false church, on the other. See J. W. van der Jagt, "Een schema uit de Scholastiek: over de ware kerk en de zuivere leer" (A diagram [or: outline] from Scholasticism, on the true Church and the pure doctrine), *De Reformatie* 71.39 (July 6, 1996): 784-87. To Walaeus, the criterion for the degrees of impurity was this: How far is this church deviating from the Scriptural doctrine?

[26] That it is not advisable to use the distinction between pure and impure or between pure and less pure is clear from the use of the adjective "pure" in "the pure preaching of the gospel" and "the pure administration of the sacraments as Christ instituted them" (Art. 29). In the latter, in particular, it is obvious: "pure" means "according to the divine rule." A sermon is "pure" (faithful to the Word of God), or "impure" (not in accordance with that Word). Here, there is no "more or less."

[27] N. H. Gootjes, "The Church in the Act of Liberation," *The Liberation: Causes and Consequences: The struggle in the Reformed Churches in The Netherlands in the 1940s*, ed. Cornelis van Dam (Winnipeg: Premier, 1995) 83. Gootjes repeated this in his final sentence: "The Act of Liberation did not want to give birth to a new denomination but wants us to stay in the communion of the ecumenical church" (91).

was written, namely, the twofold aim of (a) helping Reformed believers maintain the true-false distinction and not being ashamed of it in the midst of a complicated life, full of persecutions, and in the midst of a variety of churches, and (b) trying to attract others who, despite their "concern," are remaining in an apostate church, and urging them to maintain the unity of the Church.

Conclusions

We are now ready and able to draw some conclusions from all that we have learned so far.

The first is that we must apply to ourselves the Scripture references which, as we have seen, precede the actual text of the Confession. They exhort us to profess our faith before men. This means that, in the midst of a religious world which, generally speaking, has dropped the distinction between true and false churches, we must stand firm and maintain this confession, despite much misunderstanding and despite being accused of fundamentalism and extremism. We are obliged to do so by one of the aims of our Confession, as we have seen.

At the same time , we must return to another of the original aims of the Belgic Confession, particularly in its treatment of the Church. If we neglect its practical purpose, and especially its purpose to attract fellow-believers, we can easily fall into one extreme or another: either false ecumenism or isolationism.

Let us not forget that in its articles on the Church our Confession has all believers in view. It confesses that Christ has them all in mind, as He gathers them into one flock. He has in mind the Church of God's promise given of Abraham, which is to be gathered from "all families and all nations," the Church which, on the last day, will enter into the fullness of the Kingdom as its population. Let us remember the definition of the Church in Article 27: it "is a holy congregation and assembly of the true Christian believers." The article "the" here is very important. The Latin text even has *omnium*, which means "all."[28]

Emphasis

Whereas the Heidelberg Catechism, in Lord's Day 21, introduces the gathering of the Church as a great work undertaken by Christ, our Confession

---

[28] The Augsburg Confession of 1530 has the same: The Church is the gathering of all believers (Art. VII). The First Helvetic Confession (1530) states that the holy catholic Church is the communion and gathering of all the saints (Art. 25); and the Second Helvetic Confession (1566) declares that the Church is a community of all saints, which are all citizens of one heavenly city (Chap. XVII).

strongly emphasizes the believers' duty in this respect. We see this already at the end of Article 27, when it says that the Church "is joined and united with heart and will, in one and the same Spirit, by the power of faith," but Article 28, in particular, is full of that duty. This may explain the reasoning in these articles: Article 27 presents a definition of the Church, after which we confess that the Church has been present and will be present throughout the ages, and that it is spread all over the world, yet united in the same Spirit. Then Article 28 emphasizes the duty of all believers to maintain the unity of the Church by letting themselves be gathered into it, joining it and uniting with it. After that, Article 29 shows where this Church — the true Church, because there are also many sects and the false church — can be found, with the help of its marks.

Those who are addressed are the ones who are described in Article 27 as people who expect their entire salvation in Jesus Christ. In Article 29, we read a similar definition of what true Christians are: "They believe in Jesus Christ the only Saviour, flee from sin, fight against their weakness, and appeal constantly to the blood of Christ."

These addressees who are still outside — in the Church of Rome, for example — are able to recognize their own faith in that of others, namely the members of the true Church. This, then, should lead them to unite with the others and join the true Church, because their own faith also must be nourished by the pure administration of God's Word, the sacraments, and Church discipline.

This aim of our Confession — to invite and appeal — must not be overlooked. It may be very helpful in our approach when true believers and even other churches are put in our path by Christ, the Head of the Church. When that happens, we are in exactly the same situation in which the Confession was compiled and Articles 27 through 29, in particular, were written.

ARTICLE 27

THE CATHOLIC
OR UNIVERSAL CHURCH

*We believe and profess one catholic or universal Church,[29] which is a holy
congregation and assembly of the true Christian believers, who expect
their entire salvation in Jesus Christ, are washed by His blood, and are
sanctified and sealed by the Holy Spirit.*
*This Church has existed from the beginning of the world and will be to the
end, for Christ is an eternal King Who cannot be without subjects. This
holy Church is preserved by God against the fury of the whole world,
although for a while it may look very small and as extinct in the eyes of
man. Thus during the perilous reign of Ahab, the Lord kept for Himself
seven thousand persons, who had not bowed their knees to Baal.*
*Moreover, this holy Church is not confined or limited to one particular
place or to certain persons, but is spread and dispersed throughout the
entire world. However, it is joined and united with heart and will, in one
and the same Spirit, by the power of faith.[30]*

---

[29] Following the text of the 1984 edition of the *Book of Praise*, we maintain the capital C in the name
"the Church," as we do throughout this book.

[30] For the convenience of our readers we shall reprint relevant sections of the text of the articles
before we comment on them.

"THE CATHOLIC OR UNIVERSAL CHURCH"

The heading

This is the heading as we read it above Article 27 in the *Book of Praise*. It is not original. Headings were first included in Arent Cornelisz's edition (1566) and in the edition of 1583, and were repeated in the "Schilders edition" (or "Middelburgh edition") of 1611.

We cannot say that this heading belongs to the text of the Confession as adopted by the Synod of Dort in 1618-19. At the beginning of the seventeenth century, the Arminians were teaching things which were not in accord with the Confession, and the Synod of Dort intended to address the Arminian teachings. Since not all of the delegates of the foreign churches could read Dutch or French, Festus Hommius, who was soon afterwards appointed as one of the clerks of that synod, translated the Confession into Latin, adding many quotations from the writings of the Arminians after the relevant articles. In this way, the delegates were able to prepare themselves to contribute to the deliberations and decisions on the Arminian controversy. When, during one of the last international sessions, the Confession was read in Latin, its contents were unanimously approved as Scriptural. To Hommius's greatly appreciated efforts we owe the headings above the articles of our Confession, but, once again, they were not officially accepted by the Synod of Dort. These churches were most likely not aware that these headings were not original.[31]

Only as far as the (general) synods of the Canadian Reformed Churches and the Free Reformed Churches of Australia have accepted an official text of the Confession may the headings be considered to have been approved.[32]

---

[31] That these headings must be viewed with some reservation is evident from the different translations of Hommius's version. He himself had "*De Ecclesia Catholica*" (On the Catholic Church), whereas the 1984 and 1987 editions of the Book of Praise, interpreting the term "catholic," had "The catholic or universal Church." Older Dutch versions added the word "Christian": "Van de algemeene christelijke Kerk." It may be interesting to learn that since their latest revision the Dutch churches (Reformed Churches in the Netherlands [liberated]) have "De katholieke of algemene kerk."

[32] There is a difference between the Canadian and the Australian churches. In the 1993 edition of the *Book of Praise* the heading of Article 27 reads, "The Catholic Christian Church." This is an English rendering of the Dutch "Van de algemeene Christelijke Kerk," as found in older editions of the Dutch church service book (put in between brackets as being inauthentic). Vermeulen's edition of Vallensis' *The Belgic Confession and its Biblical Basis* follows the same older Dutch text. The reason for this change in the latest edition of the *Book of Praise* may be that the Canadian Reformed Churches, together with the Dutch churches, virtually added the word "Christian" to the received text of the Apostles' Creed. I have shown that this move is incorrect in my *Our Reformed Church Service Book* (Neerlandia: Inheritance, 1995) 88f. There I followed J. Faber, "De tekst van het Apostolicum in ons Book of Praise," *Clarion* 22.10 (May 10, 1973) and "Ik geloof de heilige katholieke Kerk," *Clarion* 22.11 (June 2, 1973).

The Free Reformed Churches of Australia have not endorsed a revised text of the creeds and confessions since Synod Albany 1987 decided to adopt the text published in the 1984 edition of the *Book of Praise*. For the Australian churches, the 1984 text is the approved text.

"WE BELIEVE AND PROFESS . . ."

An abbreviation

Article 27 begins with these words, as do all the other articles of our Confession. Each of them is introduced by the same words or by synonyms. They are abbreviations of the words with which the whole Confession is introduced in Article 1: "We all believe with the heart and confess with the mouth. . . ."

That this is so may be seen from the first Dutch edition of the Confession, published in 1562. This version adds the words "with the heart" (*van herten*) to Article 27. Although since 1619 we no longer find these words in our current edition, we must not overlook the fact that what we confess regarding the Church must live in our heart.

> Here the true believers already distance themselves from those whom Article 29 calls "hypocrites." The Scottish Confession of Faith of 1560 calls them people who "only confess God for a time with their mouths and not with their hearts."[33]

"We"

Unlike the Apostles' Creed, the Belgic Confession speaks in the plural: "We." Whereas the singular "I" in the former reveals something of its original function as a creed recited by adult baptismal candidates, the latter underlines what the original subtitle said: This Confession of Faith was "made with common consent by the believers scattered throughout the Netherlands, who desire to live in accordance with the purity of the holy gospel of our Lord Jesus Christ."

> The Belgic Confession is one of the Three Forms of Unity. Together with the Heidelberg Catechism and the Canons of Dort, it expresses our common faith. The phrase "Forms of Unity" was first used in 1622. In the previous year, the provincial synod of South Holland appointed the church of Leyden to request the professors of theology and other officials of the Leyden University to subscribe to the Belgic Confession, the Heidelberg Catechism, and the Canons of Dort. At the next provincial synod, this church reported that these persons "had been requested to subscribe to the forms of Unity."[34]

---

[33] Chapter XXV of The Scottish Confession of Faith (1560), cited in the "modern English version" produced by James Bulloch in 1960 and published in Cochrane, *Reformed Confessions*. An even more modern version has "but such being but temporal professors in mouth, but not in heart . . ." which is a more literal rendering of the original Scottish text: "Bot sik being bot temporall professoures in mouth, but not in heart . . ." (*Scottish Confession of Faith* [Dallas: Presbyterian Heritage, 1995]).

[34] J. N. Bakhuizen van den Brink, *De Nederlandse Belijdenisgeschriften in authentieke teksten met inleiding en tekstvergelijkingen*, 2nd ed. (Amsterdam: Ton Bolland, 1976) 50.

"We believe . . ."

The Church is a matter of faith. This means, first of all, that our Confession is based on what God Himself has revealed in the Scriptures. The various synonyms used in the first lines of the articles make this clear.[35]

The abbreviation of the very first line of our Confession means, in the second place, that what we confess regarding the Church can be characterized as truly Reformed. It is based on the very first proof text added to Article 1: "For it is with your heart that you believe and are justified, and it is with your mouth that you confess and are saved" (Romans 10:10).

The Reformation's principle of *sola fide* (by faith alone) plays a significant role here. We are not saved by doing the "good work" of belonging to a church, but in the way of believing what God has revealed in His Word — including what He has revealed regarding the Church. A nominal church membership does not guarantee anything; rather, we must be living members of the Church.[36]

This may explain why the lines which follow emphasize the living relation which the believers have with Christ: their entire salvation is in Him. We are thus obliged always to keep in mind that whenever we speak about the Church we are speaking about Christ! It is quite easy for us to talk about the Church as if it is just another subject. The Church, however, is the fruit of divine activity, and even of incomprehensible grace. That we belong to the Church must fill our heart with deep gratitude and even with the amazement of faith: Why has the Lord chosen me to be a member of the Church?

> In 1929 Klaas Schilder wrote, "In our day there is a desire on the part of those who are not Reformed to construct the concept of the Church from experience, from what is observable, from what appears to be realizable. This is the rationalistic, modern method of reasoning of the Church. No, the Church is a matter of faith . . . In describing the being of the Church I have nothing to do with empirical states of affairs or with the practical situation of what is achievable, but only with special revelation: the Word of God."[37]
>
> Schilder says something similar in the first of his "Nineteen Theses on the Church," first published in 1935, which reads, "That a Church exists — this one cannot see, but only believe. Every definition of the essence of the Church (supposing that it is possible to speak about such an 'essence') using that which

---

[35] "We believe and confess" (Arts. 11, 34, 35); "We believe" (Arts. 4, 7, 8, 10-12, 19-26, 28-33, 36, 37); "We confess" (Arts. 3, 18); "We know" (Arts. 2, 9); "We distinguish" (Art. 6); and "We receive" (Art. 8). These words prove most clearly that all that we confess is a respectful and grateful acknowledgment of what God has revealed in His Word. Let us put it this way: to believe, profess, or confess is the same as to know, distinguish, and receive. All that we confess has been received from God, and this is why we now know and believe and confess!

[36] Heidelberg Catechism, Lord's Day 21, Q&A 54.

[37] Quoted in J. Kamphuis, "Critische Sympathie over den Dogmatischen Arbeid van Dr. K. Schilder" (A Critical Appreciation of K. Schilder's Work in Dogmatics), *Almanak van het Corpus Studiosorum in Academia Campensi: Fides Quadrat Intellectum* (Kampen: Zalsman, 1953) 86, translated by J. M. Batteau in "Schilder on the Church," *Always Obedient: Essays on the Teachings of Dr. Klaas Schilder*, ed. J. Geertsema (Phillipsburg, NJ: Presbyterian and Reformed, 1995) 100n68.

one can see in the world here below, or on the grounds of other axioms than the Scripture has revealed, is thus a work of nonbelief or unbelief. . . ."[38]

"We profess . . ."

It is not sufficient, however, to believe with the heart all that God has revealed about the Church. The Church must also be confessed with the mouth. This is done publicly, before other people.

The proof text which undergirds the whole Confession quoted above — Romans 10:10 — and the texts which were printed after the title page and prior to the Confession itself require such a courageous public confession. Such a confession includes, if required, the attempt to explain why we are members of the Church, and even of a particular church.

This means, for instance, that in times when all kinds of unscriptural ideas about the Church and churches are propagated we should not feel ashamed to adhere to the Scripturally-based distinction between the true Church and the false church. In a world in which there is all kinds of pseudo-ecumenical talk about "inter-denominationalism" and "pluriformity," we as believers are expected to show the same courage as our fellow Christians who, in a time of persecution, stood firm in their faith that they were living members of the Church of the Lord Jesus Christ and had learned where that Church could be found.[39]

Not "in"

In some other confessions we find the word "in": "We believe in the holy catholic Church."[40] From Aurelius Augustine and John Calvin, however, the Reformed churches have learned that we believe in God — in God the Father, in God the Son, and in God the Holy Spirit — but not in the Church. When we speak of the Church, we leave out the little word "in." "Believe in" can be used for the Triune God and the three divine Persons only.[41]

---

[38] Batteau 86.

[39] When it insists that we must not only believe with the heart but also confess with the mouth what God has revealed in His Word concerning the Church, the Confession may have the Nicodemites in view.

[40] The Apostolic Tradition of Hippolytus of Rome (c.215); the Private Creed of Arius (328); the Creed of Cyril of Jerusalem (c.350); the two creeds of Epiphanius (374); the Greek version of the Nicene Creed; the received text of the Greek Church (381). More recently: the old English version of the Second Helvetic Confession, included in *The Harmony of Reformed Confessions* (1586), reprinted in Philip Schaff, *Creeds of Christendom*, 3 vols. (1931; Grand Rapids: Baker, 1983) 3:869; the Confession of Dositheus or the Eighteen Decrees of the Synod of Jerusalem (1672); the Larger Catechism of the Eastern Church or the Russian Catechism of Philaret, revised by the Synod of St. Petersburg (1839). That confessions in the Greek language have the word "in" is a matter of idiom. On the Nicene Creed see W. W. J. VanOene, "A Revision Revised," *Clarion* 46.19 (Sept. 19, 1997): 415.

[41] Calvin, *Institutes* IV.i.2: "The particle *in* is often interpolated, but without any probable ground. I confess, indeed, that it is the more usual form, and is not unsupported by antiquity, since the Nicene Creed, as quoted in Ecclesiastical History, adds the preposition. At the same time, we may perceive from

This does not mean that what we believe regarding the Church is not important. On the contrary, the Church is one of God's works. Nevertheless, we express the difference between God and His works by using or omitting the little word "in."

"ONE CATHOLIC OR UNIVERSAL CHURCH"

Proof text

At the end of the first line of Article 27 — "We believe and profess one catholic or universal Church" — we find the first reference to the biblical basis on which this article rests. The proof text is Genesis 22:18: "In your seed all the nations of the earth shall be blessed, because you have obeyed My voice."

This is a very important proof text. We should never forget it when we have the Church in mind. The Church is based on this promise given by God when Abraham had shown his willingness to offer his son Isaac in response to God's command.

In Galatians 3:16, the apostle Paul interprets "seed" as a reference to Christ: "He does not say 'And to seeds,' as of many, but as of one, 'And to your Seed,' who is Christ." Genesis 22:18 thus reveals God's great plan. The Lord took Abraham from Ur and brought him into the land of Canaan because He wanted to begin a great work of redemption which would ultimately lead to the coming of Christ, the great Seed of Abraham. This promise was really intended to work salvation in the midst of a crooked human race. The gospel of Christ's atoning death and resurrection would be proclaimed to all nations. God's work would take place in the midst of human history. It would be worldwide.

This work, then, is the Church!

Once again, this very first proof text for what we believe regarding the Church is an extremely important one. It clearly demonstrates that the Church is a divine work. The God of Abraham, the covenant LORD, is behind the gathering of the Church! He establishes it.[42] He preserves it.[43] And He also regulates its life by the instructions He gives in His Word.[44]

---

early writers, that the expression received without controversy in ancient times was to believe 'the Church,' and not 'in the Church.' This is not only the expression used by Augustine, and that ancient writer, whoever he may have been, whose treatise, *De Symboli Expositione*, is extant under the name of Cyprian, but they distinctly remark that the addition of the preposition would make the expression improper, and they give good grounds for so thinking. We declare that we believe in God, both because our mind reclines upon him as true, and our confidence is fully satisfied in him. This cannot be said of the Church, just as it cannot be said of the forgiveness of sins, or the resurrection of the body." See also J. Faber, *Vestigium Ecclesiae* (Goes: Oosterbaan & Le Cointre, 1969) 178n34.

[42] Article 28.

[43] Article 27.

[44] Articles 28 and 29.

In Abraham's Seed — that is, in Christ — the nations would be blessed. The Church exists through Him and in Him. It is not strange, therefore, that in what we call "the great commission" of Matthew 28 the Lord Jesus Christ gave the apostles the mandate to "make disciples of all nations." From the day of Pentecost on, in particular, the great work of gathering the Church from among all nations started, and the book of Acts was written to show clearly that it is all Christ's work. Did Peter not say, on the day of Pentecost, that what was happening on that day was the work of the glorified Jesus Christ (Acts 2:33)? Did not Stephen see the glory of God and Jesus standing at God's right hand (Acts 7:55)? Was not the apostle Paul called by the Lord Jesus Himself (Acts 9:4)?

Nor is it strange that Christ's name appears no fewer than nine times in Articles 27 through 29.

The Church, therefore, is a matter of faith. Only by faith in the God of the covenant and in Jesus Christ as our Saviour Who came to fulfil God's promise given to Abraham can we see the Church and genuinely live in the Church.

This relationship between Christ and the Church may explain why the Confession is able to say that there is no salvation outside the Church. This confession is based on the truth about Christ: "Nor is there salvation in any other, for there is no other name under heaven given among men by which we must be saved" (Acts 4:12).

It may explain the obligation, as confessed in Article 28, to maintain the unity of the Church. It may also explain why, after so many sects and even false churches have been established in the course of history, Article 29 insists that we must discern diligently and very carefully from the Word of God where the true Church is found.

The very first proof text presented by our Confession as soon as it starts dealing with the Church — Genesis 22:28 — thus explains all that is confessed in Articles 27 through 29! We must keep it in mind as we continue reading what our Confession says about the Church.

A blessing

In Christ, who is Abraham's Seed, all the nations of the earth would be blessed, according to God's promise. This is God's work, and the work of Christ.

Certainly, human responsibilities and activities are not excluded. This should be perfectly clear from "the great commission" and the history revealed in the book of Acts and in the apostolic epistles. If these human responsibilities and actions take the dominant place in our thinking about the Church, however, it would be easy for us to start talking about the Church in a "businesslike" way, as if it were a human affair and not a work of God's hand.

Because the Church is a divine work, we are obliged to be very careful not to put stumbling-blocks in the path of those who still do not acknowledge the Lord Jesus as their Saviour or who belong to other churches — or who belong to our own church.

Because the Church is a divine work, we have the important responsibility of maintaining and promoting the unity of the Church as far as we can.

Because the Church is a divine work that includes all nations, it is important to question whether we ourselves are the blessing we should be to our own national life.

Because the Church is a divine work, we must face the question whether the existence of so many "denominations" is a blessing for the nations. Human weakness and sin sometimes play their role in Church life, even to the extent that our attitude toward the Church is in danger of becoming negative. We must never forget that the Church is the fruit of God's promise to Abraham, and that He has fulfilled this promise and is still fulfilling it today.

This, then, guarantees what our Confession declares a little farther on, namely, that "this Church . . . will be to the end."

"One"

We have said that the Church is a divine work, and we used the singular: *the* Church. This brings us to our confession that the Church is one.

> This oneness is one of the so-called "attributes" of the Church, which must be distinguished from the "marks" of the Church. The difference can be formulated as follows: The attributes give us information about what the Church is, whereas the marks tell us where the Church can be located. Later on we shall deal further with this distinction.

It is remarkable that, unlike the Nicene Creed, the Apostles' Creed does not have the word "one" in its article on the Church. It has the term "catholic," and the close relationship between the oneness of the Church and its catholicity makes it superfluous to mention the oneness of the Church explicitly. Nevertheless many of the so-called Church fathers[45] emphasized that the Church is one,[46] as does the Nicene Creed.

> The Greek word for Church is *ecclesia*, and the New Testament has it in the singular as well as in the plural. As *ecclesiai* (plural) it refers to the local congregations; as *ecclesia* (singular) it can indicate one single local congregation or, on the other hand, the one worldwide Church.

---

[45] Unless otherwise indicated, quotations from the writings of the Apostolic Fathers are from *The Apostolic Fathers*, trans. J. B. Lightfoot and J. R. Harmer, ed. and revised Michael W. Holmes, 2nd ed. (1891; Grand Rapids: Baker, 1989).

[46] E.g., the Muratorian Canon (2nd century), Tertullian (160-220), Cyprian (3rd century).

This twofold use of the singular can be explained from the history of the Christian Church. Starting at Pentecost, the Church claimed to be the legal continuation of the Old Testament Church, which was called the *qᵉhal*, "the assembly of the LORD."[47] The term *ecclesia* was applied to this Church of Pentecost. Soon after Pentecost, other local congregations were established, each of which was also called an *ecclesia*.

Now it is true that the Bible does not present us with a dissertation on the exact character of the relationship between the local congregations and the whole Church of Christ. It does indicate, however, that the local congregation has a strong tie with "all who in every place call on the name of Jesus Christ our Lord" (1 Corinthians 1:2) and "with all the saints who are in all Achaia" (2 Corinthians 1:2).

Although it is difficult and therefore somewhat risky to try to explain this relationship, we may not be far from the truth when we say that the universal Church manifests itself in the local congregation, that the local congregation is the universal Church in that particular city, town, or locality. Article 28 states that God has established the (universal) Church in the local congregations.

When we examine the whole of what the New Testament teaches concerning the Church, therefore, it is not surprising to find that a great deal of emphasis is given to the universal Church, and we must not neglect it.[48] Do not forget the very first proof text: Genesis 22:18!

We are accustomed to place the most emphasis on the local church, but we must not forget the context in which we do so, namely the confederation of churches with its "major assemblies" such as classis, regional synod, and general synod. The autonomy of the local church must be maintained and defended in our struggle against the threat of hierarchy which so easily invades church life. The relationship of the local church and the major assemblies, however, is not the same as that between the local congregation and the universal Church, even though we live in a confederation of churches by means of which we express our belief that the Lord, in fulfilment of the promise made to Abraham, is allowing our Saviour to gather a single, universal Church.

None of this means that the Church is invisible. The relationship described above between the local churches and the universal Church makes this impossible. The concept of an invisible Church is foreign to the New Testament. "Invisible" is not the same as "unsurveyable"!

Paul's epistle to the Ephesians, in particular, emphasizes the oneness of the Church: "There is one body and one Spirit, just as you were called in one hope of your calling, one Lord, one faith, one baptism; one God and Father of all, Who is above all, and through all, and in you all" (Ephesians 4:4-6).

The oneness of the Church rests upon the unity of true faith. Oneness or unity and truth go together. Both have been given in Christ and in His Spirit and are signified and sealed in baptism. Without Christ, there is no real unity of faith, no real Church unity. This is why, speaking positively, we can also

---

[47] E.g. Deuteronomy 23:2-3, 8. The Old Testament has also another word for the Church: *'edah*. The slight difference, as well as the relationship between *qᵉhal* and *'edah*, may be formulated as follows: The Israelites as a whole are the "congregation" (*'edah*) every day; when they gather together formally, however, they form the "assembly" (*qᵉhal*). See J. Faber, *Lectures on the Church* (Kelmscott: Pro Ecclesia, 1990) 4.

[48] W. C. van Dam, *De nieuwtestamentische gemeente* (Kampen: Kok, n.d.) 10.

say that in true faith in Jesus Christ — as expressed in a Scriptural confession such as the Belgic Confession of Faith — the unity of the Church is preserved.

That this unity is under threat is true. The evil one does not easily withdraw from the scene of church life. This is why our Confession does not limit itself to a kind of definition of what the Church is, as in Article 27, but goes on in Article 28 to appeal strongly to those who, for one reason or another, have not had the courage to break with the apostate Church of Rome or who have wrongfully joined one of the many Anabaptist sects — to appeal to them to make that break and thus preserve Church unity. Then, in Article 29, the Confession explains where the Church of the Lord Jesus Christ can be located.[49]

"Catholic or universal"

The word "catholic" literally means "all-embracing," "having to do with the whole" — and thus, in the case of the world, it means "worldwide." The Confession interprets the word to mean "universal." There was a need for such an interpretation in the days of the Reformation. When they heard about "the catholic Church," many people must have thought that it referred to the Church of Rome.

Today, too, a sign such as "proposed site of a catholic school," which can be seen close to where I live, may indicate that the local authorities identify the word "catholic" with the Roman Catholic Church. The Church of Rome seems to claim the term "catholic" as its own exclusive property.[50]

This may explain why Martin Luther replaced it in the Apostles' Creed with the word "Christian." The term "catholic" was "occupied territory" to him.[51] It may also explain why it is fashionable today to use the word "ecumenical": Please, don't offend the Church of Rome![52]

The Calvinist reformers, however, insisted on keeping the word "catholic" in the text of the creeds and in their confessions. After all, did they not claim to be the same catholic Church that had existed ever since the Day of Pentecost when God began to fulfil the promise given to Abraham?

---

[49] Its oneness obliges the Church to receive any true believer, as J. R. Wiskerke says: "The Church is one in the midst of all kinds of people and for them, so that in the confession of its catholicity is included its calling to admit all believers who want to live according to God's Word — their views of other matters, nationality, and race notwithstanding — as well as the calling of all believers to join the Church" ("Verantwoorde oecumeniciteit," *De Reformatie* 33.15 [Jan. 18, 1958]: 121, our translation).

[50] The Greek Orthodox Church also lays claim to this term.

[51] The Dutch churches were partly following his example when they added the word "Christian" to the text of the Apostles' Creed. This is explained further in my *Our Reformed Church Service Book* 88f.

[52] "Ecumenical" has been the preferred term since the missionary conference of 1900, and the word has been adopted by the "ecumenical movement" embodied in the World Council of Churches since 1948. To lay claim to the word "catholic" would harm the relationship with the Church of Rome, after all!

Historical background

The use of the term "catholic" for the Church has a historical background. In order to learn this history, we must return to the term "ecumenical." Behind the word "ecumenical" is the Greek noun *ecumene*, which was the term used for the world empire established by Alexander the Great and for the political and cultural ideals of Hellenism. Soon afterwards it was also used for the Roman Empire. Every year we are reminded of this when, on Christmas Day, we hear that Caesar Augustus decreed that a census should be taken of the *oikoumene*.[53] At a later stage the adjective "ecumenical" was introduced in Church parlance. We have all heard of the ecumenical creeds and ecumenical councils.

During this time, the word "catholic" appeared on the scene as a kind of synonym for "ecumenical," although it has a broader meaning. As far as we know, the first one to use "catholic" was bishop Ignatius of Antioch.[54] Since then the word "catholic" has been given a place in the Apostles' Creed as one of the attributes of the Church.[55]

"Catholic"

More must be said about what the word "catholic" means when we apply it to the Church. As we have already learned, "catholic" was used originally in a geographical sense. It has another sense as well, though. We may remember this from the Athanasian Creed, which presents its contents — twice — as the *catholic* faith.

In this context, "catholic" does not mean only that this faith can be found throughout the world. Immediately after the phrase "catholic faith" has been introduced in its first article, the second article of the Creed states that this faith must be kept whole and undefiled. Nothing should be left out or taken from it. All that the triune God has revealed about Himself and His works[56] must be believed, and that faithfully, since otherwise one cannot be saved, as the final article states. In other words, "catholic" here indicates that the faith embraces the whole of the doctrine of the Scriptures.

The term "catholic" has more aspects yet. They all are included in the following quotation from the "Catechetical Lectures" delivered in 350 by

---

[53] Luke 2:1: "all the world." The NIV has "the entire Roman world," which is more of an interpretation than a translation.

[54] In his letter to the church at Smyrna, written in approximately 110, Ignatius said, "Wherever the bishop shall appear, there let the people be; even as where Jesus Christ may be, there is the catholic Church." "Bishop" in this context still has the original meaning of "overseer," elder (42-3).

[55] We do not know exactly when and why this happened.

[56] The first part of the Athanasian Creed is a summary of what God has revealed about Himself; the second part is a summary of the divine work of redemption in the Lord Jesus Christ, described along the same historical lines as the Apostles' Creed.

Cyril, bishop of Jerusalem: "The Church, then, is called Catholic because it is spread throughout the whole world, from one end of the earth to the other, and because it never stops teaching in all its fullness every doctrine that men ought to be brought to know; and that regarding things visible and invisible, in heaven and on earth. It is called Catholic also because it brings into religious obedience every sort of men, rulers and ruled, learned and simple, and because it is a universal treatment and cure for every kind of sin whether perpetrated by soul or body, and possesses within it every form of virtue that is named, whether it expresses itself in deeds or words or in spiritual graces of every description."[57]

So there is a geographical aspect: the Church is worldwide. There is also a doctrinal aspect: the Church embraces the whole of the biblical doctrine. There is a social aspect: all sorts of people are brought to obey the gospel. And the Church, being catholic, has a cure for any sin, for body and soul, and with its salutary doctrine it stimulates man to produce all kinds of fruits of faith.

In the same "definition" another aspect is more or less hidden. The teaching of the catholic faith by the catholic Church never stops, it says. God's work continues throughout history, generation after generation, until the name "catholic" will gloriously indicate that the full number of elect has been gathered.

> As for the latter aspect, other confessions and churches are taking the catholicity of the Church seriously when, in defining the Church, they state that it consists of "the whole number of the elect." This is what we find in, for example, Article 68 of the Irish Articles of 1615 when it says, "There is but one catholic Church . . . and because this Church consists of all those, and those alone, which are elected by God unto salvation, and regenerated by the power of His Spirit, the number of which is known only to God Himself; therefore it is called the Catholic or universal and Invisible Church."
>
> The Irish Articles were consulted during the process of formulating the Westminster Confession, which has something similar in chapter XXV: "The catholick or universal Church, which is invisible, consists of the whole number of the elect that have been, are, or shall be gathered into one . . . ."
>
> What the Westminster Confession, in particular, says is sometimes interpreted as "static," having lost the "dynamic" activity of Christ: the Church is the sum total of the elect. This, however, does not do justice to this Confession, its predecessor, and other confessions which have a similar definition. First of all, in the next paragraph the children of the believers are said to be included in the Church. Furthermore, the Confession clearly says that the elect "shall be gathered into one." The emphasis may be placed too strongly on the final result of Christ's work of gathering His Church, but the "dynamics" of the heavenly Shepherd's work of bringing all His sheep into the eternal sheepfold are really present.[58] And no one among us would deny that ultimately only the elect will be in the Church when it is fully complete!

---

[57] Cited in Faber, *Essays* 75, 90.

[58] That there is no contrast at this point between the Westminster Confession and our Three Forms of Unity has been made clear by Stuart R. Jones in "The Invisible Church of the Westminster Confession of Faith," *Westminster Theological Journal* 59 (1997): 71-85.

Implications

All of this has its implications for the stand to be taken in the midst of the present world. Geographical, historical, and social factors should cause us to expect that — except in days similar to those of King Ahab, mentioned farther on in Article 27 — we shall sooner or later discover other faithful churches of the Lord Jesus Christ — as was the case in the days of the Reformation when many efforts were undertaken to join forces in the common struggle against the Church of Rome and the Anabaptist sects,[59]and as has happened again in the last decades.

In other words, we must take the catholicity of the Church as a starting-point. The apostolic question is still relevant: "Or did the Word of God come originally from you? Or was it you only that it reached?" (1 Corinthians 14:36).

The other elements included in the catholicity of the Church will prevent us from using our own church life as the measuring rod with which we measure other believers or churches. We cannot expect other true believers and churches to be exactly as we are when we consider their different historical and cultural background. The all-important question is: Is it evident that in them also God has fulfilled the promise He gave to Abraham? This promise concerned all the families of the earth (Genesis 12:3), and thus included many historical, cultural, and even racial variations. Therefore we cannot expect the particular churches of every continent and nation to be similar. Within the true Church there is a healthy "pluriformity"![60]

The knowledge that the Church is catholic — which means that we are not alone in this world — can be very encouraging, especially in days of serious apostasy all around us.

"Apostolic"

So far, Article 27 has summed up two of what we call the attributes of the Church: its oneness and its catholicity. A third attribute is not mentioned: its apostolicity. This is the more remarkable because the Nicene Creed does mention it: "And I believe one holy catholic and apostolic Church."

---

[59] For further details regarding the relationship between the Lutherans, Zwinglians, and Calvinists, see my "Unity of Faith and Church Unity in historical perspective" in Part 2 of this book, and in *Acts of the 1994 Synod and Reports to the 1994 Synod of the Free Reformed Churches of Australia* 248ff.

[60] Klaas Schilder has taught us that we should not distinguish as others do between the catholic or universal Church and the local or national churches as if the former were invisible and the latter were visible. He refers to the Westminster Confession which, in Chapter XXV, first calls the invisible Church "catholic or universal," but immediately afterwards confesses the same of the visible Church. "The universal catholic Church is visible, for she adopts institutional forms, as may be clear from the Westminster Confession" (*De Kerk* 3:15).

Why the Church is also called apostolic needs no lengthy explanation. The Church is built on the foundation of the apostles, on their legacy as proclaimed to us in the Scriptures.[61]

The reason why Article 27 does not mention this attribute may be that Article 8 has already mentioned the foundation laid by the apostles when it says, "The doctrine of the Holy Trinity has always been maintained and preserved in the true Church since the time of the apostles."

At other places in our Confession the apostles are also mentioned.[62] Apostolicity means that the Church is built upon the testimony of the apostles. This testimony had a twofold role: in keeping with Christ's commandment in Matthew 28, the apostles' testimony functioned in missions, evangelism, and outreach, but, as a result, it also functioned to gather, establish, upbuild, and preserve the Church. After all, had the apostles not been commissioned to be instrumental in fulfilling the promise given to Abraham that in his Seed — in Christ — all the nations of the earth would be blessed? In the attribute of apostolicity, therefore, we hear the echo of God's promise in Genesis 22:18 and of Christ's command in Matthew 28:13.

When it refers in Article 29 to the true gospel and its preaching as one of the marks of the true Church, our Confession, in fulfilment of what we called its fourth aim, faithfully reflects the outreaching role of the apostolic testimony: it aims to build the Church further by calling all true believers who are still outside to join the Church.

It is crystal clear that this attribute is qualitative or normative, and it is therefore necessary to keep this character in mind when we are using the marks of the true Church as they are summarized in Article 29. This attribute of apostolicity is crucial for the interpretation of these marks: it shows us what is meant by the pure preaching of the gospel, the pure administration of the sacraments, and Church discipline.

"Holy"

Another attribute of the Church is mentioned in the next part of the first sentence of Article 27. There the Church is called "a holy congregation and assembly of the true Christian believers." Unlike in the Apostles' Creed and the Nicene Creed, this fourth attribute appears in a subordinate clause and not in the main sentence.

That this is an important attribute is clear from the fact that it is the only one that is repeated several times. We find it again in the middle section of

---

[61] Ephesians 2:20; Revelation 21:14.

[62] Peter (Art. 3); John (Art. 4); Paul (Arts. 14, 22, 23, 24); and all the apostles (Art. 35). For a further exposition of the apostolicity of the Church and for some historic material, see my *"True" and "False" — How Do We Read Article 29 of the Belgic Confession of Faith?* The Reformed Guardian 13 (Kelmscott: Reformed Guardian, 1994) 36ff.

Article 27, where it says, "This holy Church is preserved by God against the fury of the whole world." The last paragraph of the same article starts with the words, "Moreover, this holy Church is not confined or limited to one particular place or to certain persons." And Article 28 says, "We believe, since this holy assembly and congregation is the assembly of the redeemed. . . ."[63]

No special proof texts for the word "holy" are presented in the oldest Dutch edition, but in Scripture the Church is called "a holy temple in the Lord" (Ephesians 2:21). The Lord Jesus Christ is said to have had the intention of presenting the Church "to Himself as a glorious Church, . . . holy and without blemish" (Ephesians 5:27).

> Of course, this does not mean that the Church is already perfect. In Article 29 our Confession will confirm this when it says that there are hypocrites in the Church. The French Confession of 1559, from which our own Confession "borrowed" this sentence, adds that the wickedness of these hypocrites and reprobates "can not destroy the title of the Church" (Art. 27).
>
> It should be clear that this has its implications for the way in which we judge other faithful but imperfect churches. Conversely, it is to be hoped that other churches will not postpone their recognition of our own churches as faithful churches of the Lord Jesus Christ until they can no longer see any imperfections in our church life.

This leads to the question: What exactly does it mean that the Church is holy? It may be clear that holiness is not the same as purity and perfection. But what does it mean positively?

Here the Geneva Catechism of 1541, written by John Calvin, is helpful. It says that "elements of imperfection always remain and will never be entirely removed, until she [the Church] is united completely to Jesus Christ her Head, by Whom she is sanctified."[64]

Does not "sanctified" mean that something is set apart to serve the Lord, so that the Church is "a special treasure above all the peoples who are on the face of the earth" (Deuteronomy 14:2), to be exalted "in praise, in name and in honour," and to be "a holy people to the LORD" (Deuteronomy 26:19)?[65]

The Church is expected to reflect God's holiness. That God is holy means not only that He hates sin, but also that He has undertaken a unique work of salvation. The Church itself, being a fruit of this redemptive work, has been given a mandate to join in the progress of this divine work, and that is why the Church is called holy. The holiness of the Church, therefore, means that the Church must be aware of its position in the midst of the world. The awareness that the Church is a divine work, the fulfilment of God's promise to Abraham, will widen our interest and cause the Church to be active, as well, in serving the Lord in calling others to join it — the fourth aim of our Confession.

---

[63] For some historical material in this connection, see my *"True" and "False"* 40ff.

[64] Torrance, *School of Faith* 20.

[65] In this connection, we are also reminded of the phrase "sanctified in Christ" in the baptismal forms.

The unity of the attributes

The holiness of the Church demonstrates, in particular, that the Church has been given a significant place and role. It is true that this attribute is being threatened.[66] How often did the apostle Paul not see the need to warn the congregations against the danger of false doctrine?

This should show us that all four of these attributes of the Church — oneness, holiness, catholicity, and apostolicity — form a unity, a whole. Its oneness is closely related to its catholicity, its holiness to its apostolic origin.

In other words, wherever large churches or an organization such as the World Council of Churches have failed to preserve the apostolic heritage faithfully, as it has been inscripturated in the Bible, the unity it claims to possess is not the same as the oneness of the apostolic Church; it is a false unity. And the serious deviations from the same foundation make it impossible for the Church of Rome to lay claim legally to the attribute of catholicity.

Attributes and marks

As we pay special attention to what we have called the fourth aim of the Belgic Confession of Faith in the Introduction — namely to try to convince those believers who, out of fear of persecution and for other reasons, were still within the Church of Rome, as well as those others who had been confused by the Anabaptist doctrine and practices, that they should join the true Church — we find in the Confession not only a kind of definition of what the Church actually is (in Article 27), but also the attributes of the Church (also in Article 27), and its marks (in Article 29).

This raises the question: What is the relation between these attributes and the marks?

> We can learn very much from the wrong concepts developed by others and from their mistakes. In this context, it may be worthwhile to mention the name of Abraham Kuyper, who strongly influenced the thinking of many theologians and others in the Netherlands, South Africa, North America, and elsewhere for many decades.[67]
>
> Kuyper made a kind of contrast between the attributes of the Church and its marks. This contrast was based on a few other distinctions he made: the distinction between the visible Church and the invisible Church, and between the Church as an organism and the Church as an institute. It is not necessary to

---

[66] J. W. van der Jagt, "De katholieke kerk is te vinden," *De Kerk: Kort Commentaar op de artikelen 27-30 van de Nederlandse Geloofsbelijdenis*, Woord en Wereld 27 (Bedum: Woord en Wereld, 1995) 81.

[67] For a brief exposition of Kuyper's doctrine of the Church, see Batteau 74ff., and V. E. d'Assonville, "Schilder en die Kerk," *K. Schilder: Erfenis en betekenis* (Innesdal: die Schilder-komitee, 1992) 72. See also my "K. Schilder and the Church" in K. Bruning and G. van Rongen, *Dr. K. Schilder Commemorated*, The Reformed Guardian 10 (Kelmscott: Reformed Guardian, 1990).

explain the latter distinction further. But by "the Church as an organism," Kuyper understood the activities undertaken by believers apart from their institutional church life, for example in all kinds of Christian organizations in the field of politics, science, and so forth. It may be sufficient to summarize his ideas as follows: The visible Church — which may be distinguished into the Church as an organism and the Church as an institute — has its marks, but only the invisible Church has the attributes which are presented in the Apostles' Creed and the Nicene Creed.[68]

It should be clear that this concept inevitably leads to the theory of the pluriformity of the Church: the invisible Church manifests itself in a great variety of visible churches. We cannot elaborate on it here, but these ideas played a role in the controversy within the churches in the Netherlands which led ultimately to the Liberation of the 1940s. Those who objected against the (false) doctrine of the pluriformity of the Church were accused of breaking the catholicity of the Church.[69] The lesson from all of this is that the attributes of the Church and its marks ought never to be separated from one another. "One may not drive a wedge between the characteristics of the church and its marks."[70]

What the relationship between the attributes of the Church and its marks is may be shown from history. The Reformation of the sixteenth century returned to the Scriptural concept of the Church as it had been adhered to — though not always and everywhere — in the ancient Christian Church and deposited in the writings of the "Church fathers." The many quotations from the writings of these "Church fathers" in the works of Martin Luther, John Calvin, and others provide abundant proof of this.

In the ancient Christian Church, the attributes of the Church were strongly emphasized. The Church of the Reformation, however, added to these attributes the well-known marks, or at least emphasized them.[71] It did so because the situation required the believers to make a clear choice between staying in the Church of Rome and joining the Church of the Reformation. Besides, some people had already left the Church of Rome and joined one of the many Anabaptist sects. The right choice could be made by using the marks by which the one holy catholic and apostolic Church could be found. These attributes are not only God's gift to the Church; they are also a mandate. A local congregation or group of churches must show the world that the one holy catholic and apostolic Church can be found there: We have been built upon the foundation of the apostles and their teachings; we maintain the catholic faith, and therefore you should come and hear the preaching in our church(es), and see that the sacraments are administered in the Scriptural way, and notice how all of this is accompanied, supported, and confirmed by the administration of Church discipline!

We can put things the other way around as well: When we deal with the marks of the true Church, as they are summed up in Article 29, and have a good

---

[68] A. Kuyper, *E Voto Dordraceno*, vol. 2 (Amsterdam: Hovëker and Wormser, 1905) 146; A. Kuyper, *Encyclopaedie der Heilige Godgeleerdheid* vol. 3 (Amsterdam: [Hovëker en Wormser, 1894) 191. A discussion of Kuyper's views can be found in J. Kamphuis, *Verkenningen I: Kerk en Uitverkiezing* (Goes: Oosterbaan & Le Cointre, 1964) 45ff.

[69] J. Kamphuis, *Verkenningen I* 43.

[70] J. Faber, "The Catholicity of the Belgic Confession," *Essays in Reformed Doctrine* (Neerlandia: Inheritance, 1990) 78. See also K. Schilder, *De Reformatie* 13.3 (Oct. 21, 1932), reprinted in *De Kerk* 1:205.

[71] An early illustration is the following sentence in Article 7 of the *Confessio Augustiana* (1530): "The Church is the assembly of the saints in which the gospel is purely taught and the sacraments are administered in the right way."

look at the proof texts, we shall discover that the attributes are present there, too, and in particular the Church's apostolicity. Moreover, in the attributes something of the marks can be found: the Church is holy because it is entrusted with the gospel of Him Who has sanctified it, with its preaching, with its sealing in the sacraments, with its administration of God's Word as a two-edged sword.[72] God fulfils His promise to Abraham, using the Church as His instrument (e.g., in its mission work and in educating the next generations).

Not to be neglected

We must not neglect this relationship between the attributes of the Church and its marks. If we do, we may end up doing what we mentioned at the very beginning of our first chapter: taking our starting-point in our own church life and then asserting it to be the norm by which every other church is to be measured, weighed, and judged, including even those churches in which we cannot deny that the gospel is faithfully preached. The question then becomes, "Do they have what we have and do they do things in the same way that we do them?"

In the course of the twentieth century, we have been taught that the Church-gathering work of Christ is something dynamic. This means that some churches can deteriorate, whereas in other churches a reformative movement can be generated. The wind (which is symbolic of the Holy Spirit) blows where it wishes (John 3:8).

Our starting-point must be what the Scriptures teach about the Church, and they teach that there is only one Church, that this Church is holy, catholic, and built on the foundation of the apostles and their teachings. These attributes come to light in the marks.[73] After all, what exactly is pure preaching of the gospel? Article 29 does not define it. What is pure administration of the sacraments as Christ instituted them? This too must be learned from the apostles. The same answer must be given to the question: What is meant by the exercising of Church discipline? The attributes and the marks are inseparable!

---

[72] Other sections of Article 27 also point forward to the marks of Article 29: that the true believers "expect their entire salvation in Jesus Christ" is the fruit of faithful gospel preaching; that they are "washed by His blood, and are sanctified and sealed by the Holy Spirit" has to do with the administration of the sacraments, and the phrase "the true Christian believers" may be related to the use of the keys of the Kingdom of heaven, of which Church discipline is one.

[73] Van der Jagt, *De Kerk* 64-65 (in our translation): "There is a certain relationship between these attributes and the marks of the Church. It can be defined in the following sense: the attributes tell us *what* the Church is; the marks point to *where* the Church can be found. In other words, the attributes come to light in the marks. . . . We shall end up in the wrong place if we do not respect the Confession's train of thought in these articles. This happens when we begin with the true Church as we have found it. Then pointing to the true Church becomes an easy short-cut [*loopje*] which always ends up with one's 'own' church. As often as the Church-question is tabled, the answer is known in advance. One's own church is stereotypically and invariably credited with the name 'true Church.' The same is true of the false church. There is hardly any room left for reformation of *this* church or deformation of *that* church. Standard short-cuts [*geijkte loopjes*] leave no room for surprises or dangers!"

This Church!

It is this Church, with these beautiful attributes, which is confessed to those who are outside, to the hostile civil authorities in the days of the Reformation, and to the Nicodemites who did not have the courage to break with the Church of Rome or had been deceived and confused by the Anabaptist teachings and practices. Because of its beauty, it was and is worthwhile — and even essential — to join this Church. This is why the Reformed churches, in their confessions, have made it easy to locate it, join it, or faithfully remain in it!

As for ourselves, we should not forget that it is this Church which Article 29 calls the true Church. From the struggle whichour churches in Australia and North America had in the first stages of their existence to defend their own identity when urged to join others in a false unity, we have learned that there is the danger that we might apply the marks of Article 29 in a negative way — those other churches are not faithful — and, regrettably, this did indeed happen. As soon as other churches which appear to be faithful are put in our path, however, then, with a positive approach and with the help of the marks, we must see whether the Church of Article 27, the Church of the four attributes, manifests itself in them also. Our confession regarding the one holy catholic and apostolic Church must be the starting-point, for, on the basis of God's "ecumenical" promise to Abraham, we can expect that the Spirit of Christ has also worked elsewhere.

"WHICH IS A HOLY CONGREGATION AND ASSEMBLY"

Proof text

First of all, we mention the proof text for this line in Article 27. It is Ephesians 4:4, which reads, "There is one body and one Spirit — just as you were called in one hope of your calling."

There is only one Church. The Lord Jesus does not gather all sorts of congregations[74] and assemblies (plural), but only one such body. This text emphasizes the oneness of the Church. At the same time, it touches on the believers' responsibility. This verse shows us that the definition of the Church, as presented in the line "which is a holy congregation and assembly," is fully Scriptural. Christ is gathering the Church as one body. At the same time, it shows us that what we confess in Articles 27 through 29 calls for

---

[74] We are using the word "congregation" in this context in a different sense than when we speak, for example, of the various congregations of which a confederation of churches consists.

urgent action. This should become clear when we read this verse in the context of the whole chapter.

The apostle takes as his starting-point the responsibility of the believers. They have a duty toward one another: to bear with one another in love and keep the unity of the Spirit in the bond of peace (vv. 2-3). After this, he refers to the reason for such an attitude toward one another: The Church is one body under one Lord, with one faith and one baptism (vv. 4-6). The apostle reminds his first readers — twice! — of their calling by Christ. He goes on to speak of the various gifts showered upon the believers since Christ's ascension into heaven. These gifts have been given for the edifying of the body of Christ, and this applies to the offices in particular (vv. 7-16). Then the apostle returns to the responsibility of the believers: They must not behave toward one another as unbelievers do, by being unjust to each other and lying, being lazy and greedy, and so forth (vv. 17-32). Rather, they must show that they are one body.

Articles 27 through 32

This passage determines the contents of the articles in our Confession that deal with the Church: Christ gathers one Church (Art. 27), but then its members have the responsibility to help build it up, and this implies first of all that they must join together in one body (Art. 28), but also that they must be able to locate the Church (Art. 29) which possesses the offices Christ has given to the Church (Arts. 30-31) and where they faithfully function in the administration of God's Word, the sacraments, and Church discipline (Arts. 32-35).

Christ's work of gathering His Church includes all of this. Our faith in Him and love for Him make it urgent that we also maintain the unity of the Church in our attitude toward one another and promote it by our efforts to unite with other true believers and faithful churches.

We should never be content with the present, imperfect situation of the congregation or of the federation of churches to which we belong nor with the lamentable disunity among true Christians. It is of great benefit to read our Confession in the light of its proof texts!

"Holy"

We shall now deal with the terms used in this sentence individually. We have already discussed the word "holy" in connection with the attributes of the Church. It is not necessary, therefore, to repeat what it means. The one thing we need to repeat is that the term "holy" recurs later on when Article 27 speaks about "this holy Church" and when the next article refers back to "this holy assembly and congregation."

Holiness appears to be an important attribute of the Church!

"Assembly"

The term "assembly" has its background in anti-Roman polemic. In a commentary on the Belgic Confession published more than 250 years ago, we read the following question and answer:

> Q. Why do you call the Church an assembly?
> A.   Because one man alone does not constitute the Church — not even the Roman Pope. Scripture clearly speaks of the assembly of the upright (Psalm 111) and of one body consisting of many members (Romans 12:4-5).[75]

The Church of Rome has claimed for a very long time that where the priesthood is, there the Church is. As sons and daughters of the Reformation, we emphatically deny this claim. The Church is an assembly, and it is of the greatest significance for us to be well aware of this!

"Congregation and assembly"

From the proof text mentioned above, we have learned that there are two different aspects of Church life. First of all, there is Christ's worldwide Church-gathering work. He calls us, and who would not have in mind here a saying such as, "I am the Good Shepherd"? The main emphasis is on this activity of Christ. In the second place, there is our human responsibility. As believers we must let ourselves be called, and this includes various activities from our side. These two different aspects of what the Scriptures teach us about the Church may make it very attractive to see Christ's activities in the word "congregation," which contains the word *grex*, meaning "flock," and human activity in the term "assembly," the coming together of the believers. There are several indications in the various versions of the Confession, however, which show us that congregation and assembly were used as synonyms at the time when this document was compiled.

> The French version of the Confession has *congrégation et assemblée*, which was translated by Festus Hommius as *congregatio seu coetus* not *congregatio et coetus,* "or" (*seu*) instead of "and" (*et*). Article 28 in the French version reduces both terms into *assemblée*, whereas in our translation it says, "This assembly and

---

[75] Arnoldus Rotterdam, *Van Zions Roem en Sterkte*, 2 vols. (1757; Rotterdam: De Banier, 1934) 2:157 (translation mine).

congregation is the assembly of the redeemed." "Assembly" here is the equivalent of *coetus*, whereas the Latin version has *congregatio* and the Dutch *vergaderinge*.[76]

Consider also that in his booklet *The Staff*, Guido de Brès wrote a section "On the assemblies and congregations of the believers." The terms in the original French edition are the same as those in the French text of the Belgic Confession. He then wrote about the meetings of the Reformed believers which were organized at secret places in fields and forests. Both terms are simply used as synonyms according to the tradition of those days.

When Christophorus Fabritius, whom we mentioned in the Introduction, was in prison awaiting his execution, he wrote a Confession of Faith. For his definition of the Church he used one single word, "gathering" (old Dutch: *versaminge*), which is precisely the word which appears in the text of our Confession that the Synod of Dordrecht (1618-19) approved. De Brès, who translated Fabritius's work into French, rendered this single word as two different words: *assemblée* and *congregation*. Fabritius even used the same word for the false church, calling the Church of Rome "a gathering of unbelieving and unrepentant people," and in his translation de Brès again used two different words: *assemblée et congregation*. It is unrealistic to think that Fabritius and de Brès considered the Church of Rome a flock (*grex*) gathered by the Lord Jesus Christ!

That Klaas Schilder did not consider the terms *congregatio* and *coetus* full synonyms may be explained on the basis of his strong emphasis on the dynamic activity of Christ in the gathering of the Church over against the various expositions of the doctrine of the Church which had become traditional in his time and which used the familiar distinctions of visible and invisible, organism and institute, and militant and triumphant, distinctions which had led to a kind of stagnant church life.[77]

---

[76] Tertullian, one of the "Church fathers," already used *congregatio* and *coetus* as synonyms. Lepusculus Vallensis supposes that Hommius considered both terms to be a hendiadys, a single idea expressed with the help of two different words (*Belgic Confession* 198).

[77] See d'Assonville, *K. Schilder* 65-76; Faber, *Essays* 107; E. A. W. Mouissie, *Het onderscheid tussen "coetus" en "congregatio" bij Prof. Dr. K. Schilder* (Kampen: unpublished doctoral thesis, 1982); C. Trimp, *The Church as we confess it in Articles 27 to 29 of the Belgic Confession of Faith*, The Reformed Guardian 2, new series (Kelmscott: G. Van Rongen, 1998) 8f.

J. Faber also wrote: "It is even remarkable that sometimes in the Old Testament those two names are combined. We read of the whole assembly of the congregation of Israel. If you think of the slight difference between those two nouns for the church, then you could say that that noun 'congregation' indicates the people of God as they are going about their daily work. They are and they belong to the congregation. But there are certain moments when that congregation comes together. Then there is 'the assembly of the congregation.'" He refers to Numbers 14:5 and Leviticus 5:13ff. (*Lectures* 4).

"OF THE TRUE CHRISTIAN BELIEVERS"

We believe and profess one catholic or universal Church, which is a holy congregation and assembly of the true Christian believers, who expect their entire salvation in Jesus Christ, are washed by His blood, and are sanctified and sealed by the Holy Spirit.

First proof text

We have now arrived at the line in our Confession which defines those who are the objects of Christ's Church-gathering work, the true believers in Christ. There are three proof texts in Scripture on which this line is based.

The first one is Matthew 11:25: "At that time Jesus said: 'I thank You, Father, Lord of heaven and earth, that You have hidden these things from the wise and prudent, and have revealed them to babes.' "

This saying of the Saviour has a somewhat polemical tone. By the wise and learned, He may have meant, in particular, the spiritual leaders of those days. These men did not understand their own days, which were days in which great things were taking place. The context speaks of the return of the prophet Elijah and thus of reformation. It mentions the coming of the Son of man, a powerful Self-revelation of the Father, rest, an easy yoke, and a light burden laid on His followers. All of this was entirely different from the heavy burden and the hard yoke laid on the people by their leaders.

It should be clear why this text was chosen as the first proof text for this "definition" of the Church. It was used to show the contrast with the "institutionalism" of the Church of Rome, which was expressed in the old adage: "Wherever the priesthood is, there is the Church."[78] What constitutes the Church for Rome is not the "ordinary" membership but the priesthood.

In contrast to this view, our Confession sets out to comfort and encourage those who believe in the Lord Jesus as their Saviour by stating clearly that neither a high position among "the clergy" nor any kind of status can determine your place within the Church but faith only. Here the well-known slogan of the Reformation forms the background music: *sola fide*, by faith alone!

It is really striking that when Article 29 mentions the marks of Christians we read similar things: "They appeal constantly to the blood, suffering, death, and obedience of Jesus Christ, in whom they have forgiveness of their sins through faith in Him."

---

[78] In his *Tractatus Ecclesiae*, John Wycliffe already objected strongly to the "institutionalism" of the Church of Rome. Over against the adage mentioned above, he said, "The Church is the congregation of all the elect." See Jones 71.

Here those words "in Him" are of the greatest significance. They remind us of Article 22, where our Confession has already explained what true faith is, a warm communion with Christ: "This faith embraces Jesus Christ with all His merits, makes Him our own, and does not seek anything besides Him . . ." and "one who has Jesus Christ through faith, has complete salvation."

As John Calvin[79] — and, in his footsteps, Guide de Brès — emphasized, "The Gospel should not only be preached but also heard and believed. This too belongs to the marks of the Church."[80]

That the priest performs certain rites and believes certain things — the coal-burners of the Black Forest in Germany used to say, "Don't ask me what I believe, but ask the priest, for he believes for me!" — is not sufficient. The priesthood does not constitute the Church. The Church is an institute. That is true. But this institute consists of living members.

This struggle against Rome led to the concept of the "invisible Church." What was meant by that phrase is clearly explained by Philip Melanchthon, who wrote in his *Apologia Confessionis*, "We are not dreaming about some Platonic republic, as has been slanderously alleged, but we teach that this Church actually exists, made up of the believers and righteous men scattered throughout the world. And we add marks, the pure preaching of the Gospel and the sacraments."[81]

Two more proof texts

What we have been saying is confirmed by the other two proof texts: "And it shall come to pass that whoever calls on the name of the LORD shall be saved. For on Mount Zion and in Jerusalem there shall be deliverance, as the LORD has said, among the remnant whom the LORD calls" (Joel 2:32),[82] and "And it shall come to pass that whoever calls on the name of the Lord shall be saved" (Acts 2:21). In this third proof text, the apostle Peter, in his address delivered on the day of Pentecost, shows his hearers how the prophecy of Joel was fulfilled: There was a rather small group of followers of the promised Messiah, Jesus of Nazareth. They were the remnant about which Joel had spoken. When Peter called others to join them, approximately three thousand people were added to this remnant, all on the same day! He told them that for

---

[79] "Wherever we see the word of God sincerely preached and heard, wherever we see the sacraments administered according to the institution of Christ, there we cannot have any doubt that the Church of God has some existence . . . " (*Institutes* IV.i.9). "The Lord recognizes nothing as his own, save when his word is heard and religiously observed" (IV.ii.3).

[80] A reflection of what Calvin wrote about this can be found in the French Confession, Article 28: ". . . there can be no Church where the Word of God is not received, nor profession made of subjection to it."

[81] See Jones 71.

[82] The 1580 edition, used by Schaff in *Creeds* 3:428, has this text as a proof text for the phrase "There is no salvation outside of it" in Article 28.

everyone who would call on the name of the Lord there would be deliverance and the redemption they needed. (Calling on the Lord means urging Him to help in disastrous circumstances.) They had to acknowledge Jesus Christ as the promised Messiah.

Outreach

Again this shows us the outreaching character of the gospel and therefore of our Confession as well. Those who really believed in the Lord Jesus Christ as their Saviour and who called on the name of the Lord God for help but still did not have the true insight and courage to break with the Church of Rome or with the Anabaptists were encouraged even now to take the right steps. The "concerned" within the Church of Rome, who defended their position by claiming, for instance, that they felt obliged to try to reform this church, were also addressed. In Mount Zion and Jerusalem, where God is dwelling in the midst of His people — in the Church — there is redemption. Let them join the Church and enjoy the salvation offered there!

All believers

It is in this light that we must see and consider what our Confession is saying when it states that the Church is "the assembly of the true Christian believers." They all belong to Christ. Once again we draw attention to the article "the": "*the* true Christian believers."[83]

This is what Caspar Olevianus meant when, in a booklet on the Apostles' Creed, he writes, "All believers from Adam until the end of the world, are members of Him [Christ], and are one body through the Holy Spirit." Likewise, Zacharias Ursinus, in his commentary on the Heidelberg Catechism, writes, "The universal visible Church consists of all those who profess the doctrine of God's Word, in whatever part of the world they may be . . . So also the invisible Church is universal, inasmuch as all the elect of whatever place they may be, and in whatever time they may have lived, have one faith."[84] In his booklet *The Staff*, Guido de Brès says the same thing: "There is one single Church only, which is the congregation of all the elect who have been from the beginning of the world and will be until the end."[85] Christophorus Fabritius, who wrote his confession as a prisoner, preparing himself for the day of his execution as a martyr, says about the

---

[83] The Latin version even has "all" (*omnium vere fidelium Christianorum*), as we find in other confessions, as well (see footnote 28). The Latin version has "all" because Latin has no article. Festus Hommius therefore translated the article "the" (*les* in French, *de* in Dutch) as *omnium* ("all"), which has the same force.

[84] Ursinus, *Commentary* 287.

[85] C. Vonk, *De Voorzeide Leer* 3B (Barendrecht: Drukkerij "Barendrecht," 1956, 91 (our translation).

Church, "I acknowledge and confess that there is a holy universal Church (Matthew 16:18; Ephesians 5:25-27), an assembly of all believers (Acts 4:32). . . . This Church has, as members of one body, communion with Christ its only Head and all His spiritual gifts and goods (1 Corinthians 12:12), with which they must faithfully serve Him and assist the other members in love."[86] Here, as in answer 55 of our Catechism, the two parts of the covenant are honoured. Our concept of the Church — and also our preaching — becomes unbalanced as soon as we neglect the fact that "communion" primarily means communion with Christ.

This line in the Confession does not mean simply that all believers are in the Church already. The next article will say that no one ought to withdraw from it, putting himself outside the Church, content to be by himself, and that all who draw away from the Church or fail to join it act contrary to the ordinance of God.

Nevertheless, as we have said in the Introduction, in its articles on the Church our Confession has all believers in mind,[87] because Christ has them in mind: He wants them all among His flock. And on the last day He will be able to present to His Father one single flock, and this is why He calls them together on Sunday, urging them to be one. Therefore we can say that the Confession sets the norm here for all true believers, appealing to the faith of those who are still outside. "Some sheep are outside the sheepfold. They ought to be inside. Those are the ones who, according to Article 28, are obliged to join the Church."[88]

---

[86] Vonk, *Voorzeide Leer* 3B: 99.

[87] As for those who still stay outside, Article 28 leaves the judgment to the LORD, stating only that they act contrary to the ordinance of God. A number of authors refer in this connection to 1 Corinthians 5:13. Cf. F. L. Bos, *De Orde van de Kerk toegelicht met kerkelijke besluiten uit vier eeuwen* ('s-Gravenhage: Boekencentrum, 1950) 275 and H. Bouma, *De Kerkorde: regel voor vrede in de kerk*, Woord en Wereld 8 (Ermelo: Woord en Wereld, 1988) 62; J. Kamphuis alludes to this text in his *De Kerk*, Woord en Wereld 27 (Ermelo: Woord en Wereld, 1995) 57.

[88] J. van Bruggen, *Het Amen der Kerk* (Goes: Oosterbaan & Le Cointre, 1964) 133 (translation mine). Looking at the final result of Christ's Church-gathering work, which will be in full harmony with God's eternal counsel regarding the Church, other confessions follow the example set by John Calvin, who says in his *Institutes* that Scripture speaks about the Church *bifariam*, in two different ways. We dealt with this in Chapter 2 of the Introduction under the subheading "An Illustration," and in particular in footnote 22. Among the confessions which follow Calvin in this respect is the Westminster Confession of Faith, which opens Chapter XXV with these words: "The catholic or universal Church, which is invisible, consists of the whole number of the elect that have been, are, or shall be gathered into one, under Christ the Head thereof; and is the spouse, the body, the fullness of Him that filleth all in all." That the Belgic Confession does not emphasize this *bifariam* results from what we called one of its aims, to be a guide to those who are still outside. The same aspect is touched on, though, when the Confession deals with the phrase "sealed by the Holy Spirit" and cites as a proof text 2 Tim. 2:19, which says, "The Lord knows those who are His," a statement often referred to in Calvin's *Institutes* and some other confessional or doctrinal documents.

It is remarkable that the Westminster Confession is sometimes criticized because of its definition of the Church, whereas there is no criticism of the Belgic Confession which presents a similar definition. According to the Westminster Confession (and the Westminster Larger Catechism), the invisible Church consists of the elect. Our own Confession does not use the term "elect" in Article 27 but speaks of "the true Christian believers" and, in Article 29, of "the redeemed" and "those who are of the Church," whom it describes at length. Especially when we consider this from the standpoint of Christ's activity of gathering the Church — and thus of its final result — there is no fundamental difference.

True Christian believers

It may not need much further explanation that "Christian believers" means believers in Christ. Faith in Christ is essential for belonging to the "remnant" which, according to the prophet Joel, would enjoy salvation.

> In 1534, William Farel — the man who, a few years later, urged John Calvin to stay at Geneva in order to promote the Reformation further in that city — wrote a booklet called *Le Summaire*, which may be considered a kind of "miniature *Institutes*."[89] In that booklet he gave the following description of the Church: "The Church of Jesus Christ is the holy congregation of the believers who by true faith are united and incorporated into Jesus Christ, of whom they are members."[90] A living relationship with the Saviour is essential.

The little noun "true" is really striking. There are other people in the Church as well. Article 29 says, "We are not speaking here of the hypocrites, who are mixed in the Church along with the good and yet are not part of the Church, although they are outwardly in it."

It is therefore no wonder that in some confessions and other literature from the days of the Reformation we find a distinction between more pure and less pure — and even impure — churches. We shall deal with this issue later on. For the moment, it may suffice to say that our Confession, though realizing that no congregation is perfectly pure, confines itself to the essentials, counting as members only those who profess Jesus Christ as their Saviour.[91]

It is also remarkable that in its definition of the Church our own Confession is silent on the position of our children, whereas the Westminster Confession includes with a paragraph on "the visible Church, which consists of all these throughout the world that profess the true religion, together with their children."

Although the visible-invisible distinction should be understood against the background of the days of the Reformation, during which the concept of the Church adhered to and propagated by the Church of Rome had to be rejected, we must appreciate the fact that our Catechism does not use it. Furthermore, that the Belgic Confession does not mention the way in which Christ gathers His Church — and in particular that He does so throughout the generations of God's covenant people — may be understood when we see that its particular aim is to make it perfectly clear to all believers that they should be grateful for belonging to a faithful congregation, or that, for their salvation's sake, they must still join the true Church. We repeat: the Confession here is establishing the norm! On the normative character of our Confession, see Faber, *Essays* 74, and Vonk, *Voorzeide Leer* 3B: 112. Our Confession is again in complete harmony here with what Scripture says in Hebrews 13:7, which commands us to follow the faith of those who have spoken the Word of God to us, something which is impossible if we stay away from the congregation in which these deceased office bearers have served.

[89] Its full (translated) title is: "Summary and brief declaration of some Scripture passages which are really necessary for each Christian to know in order that he put his confidence in God and help his neighbour."

[90] *Le Summaire*, ed. J. G. Baum (1534; Geneva: Jules-Guillaume Fick, 1867) 31.

[91] This may raise the question: What about our children? As we saw earlier, the Westminster Confession clearly answers this question positively when it says that "the visible church . . . consists of all these throughout the world that profess the true religion, together with their children" (XXV.2). Our own Confession solves this "problem" in Article 34, when it states that "Christ shed His blood to wash the children of believers just as much as He shed it for adults," and that therefore "they ought to receive the sign and sacrament of what Christ has done for them. . . ." This sign is holy baptism. "By baptism we are received into the Church of God." That the children are not mentioned in Article 27 results from the Belgic Confession's aim in the contents of Articles 27 through 29 in particular.

"WHO EXPECT THEIR ENTIRE SALVATION IN JESUS CHRIST"

Brevity

In a few lines, our Confession now presents a brief description of what is meant by "the true Christian believers." What do they actually believe? Later on, in the context of the marks of the Christians, this description will be enlarged. Apart from this, what they believe has already been confessed previously. Articles 22 and 24 summarized this when they explained what "true faith" means. What our Confession says here in the first lines of Article 27 is a summary of that summary. A long exposition of what "the true Christian believers" confess is unnecessary here.

"Entire"

The phrase "their entire salvation" is typical of the days in which our Confession was written. It clearly underlines the adage of the Reformation: *sola fide*, by faith alone. Doing good works and obeying the rules set by the Church (of Rome) is not the source of salvation — not even of part of it.[92] This is confirmed by the proof text: "Nor will they say, 'See here!' or 'See there!' For indeed, the Kingdom of God is within you" (Luke 17:21).[93]

The salvation and happiness of the Kingdom of God[94] cannot be obtained from anyone or anything but Christ. An anti-Roman note is being sounded here. Besides, the phrase also points to the end: entire salvation will be enjoyed only after this life, when the goal of perfection will be reached.[95]

---

[92] A nice parallel can be seen in the Ten Theses of Berne (1528), which played a significant role in the Swiss Reformation. It says, "Christ is our only wisdom, righteousness, redemption, and payment for the sins of the whole world. Hence it is a denial of Christ when we acknowledge another merit for salvation and satisfaction for sin" (Thesis III).

[93] There seems to be reason to suppose that Luke 17:21 was meant to act as a proof text for the phrase "true Christian believers," because in the French version it is placed before Matt. 11:25. Schaff (*Creeds* 3:382) uses it as a proof text for the sentence which says that the Church "for a while may look very small and as extinct" — and he does so because he claims to have used an authentic manuscript of the French version, dated 1580 "with the revision of Dort," reprinted at Brussels in 1850. In both cases, Luke 17:21 would indicate the invisible (in the sense of "unsurveyable") aspect of the Church.

[94] We shall deal with the relationship between the Church and the Kingdom later on. It may be interesting to know, already at this point, that the Westminster Confession says, "The visible church . . . is the Kingdom of the Lord Jesus Christ" (XXV.2).

[95] Heidelberg Catechism, Lord's Day 44, Q&A 115.

"WASHED BY HIS BLOOD AND SANCTIFIED AND SEALED BY THE HOLY SPIRIT"

"Washed"

Our Confession goes on to refer briefly to the ground on which the true believers' expectation regarding their entire salvation rests: they are washed by the blood of Christ.

This is not the first time that our Confession mentions the blood of Christ. Earlier, in Article 21, the satisfaction made by Christ as our High Priest was confessed, and Article 26 quotes Hebrews 10:19. Here the believers are told that they have boldness to enter the Holiest by the blood of Jesus. To Christ's blood we attribute the fact that our prayers reach the heavenly sanctuary and will be accompanied by Christ's intercessory prayers.

That the knowledge of having been washed by Christ's blood does not make believers passive and acquiescent in the false assurance of "having arrived" is proved in Article 29, when it includes among the marks of Christians that "they appeal constantly to the blood, suffering, death, and obedience of Jesus Christ, in whom they have forgiveness of their sins through faith in Him."

"Sealed"

The words "washed by His blood" remind us, at the same time, of the sacrament of holy baptism. This is also the case in what follows: true Christian believers "are sanctified and sealed by the Holy Spirit." Here we are already catching a glimpse of one of the marks of the true Church! This sealing, too, has already been explained in our Confession in Article 24, and it will be developed further in Article 33 when we hear about the sacraments. There is an allusion to more than one mark even, since it is also by the preaching of God's Word as one of the keys of the Kingdom of heaven that the believers are assured of their salvation: "sealed by the Holy Spirit."

The Church is also one of the works of the Holy Spirit. This is true on a personal level: It is the Holy Spirit who works faith and regeneration in the believer's heart and life. It is also true on a corporate level. In the Apostles' Creed and the Nicene Creed, the Church is confessed in the third part which deals with the Holy Spirit and His work. In the Heidelberg Catechism, Lord's Day 21 is still under the heading of the previous Lord's Day: "God the Holy Spirit and our sanctification."

Proof text

The proof text on which all of this rests is 2 Timothy 2:19. There it says, "Nevertheless, the solid foundation of God stands, having this seal: 'The Lord knows those who are His,' and, 'Let everyone who names the name of Christ depart from iniquity.' " It is clear that this verse functions as a proof text particularly because of the first half of the double seal: "The Lord knows those who are His."

Our Confession is not the only Reformation document in which 2 Timothy 2:19 is quoted. John Calvin referred to this text in his interpretation of the Creed in his *Institutes*.[96] So do some confessions.[97] It was upon this text that they based their concept of an invisible Church, to be distinguished from the visible (aspect of the) Church.

Here in the Belgic Confession, however, this text is used with a different purpose. The apostle compares the Church to a house built on a solid foundation. This foundation has a double seal, which identifies the owner of the house and proves that it is his legal property. Belonging to this divine property, the Church, gives great certainty of faith and is a strong encouragement to the believers.

When we realize that this line has been inserted in our Confession to counteract the dependence of the members of the Church of Rome on the "graces" distributed by that church, we shall have an even greater appreciation of the tremendous encouragement it expresses.[98]

---

[96] "Hence, regard must be had both to the secret election and to the internal calling of God, because he alone 'knoweth them that are his' (2 Timothy ii.19); and as Paul expresses it, holds them as it were enclosed under his seal, although at the same time, they wear his insignia, and are thus distinguished from the reprobate" (IV.i.2). And: "It is, indeed, the special prerogative of God to know those who are his, as Paul declares in the passage already quoted (2 Timothy ii.19)" (IV.i.8).

Ulrich Zwingli mentioned the same text in the letter to the King of France which accompanied his *Fidei expositio* (1531).

[97] 2 Timothy 2:19 is mentioned in the First Helvetic Confession (1536), Art. 14; the Lausanne Articles (1536), Art. IV; the Confession of Faith used in the English Congregation at Geneva (1556), Chap. 4; the Scottish Confession (1560), Chap. XVI; and the Second Helvetic Confession (1566), Chap. XVII.

[98] The heavy burden laid upon the members of the Church of Rome is expressed in the definition presented by William Farel when he says, "This Church definitely does not consist in a diversity of decrees, laws, ordinances, and orders, imposed by the will of man, but in the true unity of faith in our Saviour Jesus Christ, which listens to His holy voice and believes it" (*Le Summaire* 31, translation mine).

"THIS CHURCH HAS EXISTED FROM THE BEGINNING OF THE WORLD AND WILL BE TO THE END"

This Church has existed from the beginning of the world and will be to the
end, for Christ is an eternal King who cannot be without subjects. This holy
Church is preserved by God against the fury of the whole world, although
for a while it may look very small and as extinct in the eyes of man. Thus
during the perilous reign of Ahab, the Lord kept for Himself seven
thousand persons, who had not bowed their knees to Baal.

"From the beginning of the world"

The previous line, "washed by His blood and sanctified and sealed by the Holy Spirit," seems to suggest that the Church came into existence only in New Testament days. After all, was not Christ's blood shed and the Holy Spirit poured out in the new dispensation? This seems to exclude the Old Testament dispensation. Our Confession, however, goes on to present the thesis that the Church has existed from the beginning of the world.

This line must be read against the background of history. According to the Anabaptists the Old Testament was a book for the Jews and is therefore abolished. It does not present a picture of "the pure congregation" which was the Anabaptist ideal regarding the Church. The covenant made with Abraham did not lead to the desired goal: a nation of all regenerated people. Consequently there is no basis for infant baptism and we cannot say that baptism has replaced circumcision. With the New Testament an entirely new beginning was made. At that point, God started His work over again, as it were. From then on, a "pure congregation" of regenerated people was created.[99]

It is against this background that our Confession states, "The catholic or universal Church has existed from the beginning of the world." Here the basis is laid for what we shall confess regarding infant baptism in Article 34 and regarding the benefit of the Lord's Supper for those who, according to Article 35, "have a twofold life" and therefore need "the support [given by this sacrament] of the spiritual and heavenly life, which believers have."

---

[99] A clear exposition of this Anabaptist thinking is presented by J. Kamphuis in his article "De 'sluier' bij het lezen van het Oude Testament gekozen" (The "veil" chosen at the reading of the Old Testament), *Nader Bekeken* 3.9 (Sept. 1996): 210-12.

Proof text

This historical background may also explain why Jeremiah 31:36 is the proof text for this sentence. It says, "If those ordinances depart from before Me, says the LORD, then the seed of Israel shall also cease from being a nation before Me forever."

This is a solemn statement made in the context of the promise of the new covenant given by a gracious God to an Israel that had seriously neglected the covenant which He had made with them.[100] In this statement, the LORD God referred to His decrees regarding the sun, moon, and stars, which had been allotted fixed times for their functioning. These decrees are unchangeable. One can count on them — or rather, on the God who had created this natural order. This, then, was the ground on the basis of which ancient Israel could trust the divine promise of a new covenant. Just as the sun shines by day, and the moon and stars are there at night, even until the end of time, the new covenant will remain in force. There will always be a new Israel, God's own nation, the Church.

This proof text, then, clearly underlines the fact that the Church will exist to the end. But what of its existence from the beginning of the world?

The answer is that we must not forget that a new covenant means a *renewed* covenant. The covenant announced by the prophet Jeremiah was a renewal of the covenant of Sinai, which in turn rested upon the covenant made with Abraham, and, going one more step back, the covenant with Abraham was a gracious renewal of the promise given to man in paradise after the Fall that there would be a mankind which would produce a Seed, and this Seed would bruise the head of its great opponent, to the benefit of the other "seed" of the first two people. Right from the beginning, there would be a family, families, tribes, and a nation which would enjoy the favour and love of a gracious God.

This may also explain why our Confession can state that this Church, this "holy congregation and assembly of the true Christian believers, who expect their entire salvation in Jesus Christ" — note the names "Christian" and "Jesus Christ" — has been in existence from the very beginning. God's grace in Christ has always been present. During the Old Testament days, faith was faith in the promised Messiah and was thus essentially no different from faith professed in the new dispensation.

The same can be said about the catholicity of the Church. The Lord God always had it in mind. He clearly showed this purpose in the promise given to Abraham, in which He told him that in his seed all the nations of the world would be blessed. And as for the apostolicity of the Church, the gospel preached by the apostles, on which Church life rests, was fundamentally the same in Old Testament days.

---

[100] Jeremiah 30:22; 31:31ff.

Comfort

The sentence in our Confession which we are considering includes a strong comfort and gives us encouragement, in particular, when the human aspect of Church life causes great concern and sorrow, when the prophesied days of apostasy seem to have arrived, or when hostility against the Church is on the increase. It is then that we can look up at the sun by day and at the moon and stars at night and remember the statement made by God in Jeremiah's days and be assured that God's plan can not be broken. "His Kingdom is forever, and therefore His Church is, too." Despite all the sins committed in the past, the Church still exists.

"FOR CHRIST IS AN ETERNAL KING, WHO CANNOT BE WITHOUT SUBJECTS"

"Eternal"

We ended the previous paragraph with a quotation from "the Luther Hymn": "His Kingdom is forever, and therefore His Church is, too." This brings us to the question: What is the relationship between the Church and the Kingdom of God?

It should be clear that we cannot avoid this question: in the line of our Confession upon which we now focus our attention, Christ is called "an eternal King," and "subjects" are also mentioned.

Proof texts

In order to be able to answer this question, we must read the proof texts to which the original Dutch version of our Confession refers: "And your house and your kingdom shall be established forever before you. Your throne shall be established forever" (2 Samuel 7:16); "His seed shall endure forever, and his throne as the sun before Me" (Psalm 89:36); "The LORD has sworn and will not relent, 'You are a priest forever according to the order of Melchizedek' " (Psalm 110:4); "He will be great and will be called the Son of the Highest; and the Lord God will give Him the throne of His father David" (Luke 1:32); and ". . . teaching them to observe all things that I have commanded you; and lo, I am with you always, even to the end of the age" (Matthew 28:20).

The historical progress shown in these texts is really striking. The first two are assurances given to David that his kingdom would last forever. This promise was even sealed by another covenant made with him. As for Melchizedek, we must not forget that he was not only a high priest but also a king, so that the promise of Psalm 110 is also applicable to David's Son's kingship. With the third text, we have arrived at the royal dignity and power of the Lord Jesus Christ, Who — according to the fourth proof text, spoken by the angel Gabriel — was David's great Son. Then follows what Christ said in the "Great Commission." He stated that He is a King indeed, the King of the universe, and that He would always be with His Church.

It is of great benefit to read the Bible in the redemptive-historical way, as the Belgic Confession of Faith does here! Scriptural doctrine does not rest on single texts but on the whole history of salvation.

An assuring syllogism

Our Confession shows that it is a product of the days in which it was compiled by making use of a syllogism. This was done more often in those days, but this time the way of drawing conclusions from Scriptural data and common sense is particularly comforting.

We can see the following syllogism in these lines:
Major premise: Christ is an eternal King.
Minor premise: A king has subjects.
Conclusion: Christ as a King will always have subjects.
In other words: There will always be a Church.

This is really comforting and encouraging. We cannot expect to be on our own in today's world. The Church of Christ is catholic.

Church and Kingdom

We return to the proof text of the previous line of the Confession. We are told in the Confession that there is a certain relationship between the Church and the Kingdom of God, and Jeremiah 31:36, though it may be a little vague, points to that relationship. It includes the word "nation," whereas one of the previous verses has "laws" (v.33).

Even the name "Church" has some political connotations. The Greek term *ecclesia* is used in Acts 19, where we are informed about a public meeting of the citizens of Ephesus to protest against the economic implications which the proclamation of the gospel of Christ could have for their city. In our Bible versions we read about an assembly, but the original Greek text has *ecclesia*.[101]

---

[101] Acts 19:32, 39, 41.

Certainly, the Christian Church — which is also called an *ecclesia* — is a special populace, living under Christ as its Head and King, but this does not exclude the fact that Church life has a political aspect.[102] This may explain why the Bible uses the terms "Church" and "Kingdom" together. For example, the Church at Philippi was assured by the apostle Paul that "our citizenship is in heaven" (Philipians 3:20). In the original, Paul uses the word *politeuma*, another word derived from *polis*.

This leads us to conclude that when, in Matthew 16, the Lord Jesus speaks about the Church for the first time and says, "You are Peter and on this rock I will build My church," He uses a word drawn from the world of politics, of kingdoms. So the name for the Church itself indicates a close connection between God's Church and God's Kingdom.[103]

At this point, we could present a long exposition on the relationship between Church and Kingdom.[104] We must confine ourselves, however, to the following thesis: The Church is the populace of the Kingdom of God. Our Confession has already stated that the true believers "expect their entire salvation in Jesus Christ." In other words, they submit themselves to Him as their Head and King.

Certainly, all authority in heaven and on earth has been given to Him, but the majority of people and the nations of the world, in general, are rebellious against His Kingdom. For that reason, He will judge them on the day of His glory, and the Church will take part in that great event.

The fact that the Church takes this special position within Christ's Kingdom, under Him as their Head, had led Him to entrust the keys of the Kingdom of heaven to the Church.[105] He has also taught His Church to pray: "Thy Kingdom come," which our Catechism interprets as meaning: "Preserve and increase Thy Church."[106]

The nations mentioned in the Lord's promise to Abraham and in Christ's "Great Commission" will bring their glory and honour into the New Jerusalem, the capital city of God's eternal Kingdom.[107] God's great plan revealed in Genesis 22:18 will be completed.

All of this makes it clear that the Church is not an end in itself, whereas the Kingdom is. Everything focuses on Christ and, through Him, on the heavenly Father. The glory of our Head and King is the ultimate aim for which the Church exists. This should stimulate us to keep our eyes more directly focused

---

[102] The word "political" here is used in its original, literal meaning; it is derived from *polis*: city, nation, commonwealth.

[103] Faber, *Lectures* 27.

[104] For those who can read Dutch, we recommend S. Greijdanus, "Kerk en Koninkrijk Gods," *Congres van Gereformeerden: Referatenbundel Amersfoorts congres 1948* (n.p., 1948) 29ff., a paper recently rediscussed within our Dutch sister churches, e.g., by H. J. D. Smit, "Kerk en Organisatie, Motieven en Achtergronden, een peiling," *Toekomst voor Gereformeerde organisaties* (Barneveld: Vuurbaak, 1994) 35ff.

[105] Heidelberg Catechism, Lord's Day 31.

[106] Heidelberg Catechism, Lord's Day 48.

[107] Genesis 22:18; Matthew 28:19; Revelation 21:26.

on this glory, even when we must deal with all sorts of Church affairs in a "businesslike" manner. There is always the danger of concentrating on the business of the Church without keeping ourselves aware of the whole purpose of the existence of the Church: Christ and His glory.

Allow me to be more direct. We must face this question seriously: Are we really eager for the day on which, in faith and gratitude, we shall experience proof of the truth of all that we profess here in the words we have been discussing? Will we be glad to meet, and even unite with, other subjects of the Head of the Church and the Lord of the Kingdom? Or do we prefer to isolate ourselves, thinking, more or less consciously, that we alone are subjects of that Kingdom?[108]

"THIS HOLY CHURCH IS PRESERVED BY GOD AGAINST THE FURY OF THE WHOLE WORLD"

"Preserved"

Our Confession seems to be basing what it says about the preservation of the Church by God on Psalm 102:13, where the poet expresses his confidence in the LORD by saying, "You will arise and have mercy on Zion; for the time to favour her, yes, the set time, has come."[109]

The poet calls himself "afflicted" in the heading of this psalm. He represents the whole covenant nation which is living under miserable circumstances. His days are consumed like smoke. He does not expect to live much longer. The LORD, however, will endure forever (v. 12), and this is the solid basis on which the psalmist makes a bold appeal to God. The LORD will never forsake His people. God preserves His Church!

"Fury"

God preserves His Church "against the fury of the whole world." The Church needs God's help in such a situation, as Psalm 46:5 indicates: "God is

---

[108] We shall be obliged to discuss the relationship between the Church and the Kingdom further when we deal with the sentence in Article 29 which alludes to the parable of the tares in Matthew 13. There we are confronted with the question of whether this parable can be used — as it is in a number of Reformed confessions — as a proof text for the existence of hypocrites within the Church.

[109] We say "seems" because there is a problem here. Vallensis puts this proof text here, following the oldest Dutch version of the Confession (1562). The French version, however, seems to use this text as the Scriptural basis for the confession of the Church's catholicity. The French version used by Schaff (*Creeds* 3:382) confirms this in part. It uses Psalm 102:13 — along with Luke 17:21, as in Vallensis's work — for the very first line of Article 27. This confusion illustrates what we said about the proof texts in the Prologue.

in the midst of her, she shall not be moved; God shall help her, just at the break of dawn."

Proof texts are often selected because of their function within a certain context. Within the context of Psalm 46 this particular verse gives comfort and encouragement. The beginning of this Psalm presents a lively picture of the fury — called "trouble" in verse 1 — that buffets the Church: the earth is being removed, the mountains are being carried into the midst of the sea. But, unlike these mountains, the city of God will not fall because the Most High dwells in her.

Christ Himself has given His Church the same assurance. After Simon Peter confessed his faith in Him as the promised Messiah, the Son of the living God, the Lord told him: "And I also say to you that you are Peter, and on this rock I will build My Church, and the gates of Hades shall not prevail against it" (Matthew 16:18). It is remarkable that in this saying — one of the few sayings in which He mentions the Church — the Lord Jesus assures us that nothing will be able to destroy His Church.[110]

"ALTHOUGH FOR A WHILE IT MAY LOOK VERY SMALL AND AS EXTINCT IN THE EYES OF MAN"

Scripture

The Church was small indeed in the days of Noah, when he and his family entered into the Ark, "In which a few, that is eight souls, were saved through water" (1 Peter 3:20b).[111]

Isaiah had to announce a severe punishment upon the apostate nation, but the LORD would preserve for Himself a remnant. Isaiah 1:9, the second proof text here, reads, "Unless the LORD of hosts had left to us a very small remnant, we would have become like Sodom, we would have been made like Gomorrah."[112] In Romans 9:29, the apostle Paul quotes Isaiah's prophecy: "And as Isaiah said before: 'Unless the LORD of Sabaoth had left us a seed, we would have become like Sodom, we would have been made like Gomorrah.' "

A remnant Church may look very small indeed. A church consisting of no more than eight people — one single family — is almost extinct in the eyes of man, yet God preserved it, creating from it the worldwide Church of Genesis 22:18.

---

[110] "The gates of death" are also mentioned in Psalm 9:13; 107:18; and Isaiah 38:10 ("the gates of Sheol"). Sometimes the realm of death is introduced as a dangerous city with towers and gates, a devouring monster.

[111] The 1580 edition, reprinted by Schaff (*Creeds* 3:428), has this text as a proof text for the phrase "there is no salvation outside of it" in Article 28.

[112] Instead of the word "remnant," the NIV has "survivors" here. Many of the Old Testament prophets speak of a "remnant," however, and it is a standard term, as can be seen from a concordance.

"THUS DURING THE PERILOUS REIGN OF AHAB, THE LORD KEPT FOR HIMSELF SEVEN THOUSAND PEOPLE, WHO HAD NOT BOWED THEIR KNEES TO BAAL"

An illustration

Our Confession gives an illustration from sacred history, referring to the passage in Scripture in which God Himself comforts Elijah: "Yet I have reserved seven thousand in Israel, all whose knees have not bowed to Baal, and every mouth that has not kissed him" (1 Kings 19:18). This statement is quoted by the apostle Paul as well when he refers to the story of Elijah and writes, "But what does the divine response say to him? 'I have reserved for Myself seven thousand men who have not bowed the knee to Baal' " (Romans 11:4).

> It is interesting to find that the same story is mentioned in the Second Helvetic Confession (1566), compiled by Henry Bullinger. It is in this context that that Confession uses the term "invisible."[113] This means that the term "invisible" was also used in the sense of "hidden." It was applied to a Church which exists in this earthly history, rather than to a Church existing somewhere above reality.

Church history confirms what we confess here. A map in an atlas of the ancient Christian Church shows us a surprisingly large number of dots, each representing a local congregation in Asia Minor, Syria, Egypt, North Africa, and Southern Spain.[114] In many of those places, the Church has become extinct. Information supplied by groups like the Middle East Reformed Fellowship (MERF), however, indicates that in many of these countries around the Mediterranean, as well as in Iran and other places, the Church is growing again, sometimes in circumstances similar to those of the time of Ahab and Elijah.

---

[113] The passage in the Second Helvetic Confession reads as follows: "The Church appears at times to be extinct. Yes, and it sometimes happens that God in His just judgment allows the truth of His Word, and the catholic faith, and the proper worship of God to be so obscured and overthrown that the Church seems almost extinct, and no more to exist, as we see to have happened in the days of Elijah (1 Kings 19:10, 14), and at other times. Meanwhile God has in this world and in this darkness His true worshippers, and those not a few, but even seven thousand and more (1 Kings 19:18; Revelation 7:3ff.). For the apostle exclaims: 'God's firm foundation stands bearing this seal, "The Lord knows those who are His,"' etc. (2 Timothy 2:19). Whence the Church of God may be termed invisible; not because the men from whom the Church is gathered are invisible, but because, being hidden from our eyes and known only to God, it often secretly escapes human judgment" (Chap. XVII).

[114] F. van der Meer and Christine Mohrmann, *Atlas van de Oudchristelijke Wereld* (Amsterdam: Elsevier, 1958) 2-4.

Some centuries ago, it is said, there was a flowering Church in China. It seems that since then it has become extinct, by apostasy or suppression from outside or both. Nevertheless, every now and then, we still hear of tiny congregations — a "hidden Church" — there, do we not?

Even though the number of churches and church members has more than once seemed to decrease dramatically, sacred history as well as both ancient and current Church history continue to assure us that the Church of Christ will exist to the end, "for Christ is an eternal King who cannot be without subjects." He Himself sees to that!

"MOREOVER, THIS HOLY CHURCH IS NOT CONFINED OR LIMITED TO ONE PARTICULAR PLACE OR TO CERTAIN PERSONS, BUT IS SPREAD AND DISPERSED THROUGHOUT THE ENTIRE WORLD"

Once more: The Church is truly catholic

Once again, the Confession underscores the catholicity of the Church. Together with Irenaeus of Lyon, we could say, "Wherever Christ is, there the Church is catholic."

In the fourth century, Pacianus, bishop of Barcelona, translated the word "catholic" by "everywhere one and the same."[115] Only later on did the decay in church life lead to the false claim of the Church of Rome, that the Church is concentrated in her, or in the Pope and his council of cardinals. The "headquarters" of the whole Church and of each congregation are not here on earth, however, but in the Jerusalem above (Galatians 4:26), where the only universal Bishop and the only Head of the Church[116] lives and reigns forever.[117]

---

[115] Wiskerke, "Verantwoorde oecumeniciteit" 121.

[116] Belgic Confession, Article 31.

[117] The same application of this passage must be made when some adherents of a certain "Israel theology" and a certain conception of the millennium expect the city of Jerusalem to play the role of the central city in the world. The Holy Spirit has His temples everywhere in the world (see John 4:21-24).

No proof text

No proof text is mentioned here. The support for this section is found in Article 31, which refers to Christ as the universal Bishop and Head of the Church and which cites Ephesians 1:22: "And He put all things under His feet, and gave Him to be Head over all things to the Church."[118]

"HOWEVER, IT IS JOINED AND UNITED WITH HEART AND WILL, IN ONE AND THE SAME SPIRIT, BY THE POWER OF FAITH"

Pentecostal unity

The unity of the Church lies in what true believers have in common: the gift of the Holy Spirit. It is not strange, therefore, that the first proof text refers to the situation in the Christian Church shortly after the day of Pentecost: "Now the multitude of those who believed were of one heart and one soul" (Acts 4:32a).

This unity was clearly demonstrated in the care for the needy. What was living in their hearts came out into the open, as did their strong desire to be united. Later on, in the Corinthian congregation, this desire was absent, even when the believers were supposed to have been showing and enjoying their unity in connection with the Lord's Supper (1 Corinthians 10:17ff.).

The same unwillingness has been demonstrated so often in the course of Church history, and it is often still present in the Church. For that reason — and also because we have adopted this beautiful, Scriptural confession regarding the Church — we are obliged to stand firm in our faith and show our desire and willingness to live up to this high calling.

This summons is the more urgent when in our modern days, in which the world seems to be becoming smaller and smaller, we are sometimes able to see clearly — with the eye of faith — that God's promise to Abraham is still being fulfilled in a surprising way.

---

[118] This text does not state explicitly that Christ is the Head of the Church, but it does introduce Him as the Head of all things. Christ's Headship over the Church is, however, implied in the phrase "which is His body" in verse 23.

One body, one Spirit, one hope

There is also a second proof text here, Ephesians 4:4, which reads, "There is one body and one Spirit just as you were called in one hope of your calling."

The Church is one body, joined and united in one and the same Spirit, and all believers have been called to the same hope. This is Christ's work through the Holy Spirit. When the apostle urges us to make every effort to keep this unity, however, this presupposes that the Church members have their own responsibilities, and this means that there is a possibility that they will not understand — let alone act according to — those responsibilities. The desire expressed in our Confession may be lacking!

Self-examination

This danger, then, calls for self-examination. Do we really believe that Christ is gathering a catholic Church and that the same Spirit who was given on the day of Pentecost is still being given to others today? In other words: Is our will regulated by the Holy Spirit? We should guard against a low estimate of the power of faith.

Here we would like to emphasize again that we should not forget the train of thought in these articles on the Church. We believe that there is only one Church, spread throughout the world, with catholicity as one of its attributes (Art. 27). Every true believer is responsible for maintaining this unity with heart and will (Art. 28). Therefore we must either stay within this Church or take action to join it in the place where we see its attributes demonstrated in its marks (Art. 29).

Our starting-point should never be the church of which we are members — whether it be our local church or the confederation of churches — because pointing to the true Church then becomes an easy short-cut that always stops at "our own" church.[119] As a result we are in danger of measuring any other church by what we find in our own church life, and then the Church is no longer a matter of faith. After all, did we not begin our confession regarding the Church with the words, "We believe and profess a holy, catholic or universal Church?" It is worthwhile for us to consider these things as we come to the end of our study of Article 27.

---

[119] Van der Jagt, *De Kerk* 65.

ARTICLE 28

EVERYONE'S DUTY TO JOIN THE CHURCH

We believe, since this holy assembly and congregation is the assembly of the redeemed and there is no salvation outside of it, that no one ought to withdraw from it, content to be by himself, no matter what his state or quality may be. But all and everyone are obliged to join it and unite with it, maintaining the unity of the Church. They must submit themselves to its instruction and discipline, bend their necks under the yoke of Jesus Christ, and serve the edification of the brothers and sisters, according to the talents which God has given them as members of the same body.
To observe this more effectively, it is the duty of all believers, according to the Word of God, to separate from those who do not belong to the Church and to join this assembly wherever God has established it. They should do so even though the rulers and edicts of princes were against it, and death or physical punishment might follow.
All therefore who draw away from the Church or fail to join it act contrary to the ordinance of God.

"EVERYONE'S DUTY TO JOIN THE CHURCH"

Heading

As we begin our commentary on Article 28 of the Belgic Confession of Faith, we must first of all deal with the heading as we find it in the *Book of Praise*. We reiterate: this heading is not original. It owes its existence to the editions of 1566, 1583, and 1611, though these had a somewhat longer heading: "That everyone is obliged to join the true Church."[120]

At the same time, we can declare this heading to be a correct summary of the contents of Article 28. It clearly expresses what we called the fourth aim of the Belgic Confession of Faith.[121]

"WE BELIEVE, SINCE THIS HOLY ASSEMBLY AND CONGREGATION IS THE ASSEMBLY OF THE REDEEMED . . ."

The ground

After the introductory words "We believe," which can be found in various forms at the beginning of any article of the Belgic Confession, the ground is given for what can be called the message of Article 28, namely that it is everyone's duty to join the Church.

This message is emphasized strongly, and it is repeated several times in a number of ways in this article. The Confession warns against a double danger: (a) that of individualism and (b) that of being bound to people who are in the

---

[120] The heading in Festus Hommius's Latin translation reads, "*De communione sanctorum cum vera ecclesia*" (On the communion of the saints with the true Church). It has the merit of running parallel to Answer 55 of the Heidelberg Catechism, which clearly indicates that believers must know themselves to be duty-bound to use the gifts received from Christ for the benefit and well-being of their fellow members of Christ, all of which presupposes that they have joined the Church.

[121] J. Kamphuis clearly underscores this fourth aim: "The Confession then also addresses those who have not (yet) joined the Church or keep themselves separate from it" (*De Kerk* 51 — our translation).

We can add to what we wrote in the Introduction about the historical context of the Confession that the Confession also has in mind people who have already shown the courage to break with the Church of Rome but have joined one Anabaptist sect or another. We shall come back to this point later. On this point, see Kamphuis, *De Kerk* 51; C. Trimp, "De communie beschermd," *De Reformatie* 68.49 (Sept. 25, 1993): 962, reprinted in his book *Kerk in aanbouw: Haar presentie en pretentie* (Goes: Oosterbaan & Le Cointre, 1998) 62ff. An English translation of this article, "The Communion Protected," can be found in *Clarion* 43.17 (Aug. 26, 1994) and in C. Trimp, *The Church.*

Church but do not belong to the Church. It intends to promote and maintain the unity of the Church in true faith.

The same Church

It is obvious that this article is speaking of the same Church as in the previous article's definition. We discover this already from this article's repetition of the phrase "this holy assembly and congregation" from Article 27. The little word "this" emphasizes this fact.[122] Those who belong to a congregation are members not only of that local church but also of the holy, catholic or universal, apostolic Church.

The text of the previous article has already made it impossible to maintain the thesis, so often put forward, that Article 27 is speaking of the invisible Church, whereas Articles 28 and 29 refer to the visible Church. When it states that the Church can be "very small" and almost "extinct," it means that in a normal situation such is not the case; normally, the Church is big enough to be seen. The same applies to the words "spread and dispersed throughout the entire world."

This sentence is more or less repeated in Article 28, when it speaks of this assembly wherever God has established it. The local congregation is an establishment of the catholic Church. It is that catholic Church manifested locally![123]

Proof texts

There are two brief series of proof texts for this part of the first sentence of Article 28. For the words "since this holy assembly and congregation," the following Scripture passage is mentioned: "I will declare Your name to My brethren; in the midst of the assembly I will sing praise to You" (Hebrews 2:12).

For the words "is the assembly," reference is made to Psalm 22:22: "I will declare Your name to My brethren, in the midst of the assembly I will praise You," and to Psalm 5:7: "But as for me, I will come into Your house in the multitude of Your mercy. In fear of You I will worship toward Your holy temple."

---

[122] Schilder, *Christelijke Religie* 92. See also d'Assonville, *K. Schilder* 68.

[123] The Rev. H. J. D. Smit is correct when he writes that Article 28 is not a mere repetition of the previous article but is intended to make its contents more concrete (*Toekomst voor Gereformeerde organisaties* 75). He went astray, however, when — according to a report published in *De Reformatie* (Mar. 27, 1993) — at a congress held at Nijkerk on March 12, 1993, he stated that Article 27 deals with the invisible Church and Articles 28 and 29 with the visible Church. Other examples can be found in Kamphuis, *De Kerk* 58.

All of these texts repeat and emphasize what we have seen in the proof texts which were attached to the same definition of the Church when it was presented back in Article 27. They shed light upon the Church from a different angle, however. Two of them have the words "My brethren," and the last text speaks of worshipping in God's temple, which is the Church.

"The redeemed"

The version of the Confession adopted by our churches has "the redeemed." Not everyone finds this past participle acceptable. Klaas Schilder preferred Festus Hommius's Latin text: *servandorum*, "those who must (or will) be saved."[124] As a matter of fact, the Latin version is not authentic, but the original Dutch text does have something similar.[125] For the moment, however, we stick to the text as it has been adopted by our churches: "the redeemed."

Redemption is not (only) a matter of the future, but also of the present, and even of the past. Those who, according to Article 27, are washed by Christ's blood and "are sanctified and sealed by the Holy Spirit" already enjoy their salvation now and may have enjoyed it for a long time. Article 29 will characterize them as people who "believe in Jesus Christ the only Saviour." They "appeal constantly to the blood, suffering, death and obedience of Jesus Christ, in whom they have forgiveness of their sins through faith in Him." Let us note the present tense of the word "have." This is not a matter of the future, but of the present!

We shall discuss this issue further below.

"AND THERE IS NO SALVATION OUTSIDE OF IT"

How should we read this line?

Our Confession presents us with a somewhat difficult sentence here. For that reason, we shall pay some extra attention to it.

The first thing required of us is that we realize that this is a kind of quotation, used in opposition to the Church of Rome which claimed that these words applied — exclusively, even! — to itself: Outside the Church of Rome there is no salvation. A second point that should not be neglected is the context

---

[124] Schilder, *Christelijke Religie* 57; see also *De Reformatie* 24.4 (Oct. 23, 1948), reprinted in *De Kerk* 3:248f.

[125] The original Dutch text has *dergenen die zalig worden* ("of those who will be saved"). This differs from "the redeemed" in our current English text. For further discussion of this issue, see under the next heading.

in which this sentence must be read, the purpose for which it has been included in our Confession. Only if we meet these two requirements will we be able to understand what exactly we are confessing with this phrase.

If we do not meet these two requirements we could easily interpret this sentence to mean that outside the true Church no one can be saved — in other words, that unless a person is within a true church, he cannot go to heaven but will be lost forever. But that is not how this sentence has been formulated. I do not think that anyone among us would like to say that, for example, only members of our own churches and recognized sister churches will go to heaven. What this sentence really means — and why it has been formulated in a careful way —should become clear from the explanation given below.

Anti-Roman polemic

In claiming that outside itself there is no salvation, the Church of Rome has thereby adopted the language used in the ancient Christian Church. What this sentence — in Latin, *extra ecclesiam nulla salus* — originally meant and how it was used and interpreted later on in Church history will be explained below for those who are interested in some details. Some conclusions drawn from that historical exposition will be presented afterwards.

Because the Church of Rome claimed the exclusive application of this sentence for itself, de Brès, following in the footsteps of others, inserted it in this article. It was his intention to make it clear that it was not Rome but the churches of the Reformation which were and are entitled to claim that they are the same as the Church of the apostolic and post-apostolic era.

It is striking, in fact, that our Confession speaks very carefully about what the consequences would be for those who remain outside the Church of the Reformation. The Council of Florence in 1429 stated that those who are not in the Church of Rome — gentiles, Jews, heretics, and schismatics — cannot be partakers of eternal life and will be cast into the fire of hell, unless they repent.[126] Our Confession goes no farther than to say, "All, therefore, who draw away from the Church or fail to join it act contrary to the ordinance of God." It does not deny that the people it has in mind — for example, the Nicodemites of those days — are believers; its intent is precisely to exhort them to join the Church. Further judgment is left to God, in accordance with 1 Corinthians 5:12-13.[127]

It is remarkable that Rome's attitude has changed slightly since then. In 1863, Pope Pius IX issued a statement in which he said that an invincible ignorance in many people outside his church could not be denied, so that for them

[126] Boniface VIII's papal bull *Unam Sanctam*, issued in 1302, opens with the following sentence: "Urged on by our faith we are compelled to believe and hold that there is One Holy Catholic and Apostolic Church and we firmly believe and clearly profess that outside of her there is neither salvation nor remission of sins." In the "Profession of the Tridentine Faith" of 1564 and in Pius XI's encyclical *Mortalum Animos* (1928), we read similar statements (Schaff, *Creeds* 2:605, 210, 209, and 625).

[127] For more about this, see our comment on the very last sentence of Article 28.

there is a possibility that they could obtain salvation by the power of divine light and grace.

Since the Second Vatican Council of the 1960s, believers outside the Church of Rome are addressed as (erring) brothers and sisters. In other words, the old rule has been replaced by another one: Everyone who will be saved has a certain relationship with the Church of Rome.[128]

Historical background

As we said earlier, the phrase we are considering is actually a kind of quotation. That means that it was used before. It has a historical background.

For those who want to be informed about this background, we shall deal with a few people who — whether explicitly or not — used, interpreted, and applied the phrase "Outside the Church there is no salvation." For those readers who will not read the next few pages, we shall summarize the various interpretations and draw some conclusions.

Origin: Origen

It is indeed true that the thesis "outside the Church there is no salvation," or something similar, can be found in the writings of some ancient Christian authors. Usually the name of Cyprian is mentioned in this context. It appears, however, that he was not the first to use this sentence. We must go farther back in Church history to trace its origin.

With apologies for the play upon words, we must say that this origin seems to be Origen (185-254), one of the so-called "Church fathers." Origen wrote some sermons on the book of Joshua. One of them was on the story of Joshua 2, where the woman called Rahab hides the spies, requests rescue from the imminent destruction of the city of Jericho, and is promised that she and her relatives will indeed be spared if they remain in her house. Origen explains this promise in an exemplaristic way by generalizing it: "Outside this house — which means, outside the church — there is no salvation."[129]

The only thing we can learn from this is that Origen made this rule into a norm: Stay within the Church or join it, for your salvation's sake! This, then, is the precise intent of our Confession: to show us the norm to which God has bound us as believers.

Cyprian

Cyprian — bishop of the church at Carthage from 247 to 254, when he died as a martyr — was a keen promoter of the unity of the Church in a time of schisms.

---

[128] Faber, *Vestigium Ecclesiae* 23.

[129] On Origen's Bible-interpretation, see Gerald Bray, *Creeds, Councils & Christ*, (London: InterVarsity Press, 1984) 79-82.

His best known work is *De catholicae ecclesiae unitate* (On the Unity of the Catholic Church). In this work he quotes the thesis *extra ecclesiam nulla salus*. In his opinion, one cannot live outside the Church because there is only one house of God, and no one can find salvation except within the Church.[130]

Another well-known saying of Cyprian is this: "One cannot have God as his Father if he does not have the Church as his mother."[131] This saying is repeated in even stronger terms when, in his 74th epistle, Cyprian writes, "A person cannot have God as a Father unless he first (Latin: *ante*, before) has the Church as a mother."[132]

So the Church comes first, according to Cyprian. This position is not surprising, since there was a strongly hierarchical trend in his thinking. This trend became clearly evident when Cyprian was confronted with the question: Can we acknowledge the baptisms administered by heretics and schismatics as valid? Cyprian considered baptism the "property" of the Church. This is why another thesis runs parallel to the one mentioned above: "outside the Church there is no baptism."[133]

Furthermore, when he states that those who put themselves outside the Church will be cast into the fire of hell, Cyprian goes much farther than our Confession does when it says that those who draw away from the Church or fail to join it act contrary to the ordinance of God. Our Confession refuses to go beyond that point.[134]

As a matter of course it is very useful to try to clarify certain passages in our confessional standards by tracing the intentions of the original authors. There are certain limits, however. The aim of a confession is to summarize the truth of God's Word, which has remained the same during all the centuries. When an allusion is made to what an ancient author wrote — as happens here in Article 28 in particular — his words can be used in a different context and therefore with a different meaning, too.

Cyprian's proof texts

We see the necessity for such changes when we examine the proof texts Cyprian provides for his use of the rule that "outside the Church there is no salvation." He refers to the Song of Solomon, which speaks of one house, one sacred bedroom, chastely preserved by the bride — a strange paraphrase of 3:4. Furthermore, he cites 6:9, "My dove, my perfect one, is unique, the only daughter of her mother" — relying on an allegorical kind of exegesis.

Cyprian also points to Noah's ark, outside of which there was only death, and to Christ's statement in Matthew 12:30: "He who does not gather with Me scatters." He cites John 10:30: "I and the Father are one," and argues that God's unity is mirrored in the unity of the Church — a more acceptable effort to base his doctrine on Scripture. He derives too much from Ephesians 4:4-5 and in particular from the words "one baptism" — remember the explanation we have

---

[130] See J. Faber, *Vestigium Ecclesiae* 23.
[131] *De unitate* 6, quoted by Faber, *Vestigium Ecclesiae* 29.
[132] Quoted in Faber, *Vestigium Ecclesiae* 79.
[133] Quoted in Faber, *Vestigium Ecclesiae* 37.
[134] J. Faber, *Essays* 108: "The Reformed believer does not attempt to occupy the place of God in the last judgment." Here Faber alludes to 1 Corinthians 5:13, as do Kamphuis, *De Kerk* 57; Bos, *Orde* 275; and Bouma, *Kerkorde* 62.

already given about his rejection of baptism as administered by heretics. According to Cyprian, the command to eat the Passover lamb inside the house and not to take any of its meat outside it (Exodus 13:46) is another proof for his thesis. Finally, he points to the robe of Christ which remained undivided when He was crucified — another case of allegorical exegesis.

Our conclusion is that it is impossible for us to read all these things into our Confession and that Cyprian cannot help us to understand the rule "outside the Church there is no salvation."

He even fuelled the ideas of the Donatists, those schismatics who considered themselves exclusively to be the true catholic Church[135] and based this idea on, among other things, the Song of Solomon: There is only one bride, only one Church!

Augustine

The next person whose name we must mention in this context is Aurelius Augustine, bishop of Hippo Regius. He too used the same thesis, though in a more balanced way.

His starting-point was that according to Colossians 1:24 the Church is Christ's body. Those who are not members of Christ cannot have the salvation which is in Christ. No one will reach eternal life unless he has Christ as his Head, and therefore he must be a member of His body, the Church. Those who are outside the Church miss the gift of the Holy Spirit and love (1 Corinthians 13). The Holy Spirit is only received in the Church. Those who are outside do not enjoy God's love. There is no salvation outside the Church, for whoever does not love the unity of the Church does not have God's love either. There is another side as well. This love can also be lacking within the Church. The empirical Church is God's threshing floor: there are also hypocrites within it. The salvation which is in Christ is not appreciated and received by each and everyone.[136]

Although Augustine used the same phrase as Origen and Cyprian, he based it more soundly on the Scriptures.

Calvin

John Calvin mentions Cyprian's name in his *Institutes* several times. He quoted quite frequently from Augustine's work. Yet it is remarkable that, when he alludes to the rule about *nulla salus*, these two names are not mentioned. This does not mean, however, that these ancient authors did not influence Calvin at this point. In Book 4 of his *Institutes,* he writes extensively on the Church. At the beginning of this book, he says, "What God has thus joined, let not man put asunder (Mark x.9): to those to whom he is a Father, the Church must also be a mother" (IV.i.1).

There is a considerable difference between Calvin and Cyprian, however. Whereas the latter started with the Church — "A person cannot have God as a Father unless he first has the Church as a mother" — Calvin mentions God the

---

[135] For a clear exposition of the teachings and claims of Donatism, see Faber, *Lectures* 12ff.
[136] Faber, *Vestigium Ecclesiae* 137.

Father first of all and only then speaks of the Church. Therefore he can also write later in the same chapter: "Let us learn, from her single title of Mother, how useful, nay, how necessary the knowledge of her is, since there is no other means of entering into life unless she conceive us in the womb and give us birth, unless she nourish us at her breasts, and, in short, keep us under her charge and government, until, divested of mortal flesh, we become like the angels (Matth. xxii.30). For our weakness does not permit us to leave the school until we have spent our whole lives as scholars. Moreover, beyond the pale of the Church no forgiveness of sins, no salvation, can be hoped for . . ." (*Institutes* IV.i.4). Therefore, one can put the well-known rule into the negative, "the abandonment of the Church is always fatal" (IV.i.4).

Cyprian's influence is also clear when, in the previous paragraph, Calvin writes: "We may add, that so long as we continue in the bosom of the Church, we are sure that the truth will remain with us. Lastly, we feel that we have an interest in such promises as these, 'In Mount Zion and in Jerusalem shall be deliverance' (Joel ii.32; Obadiah 17); 'God is in the midst of her, she shall not be moved' (Psalm xlvi.5)" (IV.i.3). Here some Scriptural proof is presented.

Augustine's influence can be traced in the Catechism of Geneva (1541), written by Calvin. There he asks why the article on the forgiveness of sins in the Apostles' Creed follows immediately after that on the Church. The answer is, "Because no man obtains pardon for his sins without being previously incorporated into the people of God, persevering in unity and communion with the Body of Christ in such a way as to be a true member of the Church."

He continues with the question, "And so outside the Church there is nothing but damnation and death?" The answer is, "Certainly, for all those who separate themselves from the community of the faithful to form a sect on its own have no hope of salvation as long as they are in schism."[137]

Returning to his *Institutes,* finally, we note that, in the context of the believer's duty to stay within the Church or to join it, Calvin strongly emphasizes the great significance of attending the worship services and listening to the preaching of God's Word.[138]

Others

The Belgic Confession is not the only document that quotes the well-known saying. It was used in various countries, even before this Confession was compiled.

In his *Godly Confession and Protestation of the Christian Faith*, John Hooper — one of the English martyrs, executed on February 9, 1555 — points to "the external and visible Church of Christ . . . a visible congregation of men and women that hear the gospel of Christ, and use His sacraments as He hath instituted them: in the which congregation the Spirit of God worketh salvation of all believers, as St. Paul saith, 'The gospel is the power of God to the salvation of the believers.' " Here the phrase from Cyprian is applied to the "visible Church"

---

[137] Torrance, *School of Faith* 21.

[138] "Pride, or fastidiousness, or emulation, induces many to persuade themselves that they can profit sufficiently by reading and meditating in private, and thus to despise public meetings, and deem preaching superfluous. But since as much as in them lies they loose or burst the sacred bond of unity, none of them escapes the just punishment of this impious divorce . . ." (*Institutes* IV.i.5).

with its preaching and sacraments, the marks of the true Church. It is used in the same context as in the Belgic Confession of Faith: "Unto the which Church I would all Christian men should associate themselves, although there may happen to be some things desired in manners and discipline."[139] We gratefully note his reference to the means of grace found in the Church: the preaching and the administration of the sacraments.

Virtually the same thing was said by Thomas Causton and Thomas Higbed before they were burned at the stake on March 26, 1555: Beside Christ, the chief cornerstone, there is no Saviour. " 'Neither is there salvation,' saith St. Peter, 'in any other name.' . . . We believe that the Church of Christ teacheth the Word of God truly and sincerely, putting nothing to, nor taking any thing from: and also doth minister the sacraments according to the primitive church."[140] Here a clear interpretation of the *nulla salus* is presented: Salvation is found wherever the marks of the true Church are manifested.

We may also mention the Scottish Confession of 1560 which has the following sentences: "Out of this Kirk there is neither life nor eternal felicity." It bases this claim on the fact that there "is neither life nor salvation without Jesus Christ" (Chap. XVI). In Chapter XVIII, it explains that this Church is known from its "notes" (marks).

Henry Bullinger, Ulrich Zwingli's successor in Zurich, wrote the following in the Second Helvetic Confession of 1566: "Outside the Church of God there is no salvation. But we esteem fellowship with the true Church of Christ so highly that we deny that those can live before God who do not stand in fellowship with the true Church of God, but separate themselves from it. For as there was no salvation outside Noah's ark when the world perished in the Flood, so we believe that there is no certain salvation outside Christ, Who offers Himself to be enjoyed by the elect in the Church, and hence we teach that those who wish to live ought not to be separated from the true Church of Christ" (Chap. XVII).

The *nulla salus* appears here again, based on that other thesis: There is no salvation outside Christ. In this respect Bullinger followed the example of Zwingli, who wrote in his Sixty-Seven Articles of 1523, "He [Christ Jesus] is the salvation and Head of all believers, who are His body and without Him are dead and cannot do anything" (Art. 7).

Some centuries later, A. Rotterdam wrote that the Church is the city of the living God (Hebrews 12:22). He does not dwell outside it. Those who want to be saved must be inside (Revelation 22:14-15). In the second place — and we recognize this! — the Church is the body of Christ with Him as its Head, and salvation cannot be found in any other body (Ephesians 4:12-16). Salvation will be enjoyed only at the marriage feast of the Lamb (Revelation 19:2). The Church is also a house of God (1 Timothy 3:15), Christ being the cornerstone (Ephesians 2:21-22). There is no peace or salvation for those who are not living stones of this building.[141]

---

[139] Iain H. Murray, ed., *The Reformation of the Church: A Collection of Reformed and Puritan Documents on Church Issues* (Edinburgh: Banner of Truth, 1965) 18.

[140] Murray, *Reformation* 21f.

[141] Rotterdam, *Van Zions Roem en Sterkte* 2:169f.

History in a nutshell

At this point, we pause to summarize the preceding historical survey. The first person who used the phrase "Outside the Church there is no salvation" was Origen (185-254). He used it to make clear that this is the norm set for us by God. For our salvation's sake we must stay in the Church or join it. It may be that he emphasized this point in defense of the Christian faith against attacks lodged by pagans such as his arch-enemy Celsus.

Cyprian, who lived in the same era, used the phrase in his plea for church unity. He even went so far as to put the Church before God: "A person cannot have God as a Father unless he first has the Church as a mother." There was a strongly hierarchical trend in his thinking: the validity of baptism depended on the faithfulness of the person who administered it ("outside the Church there is no baptism"). It is no wonder that this provided fuel to the Donatists, who were, in their own opinion, the true catholic Church of those days, as evidenced by their alleged "holiness."

Augustine, however, based this saying on the fact that the Church is the body of Christ. This means that he strongly emphasized the bond between Christ and His Church. Those who speak of the Church speak of Christ, and only in this name is there salvation.

This relationship was also essential to John Calvin's view. In the Church, the truth is proclaimed. God's promises are preached there and forgiveness of sins is distributed. All of this speaks of Christ and His treasures and gifts of grace. The Church is Christ's body.

Others who used this saying in the time of the Reformation connected it with the means of grace. In the Church, God's Word is proclaimed and the sacraments are administered in the name of Christ, who is the Head of the Church. There is no salvation except in Christ (Acts 4:12). Being outside the Church, in the thinking of Zwingli, Bullinger, and many martyrs, is virtually the same as being outside Christ.

The confessional context

After all of this it may be unnecessary to say much about the context in which this sentence must be read. This part of the first sentence of Article 28 is a kind of introduction to what this article intends to make clear, namely that the unity of the Church spoken of in Article 27 must be maintained. Every believer should be in the Church: those who are already inside must remain there, and those who are not — Nicodemites and others — should join it, for that is God's ordinance! Therefore we must read that first line in the context of what can be called the norm for every believer. This line is meant in a normative sense.[142]

---

[142] Faber, *Essays* 108.

It should be noted that those who are addressed in this article — whether members of the true Church, Nicodemites, or others — are all believers. This is the ground on which they are exhorted to do what this article so strongly emphasizes.

As for other applications of the *nulla salus* rule, we must be careful when we are using it in other situations. This is especially true with regard to our claim to be true churches. An application such as, "In our country we have not found yet another true church, so that there is no salvation in any other church except our own," can be based on ignorance and even unwillingness to deal seriously with the churches that have been placed on our path. The unsurveyability of Christ's work of gathering His Church and the catholicity of the Church in fulfilment of God's promise to Abraham should play a stronger role in our thinking and in our activities of faith.

Conclusions

From all of this material we can now draw a number of conclusions.

The first conclusion is that in the course of Church history the well-known rule, *extra ecclesiam nulla salus*, has been used rather frequently. It was not always used in accordance with the intention of the person or persons who developed this saying in ancient times, however. Cyprian used it in such a way that the Donatists could build on him when, in their narrow-mindedness, they limited the Church to their own exclusive group. From this period in Church history it should be clear how dangerous it is to make one's own church life and not the catholicity of the Church one's starting-point. Ultimately it is a matter of faith: do we really believe the catholic Church?

By way of John Calvin, this sentence ended up in the Belgic Confession of Faith. Other confessions, either official or personal, also include it.

Most of the proof texts which various people have presented for this saying are unacceptable. One exception, however, is when the thesis is based on the Scriptural concept that there is no salvation without Jesus Christ. Remarkably no reference is made in this context to Acts 4:12, "Salvation is found in no one else, for there is no other name under heaven given to men by which we must be saved."

This focus on Christ, then, is basic to a good understanding of what is meant by "there is no salvation outside of it." Surely, the Church is the assembly of the redeemed. Those who really belong to the Church have already found their salvation in Jesus Christ. Yet — as we shall soon see in the same article — these people must submit themselves to its instruction and discipline. Though they are saved, the redeemed are, at the same time, people who need support and the strengthening of their faith. They are daily in need of the forgiveness of their sins, this essential element in their salvation.

John Calvin refers to the title "mother" which has been given to the Church (Galatians 4:26), not only because "there is no other means of entering into life unless she conceive us in the womb and give us birth," but also because she "nourish[es] us at her breasts, and, in short, keep[s] us under her charge and government" (*Institutes* IV.i.4).

We need the Church, with its tasks and functions which have been established by Christ Himself, so that we "may grow up in all things into Him Who is the Head — Christ" (Ephesians 4:15).

The redeemed mentioned in the previous line in our Confession must be redeemed further![143]

Why is there no salvation outside the Church? And what does it mean to say "no salvation"? Salvation cannot be found outside the Church because there Christ's name is proclaimed. There the gospel is preached as Christ Himself and the apostles after Him preached it. In that Church, the promises of the gospel are confirmed and sealed to the hearts and souls of the people by the administration of the sacraments as Christ has instituted them.

What does it mean that there is no salvation outside the Church? It means that in a church that is built on what the apostles have preached and taught we are given guidance in the process of our salvation — the process of our daily justification and sanctification, of our growth in faith — until after this life we reach the goal of perfection. In the true Church we can hear the full gospel of our entire salvation.

This blessing is missing in unfaithful churches — or "sects," as our Confession calls them — of which the false church is an extreme example of decay. They are endangering spiritual life. The proper guidance in the process of our salvation is lacking there.

---

[143] This may explain why the old Dutch version had *dergenen die zalig worden* ("of those who will be saved"), the current version has *degenen die behouden worden* ("of those who will be saved"), and Festus Hommius in his Latin translation calls them the *servandorum* ("those who must be saved"), and why the French version, on the other hand, speaks of *des sauvez* ("the redeemed"). Those who have been saved must be redeemed further, and therefore they need the Church, their "mother," because in the Church God's grace in Christ is proclaimed and given.

I. de Wolff writes: "We have to take the words of the confession literally. The confession does not say that outside the Church no one shall be saved, but that outside of it there is no salvation. That is not the same thing. The meaning is: God does not give salvation to the world, not to the false church, which twists and violates the gospel through a lying and deceptive preaching, which is false prophecy and not a power of salvation — but to the true Church, where He wants to live with His Word and Spirit, as it is also said of that Church that is an assembly of those who are saved. Salvation, therefore, has to be sought there where *God* gives it, and that is not outside the Church but in the Church; just as He has also given Christ to be Head of the Church, and has poured out the Holy Spirit in the midst of it, and has given His Word to it, — so likewise salvation. This is the general rule. The confession does not say that those who do not do this, will not be saved. It states only that such people act 'contrary to the ordinance of God' " (*The Church: Notes on Articles 27-29 of the Belgic Confession* [London, Ontario: Inter-League Publication Board, n.d.] 15f.).

"Salvation"

Besides all of this, we should not forget to ask — and answer — the question: What is actually meant by salvation in the sentence "Outside the Church there is no salvation"?

Allow me to begin with a personal story.

In 1943, at my preparatory examination by the Classis to which I belonged, I had to deliver a "sermon" on Acts 4:12, where the apostle Peter proclaims to the Jewish Supreme Court, "Nor is there salvation in any other, for there is no other name under heaven given among men by which we must be saved." In that "sermon" I had explained that "salvation" includes more than forgiveness of sins and going to heaven. The story is about a man healed from a serious physical handicap. During the subsequent examination, one of the ministers more or less objected to my calling this "salvation" since, according to Lord's Day 21 of our Catechism, salvation consists of the forgiveness of sins.

The same reduction of the Scriptural word "salvation" takes place when we read the sentence about "no salvation" in Article 28 as if it refers to being barred from going to heaven, or anything like that.

The Belgic Confession can help us to understand clearly what "salvation" really means. This term appears elsewhere in the confession.

For a good understanding of the term, we do not need to go back any farther than to the first sentence of Article 27. There it says that the Church consists of "the true Christian believers, who expect their entire salvation in Jesus Christ." Note the words "expect" and "entire"! In other words, the believers are in the process of being saved. A process is going on! This is confirmed by what follows in Article 27: they "are washed by His blood, and are sanctified and sealed by the Holy Spirit." The process of being washed, assured, and sealed is ongoing. Certainly, it had a beginning, which was of the greatest significance.[144] This beginning, however, must be repeated time and again — just as our (first) conversion must be followed up by daily conversion. What our Confession intends to underline, therefore, is that in order to undergo this process believers must be in the Church!

As we flip through our Confession, we find some more passages which contain the term "salvation" or similar words. We should pay particular attention to Article 7. There we read first "that all that man must believe in order to be saved is sufficiently taught" in Holy Scripture. The next sentence assures us that the "whole manner of worship which God requires of us is written in it at length." "Worship" here is intended as a synonym to "salvation." Or rather: We are saved in order to worship God, as He requires of us in His Word. And by "worship" we must not understand only what we

---

[144] This may explain why the English text in the *Book of Praise* has "the redeemed." This is in harmony with the original French version which has *sauvez*. In Article 27, on the other hand, the French text has *estans lavez* which has correctly been translated in the *Book of Praise* as "are washed."

do in church — praising God in our songs, prayers, and confession. The original French word (*service*) could also be translated "service." Besides, the same article also refers to the doctrine of the Scriptures, and this doctrine includes, for example, that as a result of original sin we spoil our whole lives by committing daily sins (Art. 15), and also that "true faith, worked in man by the hearing of God's Word and by the operation of the Holy Spirit, regenerates him and makes him a new man. It makes him live a new life and frees him from the slavery of sin" (Art. 24). Slavery to sin is the opposite of serving God. In Christ we find "complete salvation" (Art. 22): justification in His blood, but also sanctification by His Spirit.[145] Article 18 emphasizes that salvation has regard not only to the soul but also to the body.

From all of this we may draw the conclusion that the salvation which cannot be found outside the Church includes more than forgiveness of (past and present) sins and the expected (future) eternal happiness in heaven and on the new earth.

This ongoing process[146] is to be kept alive by the means of grace which function in the Church. That is why the marks of the (true) Church are so important. Those who believe in the Lord Jesus Christ must time and again be washed by His blood and be assured and sealed by His Spirit. Here the preaching of God's Word is all important. We need it. It is essential to receive the assurance and seal of the sacraments. Even supervision is needed, the administration of both keys of the Kingdom of heaven. A little farther on in Article 28, this is repeated and confirmed when it says that all must submit to the doctrine and discipline of the Church and to the yoke of Christ. Then their positive contribution to the edification of their brothers and sisters is mentioned, too. They are expected to contribute to the "salvation" of their fellow-believers.

This process is what cannot be found outside the Church. Even in the sects mentioned in Article 29, pet ideas are dominant — never mind that in the false church the means of grace are no more than a bad caricature! That this process takes place in the Church is God's ordinance and He has bound us to it as the norm with which we have to comply. How He works in the hearts of those who are "outside," in other churches and religious groups ("sects," as they all are called in Article 29) and even in the false church — we would not deny that the Lord may have some children there — we must leave to Him. We know that the wind of the Holy Spirit blows where it wishes (John 3:8). The gathering of the Church is a divine work which we cannot perceive. Not everything has been revealed to us and many questions must therefore be left unanswered and perhaps should not even be asked, but we are bound to the norm, and this norm is clearly expressed in our Confession.

---

[145] Note also Article 14: "Apart from Me you can do nothing." Furthermore consider how "salvation" and similar words are used Articles 9, 17, 18, 22, 23, 24, and 26.

[146] For this ongoing process, see also the Heidelberg Catechism, Lord's Day 44, with its repeated "more and more" and "the goal of perfection."

The Second Helvetic Confession shows us in a beautiful way what it means that there is no salvation without Christ. It says, "we believe that there is no certain salvation outside Christ, who offers Himself to be enjoyed by the elect in the Church; and hence we teach that those who wish to live ought not to be separated from the true Church of Christ" (Chap. XVII).[147] In other words, Christ gathers His people in order that they may enjoy Him and all His benefits and blessings, and therefore we must be living members of His Church, for it is there that He gathers us.[148]

No proof texts?

Once again we are confronted with a difficulty. The oldest Dutch edition had no proof texts here. This could mean that in quoting this sentence from other sources the Confession intends to refer to the Scriptural proof presented by those who used it in the ancient literature. The 1580 edition of the French version of our Confession, however, has Joel 2:32 and 1 Peter 3:20 here. Because of this uncertainty we reprint them here. They render excellent proof for the English rendering of the thesis we have been considering: *extra ecclesiam nulla salus*.

In Joel 2:32 we read, "And it shall come to pass that whoever calls on the name of the LORD shall be saved. For on Mount Zion and in Jerusalem there shall be deliverance, as the LORD has said, among the remnant whom the LORD calls." And 1 Peter 3:20 says, "... who [the spirits in prison] formerly were disobedient, when once the Divine longsuffering waited in the days of Noah,

---

[147] This Confession continues: "Nevertheless, by the signs [of the true Church] mentioned above, we do not so narrowly restrict the Church as to teach that all those are outside the Church who either do not participate in the sacraments, at least not willingly and through contempt, but rather forced by necessity, unwillingly abstain from them or are deprived of them, or in whom faith sometimes fails, though it is not entirely extinguished and does not wholly cease; or in whom imperfections and errors due to weakness are found. For we know that God had some friends in the world outside the commonwealth of Israel. We know what befell the people of God in the captivity of Babylon, where they were deprived of these sacrifices for seventy years. We know what happened to St. Peter, who denied his Master, and what is wont to happen daily to God's elect and faithful people who go astray and are weak. We know, moreover, what kind of churches the churches in Galatia and Corinth were in the apostles' time, in which the apostle found fault with many serious offenses; yet he calls them holy churches of Christ (1 Corinthians 1:2; Galatians 1:2)" (Chap. XVII). We are presented with a serious warning here not to use simplistically (or rather, misuse) the rule that says *extra ecclesiam nulla salus*. We must be careful with our way of "reasoning" which concludes that those who withdraw themselves and, for example, join another church no longer have communion with Christ and do not share in His treasures and gifts. Such a thing can be said only in cases of ultimate hardening in sin when we have followed the whole procedure for discipline adopted by our churches and set forth in the Church Order and the liturgical forms. Besides, "God judges those outside" (1 Corinthians 5:13). From the days of the Reformation, this apostolic rule has been applied to these cases of withdrawal.

[148] This interpretation of the *nulla salus* clause runs parallel to that of K. Schilder, who, in his *Christelijke Religie*, emphasizes the gathering work of Christ and draws from it the conclusion that salvation can be expected only where the Lord Jesus brings and keeps His flock together. Schilder bases this understanding on the Latin version of the Confession, which (in our translation) calls the Church "the assembly of those who must be redeemed" (note the gerundive: *servandorum*). Although the Latin version is not authentic and the text of the Belgic Confession does not present a formal basis for this interpretation, it does touch the heart of the matter. See also d'Assonville, *K. Schilder* 68f.

while the ark was being prepared, in which a few, that is eight souls, were saved through water." As we shall learn shortly, this verse in Peter's first epistle is the classical proof text for the sentence under discussion.

For the following reasons, however, we can more or less sidestep the issue of the proof texts. First of all, we should remember that the two words with which this article opens, "We believe," are an abbreviation of the line with which the whole Confession is introduced: "We all believe with the heart and confess with the mouth," a line which, as we have seen, has been taken from Romans 10:10, which says: "For with the heart one believes to righteousness, and with the mouth confession is made to salvation." This faith is faith in Christ, as the previous verse says: "If you confess with your mouth the Lord Jesus . . . you will be saved." The words "no salvation" rest upon this Scriptural truth!

In the second place, we should not forget that this line in the Confession is part of a longer sentence and begins with "since." This means that it is part of a causal subordinate clause, the main clause being, "We believe . . . that no one ought to withdraw from it."

This is the new element in what the Confession wants to state about the Church. What the subordinate clause says is a repetition or summary of what we have confessed in the previous article. It offers the ground for the "message" of Article 28, saying as it were: We have now learned what the Church is — the Church is nothing apart from Christ, and He is central in every respect — and therefore it should be clear that there is no salvation apart from the Church, and therefore no one ought to withdraw from it.

In other words, if the proof texts have already been presented in Article 27, then there is no reason to repeat them. On the other hand, if Joel 2:32 and 1 Peter 3:20 act as proof texts here, they clearly confirm the interpretation given by other confessions: there is no salvation without Christ, and therefore there is none outside the Church either.

We can put things in the negative as well: What can we expect outside of the Church, in the sects — those groups that follow their leaders in their deviations from the Scriptural truth — let alone in a false church? Would we be safe as far as the preaching of the gospel, the sealing of our forgiveness, and our sanctification are concerned?[149]

---

[149] Kamphuis, *De Kerk* 46 (translation mine): "The exclusivity of 'no salvation outside of it' is rooted in the exclusivity of the Gospel of Jesus Christ, the proclamation of which has been entrusted to the Church" (De exclusiviteit van het "buiten haar is geen heil" is geworteld in de exclusiviteit van het Evangelie van Jezus Christus, dat aan de kerk ter verkondiging is toevertrouwd).
See also De Wolff, *The Church* 14f.

"THAT NO ONE OUGHT TO WITHDRAW FROM IT, CONTENT TO BE BY HIMSELF"

We believe, since this holy assembly and congregation is the assembly of the redeemed and there is no salvation outside of it, that no one ought to withdraw from it, content to be by himself, no matter what his state or quality may be.

The appeal

The first lines of Article 28, which are a subordinate clause, present a brief summary of what we confess about the Church in the previous article. They do so deliberately, with a clear purpose. They act as the ground on the basis of which an appeal is made. This appeal, then, is made in the main clause: No one should step aside or stay away from the Church.

Withdrawal

The focus here is, first of all, upon those who are members of the Church. An appeal is made to them not to withdraw from the Church. Historically, our Confession has a particular kind of people in mind and thereby shows that the Scriptural fundamentals regarding the Church are applicable to a real situation.

Guido de Brès called the attention of the believers to the false spiritualism found in the circles of the Anabaptists. These people were indeed content to be by themselves. They did not need the Church at all, for did they not have "the inner light"? Compared with the average believer, they considered themselves far superior. Therefore it is no wonder that among the Anabaptists schism after schism took place, so that in the long run they were "by themselves." They did not need anyone else, let alone the Church, to satisfy their spiritual needs! That this behaviour is a serious neglect of "the means of grace" — the preaching of God's Word, the administration of the sacraments, and even the communion of saints in its mutual support and supervision — is obvious. Even though this sentence is somewhat historical, our Confession here appears to be relevant to situations which can arise — and do indeed arise — in our day and age. Today, too, some people consider the Church to be of minor importance, and consequently they have no problem in withdrawing if they do not feel their needs satisfied in one way or another.

Home readers

John Calvin must have had the same people in mind when he wrote about "home readers" in several of his books. We repeat what we quoted from his *Institutes* earlier: "Pride, or fastidiousness, or emulation, induces many to persuade themselves that they can profit sufficiently by reading and meditating in private, and thus to despise public meetings, and deem preaching superfluous" (IV.i.5)

In his Geneva Catechism of 1541, he answers the question, "Do you mean that it is not enough for people to read it [the Word of God] privately at home, without altogether hearing its teaching in common?" by stating, "That is just what I mean, while God provides the way for it."[150]

In the days of the Reformation the warning was urgently needed: For your salvation's sake, do not withdraw from the Church with its offices and functions! The same warning is still relevant to today's situation in which some people withdraw from the Church for different reasons but mostly because they have complaints about the human aspect of church life. It is hardly superfluous to emphasize at this point how important it is to ensure that our human actions in church life do not put a stumbling block in the path of our fellow church members.

"NO MATTER WHAT HIS STATUS OR STANDING MAY BE"

The communion of saints

We confess that the Church is the communion of saints. Biblical examples show us that these saints are not all the same. In the apostolic Church there were converted Jews as well as former gentiles, with their different cultural and religious backgrounds. Sometimes this diversity led to tensions (Acts 11:2f; 15:1f.; Galatians 2:11-14). In the Corinthian congregation there were "strong brothers" and "weak brothers," and this resulted in problems (1 Corinthians 8). In the same congregation there were rich people as well as poor, which led to a kind of polarization even on the occasion of the celebration of the Lord's Supper, which was combined with the so-called love-meal (*agapè*) (1 Corinthians 11:20ff.).

In the days of the Reformation there was the same danger that the communion of saints would be damaged by class distinctions. It was therefore not for nothing that John Calvin addressed many high-placed persons such as

---

[150] Torrance, *School of Faith* 53.

kings and queens, princes and princesses, urging them to join the Reformed or promote the cause of the Reformation.

As for our Confession, a letter which accompanied its original editions urged the "lower" civil authorities to break with the Church of Rome and join the Reformed. The Confession calls everyone to the preservation of the Church as the communion of saints.

Here what we call "the fourth aim of our Confession" comes to the fore. Those who take a high position in the nation or in society are also called to honour and maintain the unity of the Church. The same is true of other groups, for example, people who are highly intelligent. Our Confession wants to prevent the infiltration into church life of a kind of "apartheid." It wants to protect the Church as the communion of saints.[151]

"BUT ALL AND EVERYONE ARE OBLIGED TO JOIN IT AND UNITE WITH IT, MAINTAINING THE UNITY OF THE CHURCH"

"All"

When we discussed the sentence in Article 27 which defines the Church as "a holy congregation and assembly of the true Christian believers," we learned from the proof texts that our Confession, just like Christ Himself, has all believers in mind. One day — the last day — they will have been gathered together into one flock. It is no wonder that this last day is sometimes characterized as the day "when even the very last one of the elect will have been added." It is no wonder either that Festus Hommius, in his Latin translation, added the word *omnium* (all) to the text: the Church is a holy congregation and assembly of *all* true Christian believers.

This concept recurs here in Article 28: "all and everyone."

We may say it again: The Confession does not deny that there are believers outside the Church, but they are urged to join it, for their salvation's sake.

Obligation

The context in which this "all" recurs, however, is different. The context here is that of human responsibility. Here we see something of a parallel with

---

[151] Trimp, "Our responsibility for the community," *The Church.*

God's covenant. In that covenant there is not only the divine work by which God seals His promises and makes them come true but also the aspect of human responsibility, obligations. Christ is gathering the one holy catholic and apostolic Church, but man has to honour this great work either by faithfully staying within the Church or by joining it.

The Church is one. This is something very significant which we have already confessed. Christ is gathering one Church only, but from our human side we can be disobedient to Him by staying away, and this is why our Confession says that we must maintain the unity of the Church. It is a matter of faith, faith in Christ. The "all and everyone" of Article 28 were defined in the previous article as "true Christian believers, who expect their entire salvation in Jesus Christ, are washed by His blood, and are sanctified and sealed by the Holy Spirit." They belong to Him. They love Him. To maintain the unity of the Church is to demonstrate this love, to honour His work.

"Maintaining"

The latest version of the Confession as adopted by our Dutch sister churches makes it perfectly clear what is meant by the last line of the sentence under discussion: "maintaining the unity of the Church." This version starts a new sentence here, which can be translated: "In this way the unity of the Church is maintained."

This is very important, because Scripture teaches us that maintaining unity is an apostolic command. In Ephesians 4:3, the apostle Paul says that we must be "endeavouring to keep the unity of the Spirit in the bond of peace." The Confession enjoins this duty on every believer but particularly on the Nicodemites who remained in the Church of Rome. They were shown that their attitude was in disharmony with this apostolic command. Even though they claimed that they — and not the Reformed — were maintaining the unity of the Church, they stayed in a community in which the apostolic teachings were no longer heard.

This point is explained further in the next sentence: "They must submit themselves to its instruction and discipline."[152]

Implications

Our churches are not the only ones involved in all kinds of contacts — and even efforts to unite — with other churches. Discussions and correspondence usually go on for a long time. This is understandable as long as it is not

---

[152] The Dutch version has joined these two sentences together. In translation it reads: "In this way the unity of the Church is maintained: they submit themselves to its instruction and discipline." This version shows us how the unity of the Church is maintained.

completely clear whether we are really united in the same faith. When there really is this unity, however, our mutual love for the Lord Jesus Christ and our common respect for His work of gathering His Church must make us well aware of the responsibilities we, as churches, have — responsibilities which oblige us to make progress.

If there are disappointments in this respect, they should not be our fault.

"THEY MUST SUBMIT THEMSELVES TO ITS INSTRUCTION AND DISCIPLINE"

They must submit themselves to its instruction and discipline, bend their necks under the yoke of Jesus Christ, and serve the edification of the brothers and sisters, according to the talents which God has given them as members of the same body.

Unity

The unity of the Church must be maintained. This is indeed how the original French and Dutch versions can be translated. From the previous paragraph, however, it should be clear that we prefer to delete the verb "must" and consider this sentence to be an explanation of how this unity is maintained: by submitting to its instruction and discipline.

This line shows us that Church unity is not something vague and mysterious. It can be seen. It can be experienced. One maintains the unity of the Church not only by joining it, but, in particular, by showing oneself to be a living member of the Church by eagerly listening to what it teaches from the pulpit, in the catechism-room, and in the home! This is done corporately, as is submitting to the discipline of the Church, which is the discipline of the gospel.

"Instruction and discipline"

When we read here that true believers "must submit themselves to its [the Church's] instruction and discipline," we could easily think that what is in view here is what we call "Church discipline." More than that is included in the word "discipline," however.

The way in which Festus Hommius translated this line in his Latin version of the Confession may make clear to us the wider sense in which the term *disciplina* was used in those days. Hommius had *doctrina et disciplina*, and this translation is in full harmony with the original meaning of the word "discipline."

This original meaning can be heard in "the Great Commission," when Christ told His apostles-to-be, "Go therefore and make disciples of all the nations, baptizing them into the name of the Father and of the Son and of the Holy Spirit, teaching them to observe all things that I have commanded you" (Matthew 28:19-20a).

In that saying of Christ we hear about both *doctrina* and *disciplina*: the nations must be told about the triune God and His works (*doctrina*) and taught what Christ had commanded the apostles (*disciplina*).[153] This, then, includes more than "Church discipline," which is only a special aspect of *disciplina*.[154]

It is therefore remarkable that we read in Article 28 about discipline and not about Church discipline — which will be mentioned in Article 29 as one of the marks of the true Church and will be explained further in Article 32.[155]

The implications which this close relationship between *doctrina* and *disciplina* has for the administration of Church discipline will be considered when we have dealt with the phrase "the yoke of Christ."

"BEND THEIR NECKS UNDER THE YOKE OF JESUS CHRIST"

Christ's yoke

The unity of faith must also become apparent in that all bend their necks under Christ's yoke. It is called "the yoke of Jesus Christ," and the mention of this name should remind every regular Bible-reader of Christ's own saying: "Come to Me, all you who labour and are heavy laden, and I will give you rest. Take My yoke upon you and learn from Me, for I am gentle and lowly in heart,

---

[153] In the days of the Reformation, *doctrina* and *disciplina* together were included in the phrase "the yoke of Christ," as we shall learn when we deal with the next line of our Confession.

[154] The close relationship between *doctrina* and *disciplina* may also explain why only two marks of the true Church are mentioned in a number of confessional documents. This is the case in the Augsburg Confession (1530), in John Calvin's Geneva Confession (1536), in his *Institutes* (IV.i.9-12), and in the Thirty-Nine Articles of the Church of England (Art. 19). In the earlier stages the doctrine was strongly emphasized and discipline was hardly, if ever, mentioned. The former term contained all that was needed in order for one to be a faithful disciple of the Lord Jesus Christ. But when it became necessary and possible to organize a well-structured Church life — resulting, for example, in the convening of synods and the compiling of Church Orders — *disciplina*, which taught the way in which Christ's disciples must behave, was given separate attention, with "ecclesiastical discipline" (usually called "Church discipline" in English translations) being a special aspect of it.

[155] The relationship between *doctrina* and *disciplina* comes to the fore once again when Article 30 says that the "Spiritual order" (in the original: "Spiritual police") must "see to it that the true doctrine takes its course."

and you will find rest for your souls. For My yoke is easy and My burden is light" (Matthew 11:28-30).[156]

Here we see the fourth aim of our Confession, as the Confession reveals the tremendous benefit gained by listening and responding to the call to join the Church. It is Christ's own call, a call full of compassion for those who are burdened by different yokes — that of the Church of Rome with its wearisome religion,[157] or that of the Anabaptist contempt of the world.

Under Christ's yoke — which is so light, compared with the yokes invented by humans— salvation and rest are enjoyed indeed!

A light yoke

What is that yoke of Christ really? Of what does it consist? Of course, we could try to answer this question by searching in detail in all Christ's sayings in the gospels. There is, however, the danger that we may be inclined to emphasize the various rules and regulations set down by Christ. In the so-called "missionary command," He refers to all things that He has commanded (Matthew 28:20). The word "rest" in Christ's saying, however, shows us that more is involved than just the rules. After all, did Christ not say that He would build His Church upon the apostles as they confessed Him to be the Son of God, the promised Messiah (Matthew 16:18)?

We can learn what the yoke of Christ is, then, from the inheritance of the apostles as we possess it in the New Testament.

Origin in history

This is how the reformers used the phrase "the yoke of Jesus Christ."

The first to do so, as far as we know, was Martin Bucer, the reformer of Strasbourg. He taught that Christ Himself is actively present in the doctrine and discipline, and in submitting ourselves to them we submit to Christ's yoke.

In the first edition of his commentary on the gospels, published in 1538, Bucer wrote that Christ's yoke consists of teaching (*doctrina*) as well as of rules for one's discipleship (*disciplina*).[158] He spoke about this theme more often in sermons delivered in 1538 at Benfeld. In them, he said that Christ's *doctrina* and *disciplina* are administered within the congregation, and their presence is closely related to the answer to the question, "What and where is the true Church?"

---

[156] De Brès may have supposed that every reader of the Confession would have this saying in mind; it does not belong to the original proof texts.

[157] In Article 29's discussion of the false church, the words "the yoke of Jesus Christ" recur as "the yoke of Christ." The Church of Rome clearly shows how the false church imposes a burdensome yoke because "it does not want to submit itself to the yoke of Christ." It has laid the yoke of the Pope upon the people!

[158] Here the term "discipline" is clearly used in the original meaning. It is the way in which disciples of Christ are expected to live. This original meaning should never be forgotten when we use the term in the context of the Church Order and the forms for Church discipline!

Believers in Christ are led to grow in Christ by teaching and discipline, by a spiritual regime.

John Calvin followed Bucer in this respect. The Pope and his bishops put a different yoke upon their people instead of Christ's easy yoke, an act which is nothing less than tyranny since they propagate a wrong view of the relationship between the forgiveness of sins and renewal of life, between justification and sanctification.

In the Preface to his *Commentary on the Gospel According to John*, written on January 1, 1553, Calvin said that he, together with others, had tried to reform the *doctrina* as well as the *disciplina*, which go together.

In his *Institutes*, he speaks of "the authority of the doctrine" and of the edification of the Church "by external preaching," and says "that there is no other bond by which the saints are kept together than by uniting with one consent to observe the order which God has appointed in His Church for learning and making progress" (IV.i.5). *Doctrina* and *disciplina* are not mentioned explicitly here but they are obviously being referred to.

In his last sermon on Ephesians, he stated that the *communis doctrina* (the common doctrine) is the bond of unity. The unity of the Church is established wherever everyone submits to the *doctrina* and *disciplina* of the Church and so bends his neck to the yoke of Christ.

Finally, even on his deathbed Calvin spoke of *obsequium doctrinae*: the doctrine must be obeyed.[159]

Our Confession

To John Calvin we owe what we read in Article 28 of the Belgic Confession when it says that believers "(must) submit themselves to its instruction and discipline, [and] bend their necks under the yoke of Jesus Christ."

Calvin used the same terms: "bend their necks to the yoke of Christ." This phrase, however, was not derived directly from Calvin. A "detour" was made by way of the Confession of Faith adopted by the French Churches in 1559 — after John Calvin had given some advice. In this French Confession we find almost the same sentence: believers are expected to "submit to the public teaching, and to the yoke of Christ" (Art. 26).

Bucer, Calvin, and de Brès clearly saw that the yoke of the Pharisees had been brought back to life again in the yoke which the Pope had laid upon his people. It did not give rest to the souls, whereas the real yoke of Christ does. That yoke is His doctrine of salvation and the *disciplina* that is intended to keep the people in the salvation obtained for them.

So what our own Confession says about the "yoke of Christ" and about "discipline" in Article 28 has been derived, by way of the French Confession, from John Calvin and, going even farther back, from Martin Bucer, who led

---

[159] This summary of Bucer's and Calvin's interpretations of "the yoke of Christ" has been derived from W. van 't Spijker, ". . . Den hals buygende onder het jock Jesu Christi . . . ," *Bezield Verband* (Kampen: Van den Berg, 1984) 206-219. See also my *"True" and "False"* 52-54.

the people of his own day and us, as well, back to the Scriptures, to what Christ said about His easy yoke and light burden and to the two aspects of that yoke, *doctrina* and *disciplina*.

It should be clear that Article 28 should be read and applied in this way, and when Article 29 speaks of Church discipline — and when it does so it adds the word "Church" — we must not forget that Church discipline is a special aspect and application of discipline in the more general sense of the word.[160]

Implications

The "yoke of Christ" may also include a Scriptural church order — as the French Confession indicates when, immediately after it has mentioned the yoke of Christ, it refers to a good church order. Submission to this yoke or refusal to do so is the unbridgeable gulf between the true Church and the false church, as Article 29 of our Confession will explain.

Christ's yoke is light — the yoke of living in a Reformed congregation with its truly Reformed administration of God's Word, the sacraments, and Church discipline. Therefore it follows that life in a truly Reformed confederation of churches is not a heavy burden. It is incumbent on us, with our human responsibility, not to change this into synodocracy, consistoriocracy, ministeriocracy, and other forms of hierarchy.

Conclusions

Furthermore, we can draw a number of conclusions from all of this.

1. Because being a disciple of the Lord Jesus Christ includes gratefully receiving the *doctrina* and *disciplina* as they are taught and administered in Church, the *doctrina* and *disciplina* constitute the three marks whereby the true Church is known (since discipline, taken in its original meaning, also includes the administration of the sacraments as something which belongs to all the things that Christ commanded His disciples).

2. Church discipline is a special aspect of discipline in the general sense of the word. In turn, *disciplina* rests upon *doctrina*, which it often accompanies, as can be seen even in Article 28 of our own Confession. Therefore we must

---

[160] We can recognize the development from "discipline" to "Church discipline" in other Confessions, as well. After summing up the marks of the true Church, the First Helvetic Confession of 1534 deals with the "discipline" of Christ in Article 14 as we see it in the "rites" (German: *Ordnungen*) or ceremonies (we could think here of the institution of the two sacraments). In the same year, the term "discipline" was used in the specialized sense of Church discipline in the Geneva Confession, when it speaks of "discipline of excommunication" (Art. 19). The Confession of the English Congregation at Geneva (1556) has "ecclesiastical discipline" in Article 4, as does Chapter XVIII of the Scottish Confession of 1560. In the more general sense, however, the word "discipline" is again used in Chapter XVII of the Second Helvetic Confession of 1566.

not isolate Church discipline from the *disciplina* and *doctrina*. A reflection of this close relationship can be found in the emphasis which is put on the many admonitions which the Forms for Church discipline require. In Scripture, "to admonish" is to remind someone of and call someone back to the normal situation, back to the rule — to what the person concerned has been taught as a disciple of Christ, namely that he take upon himself the yoke of Christ. The way in which we administer Church discipline must be determined by the great context in which Christ has put it. Then the adopted rules for its administration will be applied in their proper Scriptural context, and no legitimate complaints about "lack of love" will be heard from the side of those who must be disciplined.

3. It should now be clear why our Confession refers to what Christ said about His yoke in Matthew 11:29-30. Those who submit to that yoke are not heavily burdened, unlike the people who allowed themselves to suffer under the yoke of the Pharisees and Scribes in the days when Christ was on earth and the many people who were — and still are — sighing under the human inventions and laws introduced (by the Pope) into the worship of God, which bind and compel the consciences (Art. 32).

4. All of this determines the structure of our church life as well. Christ is the only universal Bishop and the only Head of the Church (Art. 31). The Pope's claim to be the apostle Peter's successor as Christ's vicar here on earth is unacceptable. We do not need such a representative. Christ Himself — as we have learned from Martin Bucer — is actively present in the instruction and discipline of the Church!

"AND SERVE THE EDIFICATION OF THE BROTHERS AND SISTERS, ACCORDING TO THE TALENTS WHICH GOD HAS GIVEN THEM AS MEMBERS OF THE SAME BODY"

Communion of saints

We confess that the Church is the communion of saints. This means that it can lay claim to all the talents of its membership.

Whereas the previous line encourages those believers in Christ who are still outside to join the Church for their own salvation's sake, this line makes a positive appeal to them: the Church needs them. True believers are expected to be active in edifying one another.

Family language is used here: "brothers and sisters." We are very familiar with these terms — perhaps even too familiar, so that this kind of language no longer appeals to us. "Brothers" and "sisters" are terms used in the Scriptures, however. The Lord Jesus Himself addressed His followers in this way.[161] This was not even a new tradition, since the term "brothers" was often used in synagogue addresses,[162] the women not being taken into consideration. The Saviour, however, included the female believers as well, as did the Christian Church in the days of the apostles,[163] although at most places in the New Testament only the brothers are addressed.[164]

Proof text

The proof text on which our Confession is based at this point is Ephesians 4:12, "to prepare God's people for works of service, so that the body of Christ may be built up." It is true that the context indicates that this verse is speaking of those who have been entrusted with a special office in the Church. Verse 11 mentions apostles, prophets, evangelists, and pastors and teachers. But building up the Church is everyone's duty and privilege.[165]

The same apostle makes this perfectly clear when he tells the Christians in Rome that, as in one body there are many members and all these members do not have the same function, so it is within the Church, which is the body of Christ. Therefore the various gifts must be used (Romans 12:4-6). And together they are one body (1 Corinthians 12:14ff.). None of the members can be lacking.

The edification of the congregation is a favourite theme in the apostle Paul's epistles. He considered it to be his own task,[166] but it is also a community task (1 Thessalonians 5:11) which takes place through exhortation, encouragement, and stimulation.

It is remarkable that the same term is used here which characterized the addresses delivered in the synagogue meetings (Acts 13:15). It is also the name which the author of Hebrews gives to his own writing (Hebrews 13:22). The various aspects of this epistle make it clear what "edifying" the congregation consists of: comfort, encouragement, exhortation, and even admonishment, and all of this — as may be seen from the contents of Hebrews — by confronting one another with the gospel of the only Saviour.

---

[161] Matthew 12:50; Mark 3:35
[162] Acts 13:15, 26, 38
[163] 1 Corinthians 7:15; James 2:15
[164] e.g., Romans 1:13; 7:1; 10:1; 13:1; etc.
[165] As for the offices in Church, the Tetrapolitan Confession — written for the Diet of Augsburg (1530) by Martin Bucer with the help of Wolfgang Capito and Caspar Hedio in the name of the four imperial cities of Strasbourg, Constance, Memmingen, and Lindau — includes the following beautiful sentence in Chapter XIII: "Concerning the ministry and the dignity of the ecclesiastical order we teach, first, that there is no power in the Church except for edification."
[166] 2 Corinthians 10:8; 12:19; 13:10f.

Our approach to those outside: individually

Those who have not yet joined the Church are also called to this Christian task. It is true that Article 28 seriously warns them: "All therefore who draw away from the church or fail to join it act contrary to the ordinance of God." This warning is given in a Scriptural way, however. In Scripture, to admonish someone does not mean to tell him off, but to call him back to the rule set by God — in this case to God's ordinance regarding the unity of the Church.

Article 28 does just that: those who have not joined the Church are called back to the rule. The article has just said that there is no salvation outside the Church. For that reason, it is imperative that they join the true Church, for there their faith will be nourished by the pure administration of the gospel, the sacraments, and supervision or discipline. The Belgic Confession itself approaches the people concerned in a positive way.

We are not finished with these people when we observe that they are unfaithful in their relationship to the Church and in particular when we add that they are therefore not good Christians. First of all, we must always observe others' faults with modesty. After all, what about our own faults and imperfections? Furthermore, it is exactly this point of weakness in them — a dangerous point indeed — that should fill us with the desire to show them the way.

In other words, a positive approach is required and not the negative attitude which declares that they are wrong in regard to their relationship to the Church and that is the end of the matter!

Our approach to those outside: collectively

Our Confession is directed to all those who, together with us, believe in the same Lord as their Saviour. This focus has its implications for our approach to other churches as well. The call to maintain the unity of the Church can be made only on the basis of common faith. Whether this faith is expressed in different confessions and catechisms is of secondary importance so long as the contents do not differ substantially. Therefore, we must approach the other churches which the Lord God places in our path in the same positive way.

The first thing we must investigate in such a situation is whether these churches have a Scriptural confession and whether they really adhere to it. If so, then we can exchange further information and discuss points of difference. The matter of common faith is first and foremost, however, because only on this basis can differences be discussed and resolved.

In this connection we must take into account what Scripture teaches us about the way in which the Lord Jesus Christ, either in person or through His apostles, dealt with churches which clearly showed that they had not yet reached the goal of perfection.

In line with 1 Corinthians and Revelation 2 and 3, great Church leaders can still give us good guidance. For example, Aurelius Augustine states that the Church is God's threshing floor, where the chaff must be separated from the wheat, and John Calvin, in his *Institutes*, says that every church shows imperfections, one church even more than the other: "even in the administration of word and sacraments defects may creep in which ought not to alienate us from its communion" (IV.i.12).[167]

The point is not whether other churches are without any imperfections — what about our own churches? — but whether we confess the same God and the same divine works of the Triune God.[168]

---

[167] See also footnote 24.

[168] For "the same divine works of the Triune God," we may refer to the Heidelberg Catechism which, in Lord's Day 8, sums up the works of the three divine Persons by speaking of "God the Father and our creation," "God the Son and our redemption," and "God the Holy Spirit and our sanctification." In Article 9, the Belgic Confession gives a somewhat more elaborate definition: "The Father is called our Creator by His power; the Son is our Saviour and Redeemer by His blood; the Holy Spirit is our Sanctifier by His dwelling in our hearts." A substantial part of our Catechism — actually the whole of it, as well as the whole Belgic Confession — deals with each of the three divine Persons and His work. The Church, in particular, belongs to the works of the Son of God (Lord's Day 21) and to those of "God the Holy Spirit and our sanctification" (Lord's Day 20).

It should be clear that what we are saying does not mean that the common faith which we would like to discover that we share with other people and other churches can be written on a thumbnail. We refer also to what Dr. J. Faber writes in *The Liberation: Causes and Consequences* 115: "Basically, the doctrine of the Christian church is found in the Apostles' Creed. It is the summary of the gospel; it is the confession of God's covenant promise. These are the articles of our undoubted catholic faith. Therefore in our Reformed church life in Canada the Apostles' Creed had such a prominent place in the questions at baptism and public profession of faith. It underlined that what is taught in this christian church is not a denominational specialty but unfolding the catholic faith."

For confirmation of all of this, we must realize that the true Church was already introduced earlier in our Confession, in Article 9. There it says, "The doctrine of the Holy Trinity has always been maintained and preserved in the true Church since the time of the apostles to this very day, over against Jews, Muslims, and against false christians and heretics such as Marcion, Mani, Praxeas, Sabellius, Paul of Samosata, Arius, and such like. . . . In this doctrine, therefore, we willingly receive the three creeds, of the Apostles, of Nicea, and of Athanasius. . . ."

"TO OBSERVE THIS MORE EFFECTIVELY, IT IS THE DUTY OF ALL BELIEVERS, ACCORDING TO THE WORD OF GOD, TO SEPARATE FROM THOSE WHO DO NOT BELONG TO THE CHURCH"

To observe this more effectively, it is the duty of all believers, according to the Word of God, to separate from those who do not belong to the Church, and to join this assembly wherever God has established it. They should do so even though the rulers and edicts of princes were against it, and death or physical punishment might follow.

"This"

This sentence mentions another duty of the believers, that of separating from those who do not belong to the Church.

It seems as if this line contradicts what we confessed before — the duty of all believers to unite with the Church and maintain its unity. Are not "unity" and "separation" contrasting things?

To answer this question, we must not forget what was stated immediately prior to this sentence. What is to be observed more effectively is "the edification of the brothers and sisters, according to the talents God has given." This, then, is a significant aspect of maintaining the unity of the Church. Are not the believers members of the same body?

Church unity is taken in a practical sense here. Together the believers listen to the instructions given in Church, the *doctrina*; together they let themselves be told the *disciplina*, the way the disciples of Christ are expected to live; together they do their utmost to edify one another, each of them exercising his or her God-given talents for that purpose.

Separation

It is in this context that the duty to separate is mentioned. Non-separation — being involved in a church life dominated by those who do not belong to the Church — makes it impossible to enjoy the freedom of living in an atmosphere in which church life can be further edified. Time and energy are, at best, spent in a hopeless struggle against hierarchy. The rules set by those who dominate the scene can even make the believers completely passive. Separation restores one's freedom to take a fruitful place in the midst of the Church.[169]

Here again the Confession makes a strong appeal to those who are still in the Church of Rome, an appeal to break with that church and enjoy their Christian freedom. Freedom is not only a matter of being free from certain (bad) things but also of being free to do and enjoy certain (good) things.

"Those who do not belong to the Church"

The first sentence of this article addresses the Anabaptist "home readers" and then turns to the Nicodemites and urges them to maintain the unity of the Church by joining the (Reformed) brothers and sisters. The second paragraph adds even more weight to this exhortation by showing them the way to do this: by separating from those who do not belong to the Church.

It should be clear, in the light of the historical context in which it was written, that the Confession is referring here to the Pope and his council of bishops. In other documents, the Pope was even called the antichrist.[170] We may understand this harsh judgment when we set those who do not belong to the Church over against those who do belong to the Church.[171] In Article 27, the latter were described as "people who expect their entire salvation in Jesus Christ." Note the word "entire"! In Article 29, they are characterized as people who "appeal constantly to the blood, sufferings, death, and obedience of Jesus Christ, in Whom they have forgiveness of their sins through faith in Him."

The very last words here are of the greatest significance: "through faith in Him." In them we hear the adage of the Reformation: *sola fide* (by faith alone),

---

[169] In Guido de Brès's original text this was even more strongly expressed: "Here then lies the duty of all believers, according to the Word of God, namely to separate. . . ."

[170] The best known illustration may be the Preface to the Heidelberg Catechism, written by Elector Frederick III of the Palatinate, in which he wrote that catechism has "been maintained in the Christian Church, until the horrible Satan, through the antichrist the Pope, had abolished it." For the original German text, see Wilhelm Niesel, *Bekenntnisschriften und Kirchenordnungen der nach Gottes Wort reformierten Kirche*, 2nd ed. (Zurich: Evangelischer Verlag A.G. Zollikon, 1938) 148.

[171] In his *Answer to Sir Thomas More's Dialogue*, William Tyndale also includes those who followed the Pope and his bishops in this category. He wrote, "And whosoever goeth unto God, and unto forgiveness of sins, or salvation, by any other way than this, the same is an heretic out of the right way, and not of Christ's Church," and, "if a man be none of Christ's, he is not of His Church" (Murray, *Reformation* 16).

Earlier, Ulrich Zwingli had made it crystal clear who are of the Church and who are not of the Church. In what is called "the first creed of the Reformed Churches" — his Sixty-Seven Articles, published and defended at a religious conference held in Zurich on January 29, 1523 — he said, "All those who are living in the Head, are members and children of God, and this is the Church or communion of saints, a housewife of Christ: the catholic Church" (Art. 8). "On the other hand, just as the living members cannot do anything without the guidance of the head, so can no one do anything in the body of Christ without its Head, Christ" (Art. 9). In other words, only those who have true communion with Christ and let themselves be guided by Him belong to the Church, and all others are not of the Church. That Zwingli applied this judgment to the Church of Rome, and particularly to the Pope and the bishops, becomes clear later on in these articles (Schaff, *Creeds* 3:197-200).

which also implies *sola gratia* (by grace alone), and therefore *sola scriptura* (by the Scriptures alone).

What does the Church of Rome teach over against this? Apart from God's grace, one needs the merits earned by doing good works. Even the "eucharist" (the original name of the Lord's Supper) has been changed into such a good work, since it is an offering presented to God. To God's revelation in the Scriptures is added new revelation in "tradition," the decisions made by councils, the sayings of popes, and so forth. All of this is imposed upon the church members with an unscriptural power, and it is claimed that the Pope has been entrusted with the keys of the Kingdom of heaven, which includes the authority to condemn those who do not perfectly submit to the rules he has issued. The Church of Rome is dominated by persons who do not adhere to the Scriptural doctrine.

We can now also understand why this sentence in Article 28 played a role in the Secession of 1834. Those who expected "their entire salvation in Jesus Christ" — in contrast with the liberal theology of those days, which was imposed upon the church with unscriptural power — had to separate from those who did not belong to the Church, from those who did not submit to the only Head of the Church, Who is also the only Saviour.

Separation is still the duty of the believers in a similar situation.

In today's situation, "separation" may be a dirty word because it is branded as "splitting the church." God-fearing people who separate from those who do not belong to the Church can be at peace and have a clear conscience, however, for by such a separation one does not leave the Church but remains within the Church, even when one is compelled to give his church a different name from now on. The real "separatists" are those who remain in the apostate church!

At the same time, all sorts of splits and schisms for other reasons appear to be wrong. The situation among the Anabaptists of the sixteenth century with their many sects should be a clear warning. This means that if there is not such a serious deviation from the gospel but rather faithfulness to it, any effort must be made to restore Church unity. Our love for the Head of the Church must lead us to this.

Proof texts

All of this is confirmed by the proof texts to which the original edition of our Confession refers after the phrase "those who do not belong to the Church."

At first glance, the first proof text does not seem relevant. It is Isaiah 49:22 (NIV), which reads as follows: "This is what the Sovereign LORD says: 'See, I will beckon to the Gentiles, I will lift up My banner to the peoples; They will bring your sons in their arms and carry your daughters on their shoulders.' "

As soon as we see the context in which these words are spoken, however, we come to the conclusion that the framework in which the matter of separation is placed is very significant. The prophet passes on the information he received from the LORD concerning a great act of grace undertaken by God. The LORD will take the remnant of His people from among the nations to which He had carried them away into exile, and these nations will even cooperate in letting God's people return to their own land. Even their kings will act as foster fathers (Isa. 49:23).[172] Separation from those who do not belong to the Church is here characterized as something caused by God, first of all. He makes them "return" indeed. He instigates a reformation.[173]

The second proof text is Isaiah 52:11-12 (NIV): "Depart, depart, go out from there! Touch no unclean things! Come out from it and be pure, you who carry the vessels of the LORD. But you will not leave in haste or go in flight; for the LORD will go before you, the God of Israel will be your rear guard."

The same element is present here that we saw in the first proof text: the LORD is present; your separation has His divine approval and it is even His own work. This, then, is the strong encouragement added to the urgent appeal: "Depart, depart, go out from there!" Again the company of those who do not belong to the Church is identified with Babylon. The LORD opens the door to escape and enjoy freedom. Hence his command: Depart!

The third proof text strengthens this urgent appeal: "With her the kings of the earth committed adultery and the inhabitants of the earth were intoxicated with the wine of her adulteries" (Revelation 17:2). The new element here is that not separating from an apostate church means sharing in its sins and punishment.[174]

In His grace the LORD offers freedom. He did so in the Old Testament days; He still does so today whenever His Church has been taken captive by strange powers — even from the inside. A separation from these powers is an act of gratitude for the new opportunity offered by the LORD to enjoy the liberty of the children of God, the freedom to be a real Church!

The words "according to the Word of God" here refer to a few proof texts which put necessary secession into a great light!

---

[172] On this text the reformers based their appeal to emperors, kings, princes, and others in authority to judge favourably concerning the churches of the Reformation and terminate their participation in the persecution undertaken by the Church of Rome. For instance, in his public reply to Pope Paul III's "fatherly admonition" at the address of Emperor Charles V, John Calvin based his appeal to the civil rulers on this text. See J. N. Bakhuizen van den Brink, *Protestantse Pleidooien* (Kampen: Kok, 1962) 2:218.

[173] This may remind some readers of a treatise written by Martin Luther in 1520, *Praeludium to the Babylonian Exile of the Church*. In this work he showed that the Church had been taken captive, in particular in the (seven) sacraments imposed by Rome. Although we cannot prove that there is a direct line from Luther to the use of this proof text in our Confession, it appears that Luther and de Brès breathed the same Scriptural air.

[174] Schaff (*Creeds* 3:418) has Revelation 17:14 here: "They will make war against the Lamb, but the Lamb will overcome them because He is Lord of lords and King of kings — and with Him will be His called, chosen and faithful followers."

"AND TO JOIN THIS ASSEMBLY WHEREVER GOD HAS ESTABLISHED IT"

Context

It seems as if this line repeats what we confessed earlier in this article, namely that "all and everyone are obliged to join . . . this holy assembly and congregation." Yet there is a difference. The first paragraph emphasizes the believers' obligation not to keep themselves separated from the Church — a separation which is a voluntary matter, as we have seen — but this line stresses the same duty in the context of an involuntary separation: separation is necessary because church life is dominated by those who do not belong to the Church.

It should be clear that this line was written in the century of the Reformation. Separation from the Church of Rome had already taken place and Reformed churches were established. Once again those who had not yet broken with the apostate church were encouraged to take that step and join the Reformed.

Here the fourth aim of our Confession is obvious.

Proof texts

Our Confession bases this summons to join this assembly on two texts. The first one is Matthew 24:28: "Wherever there is a carcass, there the vultures will gather."

I must admit that I cannot see the point to be proven in this saying of Christ.[175] Even today's commentators differ, although they do have this in common, that they understand this saying as an assurance that God's judgment will come in due time.

> De Brès may have been following John Calvin, who interpreted this saying of Christ as follows: "If the birds are so wise that many come together from distant regions over one corpse it would be shameful for the faithful not to be drawn to the Author of life, from whom alone they take true nourishment."[176]

---

[175] It cannot be a printing mistake since the French text, too, has Matthew 24:28 among its proof texts.

[176] John Calvin, *A Harmony of the Gospels Matthew, Mark and Luke*, trans. A. W. Morrison, eds. David W. Torrance and Thomas F. Torrance, vol. 3, Calvin's New Testament Commentaries (Grand Rapids: Eerdmans, 1972) 92. One useful element in this interpretation is Calvin's emphasis that Christ gathers the believers around Himself. More about this proof text can be found in W. van 't Spijker, "Waar de gieren zich verzamelen" (Where the eagles gather together), *Onthullende woorden*, eds. J. W. Maris and G. L. Peels (Leeuwarden: Jongbloed, 1997) 140-155.

There is, however, a second proof text, Hebrews 10:25: "Let us not give up meeting together, as some are in the habit of doing, but let us encourage one another — and all the more as you see the Day approaching." Whereas we are used to confronting those who are not faithful in attending church with this text, our Confession uses it in the wider context of the believers' duty to join the holy catholic Church "wherever God has established it."

"Wherever"

One of the implications of taking the step of breaking with those who do not belong to the Church was that these believers would join a "church under the cross," a congregation in hiding, meeting at secret places because of ongoing persecution. We hear this implication in the word "wherever."

Nevertheless, the Confession says, it is the duty of all believers to take this cross upon themselves. Belonging to this assembly is too important to neglect! At the same time, we find confirmation here of what we emphasized at an earlier stage: the Church of Article 28 is the same as the Church of Article 27. The one holy catholic and apostolic Church manifests itself in the local church, even when that congregation must go into hiding!

This is also confirmed when we consider that in the same word "wherever" we hear a reminder of what the long subtitle of our Confession said: "Confession of Faith, Made with common agreement of the believers, scattered throughout the Netherlands, who desire to live in accordance with the purity of the holy gospel of our Lord Jesus Christ."

"Wherever" implies "scattered"! To make the step from Rome to Reformed was no little thing. Yet it was no less than every believer's duty. The purity of the holy gospel makes it worthwhile!

"THEY SHOULD DO SO EVEN THOUGH THE RULERS AND EDICTS OF PRINCES WERE AGAINST IT"

Unconditional

In our modern day we cannot imagine the cruelties and tortures the believers had to undergo some four centuries ago. Or should we not rather say: In our Western society we cannot imagine things like these? After all, every now and then the media inform us about hostility against Christians in various countries.

The simple fact that the world proclaimed 1995 to be the "year of tolerance" is significant. Intolerance, including intolerance with regard to religion, is on the increase — and not only from the side of some extreme Islamic groups. Nevertheless, all believers have an unconditional duty, and this duty is present at all times.

Proof texts

Hostility against the Christian faith was no new thing in the days when our Confession was written. The proof texts for the sentence under discussion make this clear.

The first text, Acts 17:7, informs us about what the Jews of Thessalonica said when they could not find Paul and Silas: "Jason has harboured them, and these are all acting contrary to the decrees of Caesar, saying there is another king — Jesus." Then there is Acts 18:13: "This fellow," they charged, "persuades men to worship God contrary to the law." The final proof text is Acts 4:17: "But so that it spreads no further among the people, let us severely threaten them, that from now on they speak to no man in this name."

From the first text it is clear that Caesar's decrees and those of the rulers and princes in the days of the Reformation are being placed on the same level: Christian faith clashes with them, yet one ought to stand firm in this faith. The same can be said of the other two texts. They all show us that a firm choice must be made for Christ and against the prevailing ideas of the day, whether they are certain philosophies or other religions.

"AND DEATH OR PHYSICAL PUNISHMENT MIGHT FOLLOW"

An illustration

Here the original edition of our Confession refers to the story of the apostles Peter and John who bravely defied the Jewish supreme court's command no longer to speak to anyone in Jesus' name. At that point, we read: "But Peter and John replied, 'Judge for yourselves whether it is right in God's sight to obey you rather than God' " (Acts 4:19).

The choice between the false church and the true Church, between an easy life and persecution, is nothing less than the radical choice for God or against Him.

Is it easy?

Is it an easy thing to tell others what their duty is regarding the Church even in days of persecution? Let us not forget that this Confession was written in secret by a man who was himself sought as a heretic and who ended his life as a martyr. Nor let us forget that this was the common confession of believers, "scattered throughout the Netherlands," scattered because they were under persecution for Christ's sake.

In the future, a similar choice for the true Church may again become risky, although death or physical punishment are not so close at hand in today's Western society. Nevertheless we must be faithful — in our choice regarding the Church, as well. Ultimately it is a choice against the spirit of the age and for God and His Christ!

"ALL THEREFORE WHO DRAW AWAY FROM THE CHURCH OR FAIL TO JOIN IT ACT CONTRARY TO THE ORDINANCE OF GOD"

The conclusion

Here the Confession draws the conclusion from all that we confess in Article 28. Historically our Confession had two different groups in mind. The first consisted of people who considered the Church to be of minor importance, the "disorderly" ones, who were content to be by themselves, because they had "the inner light." Those Anabaptist sectarians did not need the Church at all.

The second group consisted of the Nicodemites, those who, for lack of spiritual strength, were still within the Church of Rome, although they strongly sympathized with the Reformed because they were "concerned" about the situation in their own church.

Both groups shared a wrong view of the Church and consequently a wrong attitude toward it.

The verdict

That both groups are wrong is the obvious conclusion from all that we have confessed about the Church in Articles 27 and 28.[177] They act contrary to

---

[177] For this reason, no new proof text is mentioned in this last sentence of Article 28.

the ordinance of God.[178] Festus Hommius translated the French word *ordonnances* as *mandatum*, "mandate."

Our Confession does not go any farther than that. It does not desire to take God's judgment seat.[179] Its message is clear, however: Every believer is obliged to join the Church, to remain in it as long as it can be called the holy catholic and apostolic Church, and to separate from it if it is clear that those who do not belong to the Church have gained power in church life to the extent that it is dominated by their apostate ideas and not by the Word of God and that the Lord Jesus Christ has been pushed from His place as the Head of the Church.

Norms

It is true that the terms in which our Confession is formulated are those of the time of its compilation. Nevertheless what we confess here are Scriptural norms, norms that are applicable at all times. Are there not many "concerned" in the various churches that deviate from the biblical truth? And are we not living in days of increasing individualism? What a great thing it is that the Church still exists today because "Christ is an eternal King Who cannot be without subjects"! How wonderful it is when we can say with a clear conscience: our churches present that Church, and we are members of it by the grace of God!

---

[178] The French Confession of 1559 has "they do contrary to the Word of God" (Art. 26) and bases this conclusion on Acts 4:19-20 and Hebrews 10:25.

[179] De Wolff, *The Church* 19: "The confession does not judge the heart at this point, and therefore neither all kinds of hidden motives which might be present. Is not-joining a result of faulty upbringing and lack of insight and therefore an error? Or is there a deeply concealed enmity against the pure Gospel, even though one may present and consider oneself as a believer and is considered as such by other people, so that one misleads oneself? Do people live so superficially that they are indifferent to Christ's Church work? The Church does not pronounce judgment for the purpose of discipline or even in order to exclude from the kingdom of heaven, in accordance with 1 Corinthians 5:12, 13, where the apostle denies that the Church may act in this manner regarding those who are without. These will one day have to give account to the Lord, Who shall judge righteously. It is only mentioned in general that those who do not join themselves to the true Church, act contrary to the ordinance of God."

Kamphuis, *De Kerk* 57 (translation mine): "It is often pointed out that the Confession speaks in a reserved way here. It does not offer a judgment on *the eternal state* of those who act in this way. This is correct! The Confession does not sit in the seat of the heavenly Judge. But it does speak in a decided way! There is a calling to 'separation,' and this calling applies to 'all believers' " (Dikwijls wordt erop gewezen, dat de belijdenis hier terughoudend spreekt. Ze geeft geen oordeel over "de eeuwige staat" van wie zo handelen. Dat is terecht opgemerkt! De belijdenis gaat niet op de stoel van de hemelse Rechter zitten. Maar ze spreekt wèl heel beslist! Er is een roeping tot "afscheiding" en deze roeping geldt "alle gelovigen").

Van Bruggen, *Het Amen der Kerk* 142 (translation mine): "Our article nowhere says that those who nevertheless withdraw from the communion of the Church cannot be saved, but that they 'act contrary to the ordinance of God' " (Ons artikel zegt ook nergens dat wie zich toch aan de gemeenschap der kerk onttrekt niet zalig kan worden, maar dat die "tegen de ordinantie Gods doet"). See also his *Annotations to the Heidelberg Catechism*, trans. A. H. Oosterhoff (Neerlandia: Inheritance, 1991) 150: "When believers neglect to follow this prescribed course, they cause untold spiritual damage to themselves."

F. F. Venema, *Wat is een christen nodig te geloven?* (Groningen: De Vuurbaak, n.d. [1971]) 212 (translation mine): "But whoever does not join the true Church acts contrary to the ordinance of God. This does not mean that such a person cannot be saved. But such a person is on the wrong path and often also on a dangerous path (1 John 4:1)" (Maar wie zich niet bij de ware kerk voegt, doet tegen de ordinantie Gods. Dat wil niet zeggen, dat zo iemand niet behouden kan worden. Maar zo iemand is toch op een verkeerde weg en vaak ook op een gevaarlijke weg, 1 Joh. 4:1).

Faber, *Essays* 108: "And in the Belgic Confession the phrase *extra ecclesiam nulla salus* is taken up in a normative sense. The Reformed believer does not attempt to occupy the place of God in the last judgment . . ."

ARTICLE 29

THE MARKS OF THE TRUE CHURCH

We believe that we ought to discern diligently and very carefully from the Word of God what is the true Church, for all sects which are in the world today claim for themselves the name of Church. We are not speaking here of the hypocrites, who are mixed in the Church along with the good and yet are not part of the Church, although they are outwardly in it. We are speaking of the body and the communion of the true Church which must be distinguished from all sects that call themselves the Church.

The true Church is to be recognized by the following marks: It practises the pure preaching of the gospel. It maintains the pure administration of the sacraments as Christ instituted them. It exercises Church discipline for correcting and punishing sins. In short, it governs itself according to the pure Word of God, rejecting all things contrary to it and regarding Jesus Christ as the only Head. Hereby the true Church can certainly be known and no one has the right to separate from it.

Those who are of the Church may be recognized by the marks of Christians. They believe in Jesus Christ the only Saviour, flee from sin and pursue righteousness, love the true God and their neighbour without turning to the right or left, and crucify their flesh and its works. Although great weakness remains in them, they fight against it by the Spirit all the days of their life. They appeal constantly to the blood, suffering, death, and obedience of Jesus Christ, in Whom they have forgiveness of their sins through faith in Him.

The false church assigns more authority to itself and its ordinances than to the Word of God. It does not want to submit itself to the yoke of Christ. It does not administer the sacraments as Christ commanded in His Word, but adds to them and subtracts from them as it pleases. It bases itself more on men than on Jesus Christ. It persecutes those who live holy lives according to the Word of God and who rebuke the false church for its sins, greed, and idolatries.

These two churches are easily recognized and distinguished from each other.[180]

---

[180] It is true that the way in which both the true Church and the false church are printed in the *Book of Praise* is generally correct: they are not put on the same level, for the former is honoured with a capital C and the latter is not. We have not, however, followed the *Book of Praise* in printing the word "Churches" with a capital C in the last sentence. This printing allows too much honour for the false church.

"THE MARKS OF THE TRUE CHURCH"

Correction

The heading we have given here is not the one we find in our *Book of Praise*. There it says, "The marks of the true and the false church." This heading, however, is not correct.

Our readers may remember that the headings above the articles of our Confession are not original, let alone authentic. The original French and Dutch versions did not have any headings. They were added in later editions, such as those published in 1566 (Arent Cornelisz), 1583, and 1611. Above Article 29 they had, "On the difference and the marks of the true and the false church," a heading which was used until recently, when our Dutch sister churches changed it to "The marks of the true Church, of its members, and of the false church."

Festus Hommius formulated his own headings in the Latin version which he prepared for the delegates of the foreign churches to the Synod of Dordrecht (1618-19). Above Article 29 he wrote "On the marks of the true Church."

This is a correct summary of the contents of Article 29. In its first sentence we see that the emphasis is on the true Church and from what we learned from the previous article we understand that this emphasis is in perfect harmony with what we called the fourth aim of our Confession, namely to assist those believers who are still outside in finding the one holy catholic and apostolic Church. They must learn to discern the Church.

Furthermore, this article makes a distinction — not between the true Church and the false church, but between the true Church and the sects, of which the false church is an extremely bad example. Hommius's heading is more to the point and therefore we have replaced the heading in the *Book of Praise* with it.

> The National Synod of The Hague (1586) discussed an instruction to have every office bearer and teacher subscribe to the Confession "in order to maintain the pure doctrine against all sects." More than three decades after the publication of the Belgic Confession, the true Church was still confronted with the sects, and not only with the false church, namely that of Rome.[181]

With that we have arrived at the first line of this article.

---

[181] Rutgers, *Acta* 543.

"WE BELIEVE THAT WE OUGHT TO DISCERN DILIGENTLY AND VERY CAREFULLY FROM THE WORD OF GOD WHAT IS THE TRUE CHURCH"

We believe that we ought to discern diligently and very carefully from the Word of God what is the true Church, for all sects which are in the world today claim for themselves the name of Church.

The French Confession

First of all, before we deal with this sentence, we shall read the Confession of Faith which the Reformed churches in France adopted in 1559 and to which John Calvin contributed. We do so because Guido de Brès used this Confession as an example. This document influenced the contents of our own Confession and even its formulation.

A clear illustration of this influence can be seen in Article 28, where we confess that it is the believers' duty to join the Church "wherever God has established it." This line is based upon Article 26 of the French Confession: "We believe that no one ought to seclude himself and be contented to be alone; but that all jointly should keep and maintain the union of the Church, and submit to the public teaching, and to the yoke of Jesus Christ, wherever God shall have established a true order of the Church; even if the magistrates and their edicts are contrary to it. For if they do not take part of it or if they separate themselves from it, they do contrary to the Word of God."[182]

As we can all see, it looks as if de Brès copied this article with only a few changes.

Abbreviation

It is not our intention to elaborate on this influence. What we have in mind is that the French Confession speaks of the "true order of the Church." This is not the only time that it uses this longer phrase. In the previous article, Article 25, it did the same. There it said, "Now as we enjoy Christ only through the gospel, we believe that the order of the Church, established by His authority,

---

[182] The original texts of the French Confession and (the French version of) the Belgic Confession are even more alike than are Cochrane's translation and the English version in the *Book of Praise*.

ought to be sacred and inviolable, and that, therefore, the Church can not exist without pastors for instruction . . ."[183]

Then, after speaking twice of the "true order of the Church," the Confession says in Article 27: "Nevertheless we believe that it is important to discern with care and prudence which is the true Church, for its title has been much abused." So it appears that "the true Church" is an abbreviation of "the true order of the Church."

Since we note that even in the first sentence of Article 29 of his Confession de Brès borrowed heavily from the French Confession of Faith, we can keep the longer "the true order of the Church" in mind as a phrase which helps us understand what is said in this article.

Clarification

This point may clarify the important issue of the relation between the catholic, apostolic Church and the local church or a confederation of churches.[184] For this purpose we must return to the French Confession.

A number of articles in that Confession deal with Christ, His perfect sacrifice, intercessory prayers, and other works of grace. Then Article 25 says that we enjoy Christ only through the gospel. This article thus refers to what happens locally, to the gospel preaching as it takes place in the local church. In the local congregation we can see the one holy catholic and apostolic Church in a well-ordered form.

The catholic Church must always be in our mind and have our love when we are involved in the life of the congregation of which we are members or in that of the confederation of churches to which our congregation belongs.

Put briefly, the local church is the catholic Church in its well-ordered and structured form. By being a member of the local church one is a member of the catholic Church. By joining the local congregation one joins the holy, universal, apostolic Church, gratefully acknowledging that one has been taken up in God's great divine work of fulfilling His "ecumenical" promise to Abraham.

To be aware of this relationship can be very beneficial. For example, it can protect us against the danger of using "our own church" or "our own churches" superficially as the norm by which we judge other churches. In this respect the

---

[183] This statement may be based on the Geneva Confession of 1536, which says, "Where the Gospel is not declared, heard and received, there we do not acknowledge the form of the Church" (Art. 18).

[184] In the literature the latter are often called "a particular church" or "particular churches." See the Westminster Confession XXV.4, which follows, among others, Chapter XVIII of the Scottish Confession of 1560 with its "particular Kirks" and Chapter XVII of the Second Helvetic Confession of 1566. Somewhere in Craig's Catechism (1581) the question is asked, "May we leave the particular church where the Word is remained?" (Torrance, *School of Faith* 121).

knowledge that "the true Church" may be considered an abbreviation of "the true order of the Church" can be helpful.[185]

"We believe"

Furthermore it should be clear that it is not for nothing that this article begins with the words "We believe." The Church — the true Church — is a matter of faith, and it is such in its well-ordered form, too.

"Discern"

When we dealt with the heading of this article, we translated the heading added in the editions of 1566, 1583, and 1611 as "On the difference between and the marks of the true and the false church." This is actually not an altogether satisfactory rendering, however. The word translated "difference" is intended to refer to what is said in the first sentence, namely that we must discern "what is the true Church." We must learn from the Word of God to distinguish the true Church. Again this is an act of faith for which the Bible is the only source. This discernment must be carried out "diligently and very carefully" since there is not only the false church but also the many sects which are in the world, of which the false church is an extreme example. From what we shall learn about these sects below, it should become clear that it is not always easy to see at which particular point they follow the ideas of their leadership and not the Scriptures.

The word "diligently" assures us that we must exert ourselves, gather some reliable information, and, by carefully studying the matter and comparing it with the Scriptures, reach certain conclusions. We must do all of this "very carefully." The text actually says, "with prudence," which means with discretion and circumspection, not rapidly and superficially. Only then, when we have taken our time, will it become clear to us which is the true Church that is entitled to bear that name.

As for the false church — which is indeed an extreme example of a sect, characterized by its basing itself "more on men than on Jesus Christ" — it is much easier to recognize it and distinguish it from the true Church, as the final sentence of this article says.[186]

---

[185] In the Belgic Confession the term "order" does not appear before in Article 30. It is used there in a somewhat narrower and more organizational sense, as is particularly the case in Article 32 which makes us think of a "Church Order." Nevertheless I am of the opinion that reading the French Confession with its abbreviation of "the true order of the Church" into "the true Church" is helpful.

[186] Even as far as the false church is concerned, the Scottish Confession states that we can be deceived by it. It says in Chapter XVIII: "So it is essential that the true Kirk be distinguished from the filthy synagogues by clear and perfect notes lest we, being deceived, receive and embrace, to our own condemnation, the one for the other."

Proof text

Before we deal with the reason our Confession gives for the words "diligently and very carefully," let us first take note of the proof text for this part of the sentence.

It is rather long, the whole of Matthew 13.[187] We quote only verses 24-29 and verse 38,[188] which read as follows: "Another parable He put forth to them, saying: 'The Kingdom of heaven is like a man who sowed good seed in his field; but while men slept, his enemy came and sowed tares among the wheat and went his way. But when the grain had sprouted and produced a crop, then the tares also appeared. So the servants of the owner came and said to him, "Sir, did you not sow good seed in your field? How then does it have tares?" He said to them, "An enemy has done this." The servants said to him, "Do you want us then to go and gather them up?" But he said, "No, lest while you gather up the tares you also uproot the wheat with them."' . . . The field is the world, the good seed are the sons of the Kingdom, but the tares are the sons of the wicked one."

This proof text undergirds the terms "diligently and very carefully" in the first sentence of Article 29 because at first sight tares can easily be mistaken for wheat.

In "the sons of the Kingdom" and "the sons of the evil one," de Brès must have understood two different churches, the true Church and the sects — which sometimes show a strong resemblance to the true Church. We shall discuss whether this is a correct reading and application of this parable when we deal with the sentence which mentions the hypocrites.

Here our Confession refers to the Scriptures. Apart from the general proof text quoted above, it does not provide any other Scripture passages. The reason for this is that a sufficient number have been presented for the previous articles. The Word of God offers abundant help to show every believer where he can find the proper location of the Church.

The proof texts on which our Confession rests should therefore be printed in every edition. This will help our Confession achieve the aim that is so dominant in the articles on the Church. Nicodemites are still all around us, and the duty of faithful churches to unite still rests upon them!

---

[187] The French version quoted by Schaff (*Creeds* 3:419) has Matt. 13:22.

[188] In so doing, we follow Vallensis.

"FOR ALL THE SECTS WHICH ARE IN THE WORLD TODAY CLAIM FOR THEMSELVES THE NAME OF CHURCH"

Proof text

First of all, we shall focus our attention on the proof text for this sentence. It is Revelation 2:9, which contains Christ's word to the church in Smyrna: "I know your works, tribulation, and poverty (but you are rich); and I know the blasphemy of those who say they are Jews and are not, but are a synagogue of Satan." The point being made by the use of this text here is that there was a group of people in Smyrna who claimed for themselves the name "Jews" — a name of honour, in this case.[189]

In Scriptural times the situation was already fundamentally the same as in the days when our Confession was written — and today as well. Already then people could easily be confused by the attractive but false pretence of that same group.

Today

We deliberately read the proof text first. From it, we can learn that when our Confession states that "today there are many sects which claim for themselves the name of Church," this statement cannot be restricted exclusively to the time when the Confession was written, as if the situation is different in our own day.

We aim to pay special attention to this point because every now and then we are confronted with the assertion that the true Church-false church distinction is outdated. According to this opinion, the distinction may have been functional some four centuries ago but not now in today's "ecumenical" climate. The same objection can be heard among people who belong to a church which still includes the Belgic Confession among its subordinate standards in a merely formal sense.

One writer refers to Article 29 and says that it was applicable to the situation in the time it was written, because it refers to the many sects which are there "today," by which the days of the mid-sixteenth century were meant. According to this writer, de Brès intended to be very careful to write

---

[189] "They stand in implied contrast to true Jews who are committed to God and His will (cf. Romans 2:18ff). It does not have to follow, however, that the latter are Christians" (W. Gutbrot, *Theological Dictionary of the New Testament*, abridged ed., trans. and ed. Geoffrey W. Bromiley [Grand Rapids: Eerdmans, 1985] 375. For a lengthier discussion, see also W. Gutbrot, *Theological Dictionary of the New Testament*, ed. G. Kittel, trans. and ed. Geoffrey W. Bromiley, 10 vols. [Grand Rapids: Eerdmans, 1964-1967] 3:369-391).

specifically about his present day situation and to abstain from setting a norm for the future.[190]

Formally, it is correct that the text of the Confession refers to the situation of the sixteenth century, but the proof text demonstrates that it would be quite wrong to draw the conclusion that no norm is set for the future and that the true-false distinction is therefore no longer applicable.[191]

The same may also be seen when we focus our attention on the little word "sects."

Sects and false church

In the opening sentence of Article 29, the true Church is mentioned together with the sects. Later on in this article it will be accompanied by the false church. The question then arises: Are we dealing with two different entities — the false church and the sects — or are these two different names for one and the same body?

Both sentences in which the sects are mentioned seem to suggest that they are indeed the same, since they say that the true Church must be distinguished from those sects. Then, as soon as an elaborate exposition has been presented as to how the true Church — together with those who are of the Church — can be recognized, the false church is introduced, more or less suddenly, and the article ends with the conclusion that the true Church and the false church "are easily recognized and distinguished from each other."

It appears as if everything supports the thesis that the sects and the false church are the same.

This view seems to be confirmed when we read in Calvin's *Institutes*: "And certain of their sect are so impudent as to dare openly to boast. . . ." (IV.v.17). The singular "sect" is no printing mistake, for in this paragraph Calvin is dealing with the Church of Rome.

The heading again

Are the sects and the false church the same? We are convinced that a thorough consideration of this question will be very beneficial. It will provide us with a better insight into today's situation and produce the fundamentals for the correct way to evaluate other churches.

---

[190] This opinion was expressed in *Contact*, a magazine published in the Netherlands a few decades ago, and is quoted and rejected by Kamphuis in *Verkenningen* I 8f.

[191] "There are movements and groups in this country that do not in the least desire to be called 'church.' They consciously want to be religious societies in which like minded Christians may express their religion. Their liturgy is a sort of 'happening,' and their doctrine is an assortment of truths (or what looks like it) grouped around certain preferential ideas" (Trimp, *The Church* 58).

Our starting-point is the very first sentence of Article 29, when it says that it is "from the Word of God" that we ought to discern the true Church, for all the sects "claim for themselves the name of Church." This idea is repeated in the last line of the same paragraph, where it states that the true Church is to be "distinguished from all sects that call themselves Church." The false church is not yet mentioned here. It is spoken of only at the end of the article.

For this reason we can be happy that the heading which is printed above Article 29 in the *Book of Praise* is not original and furthermore is incorrect. This article does not deal only with the marks of the true Church and the false church. It is about the local address of the holy, catholic, apostolic Church. Where can this Church be found and consequently joined, since the appearance presented by the many sects (or "churches" — for that is what they call themselves) is so confusing?

This question can therefore be answered only by God's Word.

Embarrassment

The heading in question may have caused the frequent misreading of this article. People fail to notice that sects are mentioned — twice — at the beginning, while the false church is introduced only later. True Church and false church have been put next to each other, whereas what is actually being contrasted here is the true Church and the sects. The necessary choice is not one between the true Church and the false church, but a more general and wider one: between the true Church and all kinds of sects.

It is therefore no wonder that a degree of embarrassment among us is evident. Can we say that every church which is not a true Church must be condemned as a false church? Many people are hesitant to answer this question in the affirmative. On the other hand, they do not have the courage to draw the opposite conclusion: Every church that cannot be called false must be a true Church.

We can be happy that this kind of "logical reasoning" has never found expression in official statements made by our churches and our sister churches overseas.[192]

More is confessed in Article 29 than just the difference between the true Church and the false church. Full emphasis is placed on the difference between the true Church and the sects. It is in this context that the false church is introduced at the end of the article.

The article, then, says that diligence and prudence are needed to distinguish the true Church because the situation can be extremely confusing since all kinds of sects cover themselves with the name of church.

This raises the question: What exactly must we understand by "sects"?

---

[192] Every now and then, some people may have expressed extreme personal opinions. I remember one instance when the writer of a youth column called all the ministers of other churches "strangers" and "hirelings," but this youthful, immature way of thinking may have been overcome since then.

Sects

In the Scriptures, the word "sect" is used of a group or a school — for instance, that of the Sadducees or of the Pharisees, which were groups among the Jews.[193] The followers of Christ were called the "sect of the Nazarenes" or "this sect."[194] In this sense the word does not have an unfavourable sound — and no wonder, because the Greek word is derived from a verb that means "to choose."[195]

In other places, however, it does have an unfavourable meaning — for example, when it stands for a group which is following a leader in his false teachings, in which case it also means "heresy" (Galatians 5:20).[196] In this sense, the existence of a sect can even lead to the establishing of a counter-church.[197]

Apart from its "neutral" use, the word "sect" is used for the followers of those who, at one point or another, have falsified the Scriptural doctrine and created a separate group,[198] either outside the Church or within it — but if within, then in such a way that an *ecclesiola in ecclesia* (a little church within the church) is established.

It may be true, as John Calvin said, that the Church of Rome can also be called a sect because it consists of supporters of the Pope and his false doctrines and is incompatible with the nature of the Church, and therefore is a counter-church. Nevertheless, the term "sects" covers a much wider field than just the Church of Rome.

Our conclusion, therefore, must be that the sects at the beginning of Article 29 cannot be identified with the false church of the last section.[199]

---

[193] Acts 5:17; 15:5.

[194] Acts 24:5; 28:22.

[195] The same is true of the English word "sect," which is derived from a Latin verb meaning "to follow."

[196] John Calvin uses the word "sect" in this sense in the Geneva Catechism (1541), as does Martin Luther in his Larger Catechism (1529).

[197] This can be seen as a danger in 1 Corinthians 11:19 and 2 Peter 2:1-2. So H. Schlier, *Theological Dictionary of the New Testament*, abridged ed. 28 (1:180-85 in the original edition).

[198] Roman Catholics used the word "sect" in the same sense for the Calvinists. In a letter written by Giovanni Michieli, Venetian ambassador at Paris, we read, "You would never believe the active correspondence carried all over the kingdom by the principal minister of Geneva, named Calvin, a Frenchman from Picardy, a man who has acquired an extraordinary authority over his sect by his life, his learning, and his writings" (Janet Glenn Gray, *The French Huguenots: Anatomy of Courage* [Grand Rapids: Baker Book House, 1981] 62).

[199] Further proof for this conclusion can be found in the records of the National Synod of The Hague (1586), which had to deal with a complaint that the sects were increasing daily and with the suggestion that the churches try to arrange discussions with their members. In this context these people's objections against taking an oath are mentioned, which proves that by these sects Anabaptist groups are meant (see Rutgers, *Acta* 543f).

History

For this reason, Henry Bullinger could include paragraphs introduced by the word "The Sects" in several chapters of the Second Helvetic Confession. In these paragraphs, he refutes the doctrines and practices of a large number of sects.[200]

A few years earlier, Christophorus Fabritius, the martyr, wrote a confession in which he distinguished the true Church "from all churches and congregations, sects, errors, and heresies." In the Dutch translation, de Brès added the word *rotten*, which may have meant "heresies, groups in decay."[201]

In 1552, Marten Micron, one of the ministers of the London congregation of Reformed refugees, wrote a treatise in which he dealt with the motives of the Nicodemites, the people who were staying in the Church of Rome. According to him they had a variety of excuses, one of which was that by staying in "Babylon" they were able to teach others the biblical truth. Another reason was that in any church there are faults and defects, so that it would be very difficult to find a satisfactory alternative. Micron replied: "There are substantial differences in the defects of the various churches: some of them do not have the right foundation, Jesus Christ. They err either as far as His Person is concerned or regarding His divine and human natures, His power and the glory of His Kingdom, priesthood, His being a Prophet — and one must avoid all of them as much as the Jewish, Turkish, and Papist and suchlike churches."[202] It is clear that Micron had the Anabaptist sects of his day in mind. He placed them on a level with apostate communities such as Judaism, Romanism, and Islam.

Decay

Although we have dealt with a large number of sects and false churches, it should be clear that they were not all on the same level.[203] Nevertheless there was one thing they all had in common: in one way or another they deviated from Scriptural doctrine, leaving them unable to lay legitimate claim to the name "church." Those who reject the teachings of the apostles at any point cannot say, "We are the apostolic Church." Despite the different degrees of

---

[200] E.g., Pelagians, Jovinians (Chap. VIII), Manichaeans (IX), Arians (XI), Nestorians, Monothelites or Monophysites (XI), Ebionites, Nazarites or Mineans (XIII), Messalians (XIX), Tatians, Encratites, the disciples of Eusthathius (XXIV). At one place he even points out that within the Church there has often been a number of sects (XVII).

[201] Going a little farther, he translates the French *membres pourris* by *verrotten lidmaten*, "decayed (rotten) members." See Vonk, *Voorzeide Leer* 3B:99, 103; Doekes, "Reformatorische Onderscheiding" 265. The Dutch and German word *rotten* was commonly used for "heresies" or "gangs." This is how Ulrich Zwingli used the term in the German version of his Sixty-seven Articles, and it is what John Calvin, in a letter to a Polish archbishop, called the Church of Rome — in other words, "an old piece of dirt" (Schwarz 3:984; 711, 1147, 1181). In the *Formula Concordiae* (1576) the Latin word for "heresies" is translated into the German *rotten*. Here "heresies" and "sects" are almost synonyms, although the latter refers to a group.

[202] Cited in Doekes, "Reformatorische Onderscheiding" 268 (translation mine).

[203] That there are other serious instances of sects besides the Church of Rome is clear from the French Confession which says, "We detest all visionaries who would like, so far as lies in their power, to destroy the ministry and preaching of the Word and sacraments" (Art. 25). This confession has in mind some Anabaptist extremists. There were many sects among the Anabaptists, the one more seriously deviating from the biblical truth than the other.

decay, as far as their particular doctrine is concerned they must all be called "sects," including the Church of Rome.[204]

Some communities, however, are much worse than others. Among them at the time of the Reformation was the Church of Rome — and it still is today. When we take into account its degree of decay, we must call it a false church, and, because the Church of the Reformation was involved in a fierce struggle against this church and our Confession was aimed at convincing the "concerned" within this church that they should leave it and join the Reformed, the false church receives special attention in Article 29.

In any church there are faults and defects and it may therefore be difficult to distinguish the true Church from other churches (sects). The choice is much easier as far as the false church is concerned, however. Because deviation from the biblical doctrine is so much more serious and the decay almost total in the false church, the question arises: Is there anything left of the things that are characteristic of a church, the faithful administration of the gospel, the sacraments, and discipline? The answer is in the negative. Besides, the false church even persecutes those who want to live according to the Word of God!

The false church, then, is an example of an extremely bad sect.[205]

Our Confession

Let us now return to our Confession and be grateful that it can solve many a problem we have caused ourselves because we did not read Article 29 correctly and perhaps did not go any farther than the unauthorized and incorrect heading " marks of the true and false church."[206]

---

[204] That this is how we must read the first sentence of Article 29 is proven by the Synods of 1578, 1581, 1586, and 1618-19, which dealt with the conditions for admission to the ministry set for "novices, priests, monks, and those who have left any other sect."

[205] Van der Jagt, *De Kerk* 67: "Not every sect is a false church, but the false church is a sect indeed" (Alle secten zijn geen valse kerk; de valse kerk is wel een secte). It was surprising to learn that Van der Jagt, following a different route, came to the same conclusions. His contribution is therefore very helpful in breaking through the false dilemma that whatever is not a true Church must be a false church, and — the other way around — whatever is not a false church must be a true Church. In other words, the true-false scheme cannot be applied to every situation, but the real question is: Where can we find the true Church in a world full of deviation from the Scriptural doctrine, a deviation in various degrees?

As for the latter point, what we are saying here parallels what Antonius Walaeus wrote in his contribution to the *Synopsis Purioris Theologiae*. Walaeus made the distinction between the pure (*vera*, true) Church and other churches which are impure in various degrees, as Van der Jagt explained in his article "Een schema uit de Scholastiek."

[206] We must also be grateful that our Confession does not limit itself to the true-false distinction but puts the false church in the context of "the sects." This is different from other confessions, such as the Scottish Confession, which has as the heading above Chapter XVIII, "The notes by which the true Kirk shall be determined from the false and who shall be judge of doctrine." In the text of this chapter it speaks about "the notes, signs, and assured tokens whereby the spotless bride of Christ is known from the horrible harlot, the false church." This difference most likely came about because the Anabaptists were not as strong in Scotland as they were in the Netherlands and because the Reformed in Scotland had suffered at the hands of the Church of Rome from persecutions stirred up by kings and queens who were hostile to the Reformation.

Not every other church is a false church. There are degrees in apostasy and decay. Other churches must be judged according to the measure of their decay. This means that some churches can be contacted and addressed, whereas others cannot or can hardly be addressed.

It also means that there may be churches which have a Scriptural Confession and actually adhere to it but show a few weaknesses or deficiencies. As for them, the biblical examples of Corinth and some of the seven churches of Asia Minor can help prevent us from rejecting them outright or ignoring them. In extreme cases, such as the false church, we cannot say, "Here is the holy, catholic, and apostolic Church," but in other cases diligence and prudence must be used, and the all-important question is: Do those churches, which we cannot reject as false churches, take anything from — or add something to — what we confess in our creeds, on the basis of God's Self-revelation in the Scriptures, concerning the triune God and His works?[207]

"WE ARE NOT SPEAKING HERE OF THE HYPOCRITES, WHO ARE MIXED IN THE CHURCH ALONG WITH THE GOOD AND YET ARE NOT PART OF THE CHURCH, ALTHOUGH THEY ARE OUTWARDLY IN IT"

Text

First of all, we would like to focus our attention on a couple of inadequacies in the English translation as we find it in the *Book of Praise*. The

---

The Confession of Faith of the English Congregation at Geneva (1556), however, mentions "Papists, Anabaptists and such rascals" in Article 4. The First Confession of Basel (1534) declares that the "Christian Church has no fellowship with sects and the rules of religious orders which are determined to distinguish between days, food, clothing, and ecclesiastical pageantry" (Art. 5).

The Genevan Confession (1536), written by John Calvin or by both of them, runs parallel to our own Confession when it says in Article 18, "On the other hand, where the Gospel is not declared, heard, and received, there we do not acknowledge the form of the Church. Hence the churches governed by the ordinances of the Pope are rather synagogues of the devil than Christian churches."

[207] The Tetrapolitan Confession of 1530 formulates the criterion as follows: "those who propose what differs from Christ's doctrines, even though they be within the Church, nevertheless, because preoccupied with error, they do not proclaim the voice of the Shepherd, undoubtedly cannot represent the Church, the bride of Christ. Therefore they are not to be heard in His name, since Christ's sheep follow not the voice of a stranger" (Chap. XV).

original French or Dutch should not have been translated by "hypocrites" only but by "the company of the hypocrites."[208]

The term "outwardly" reminds us of the "synodical" theory that the non-elect are only "outwardly" in the covenant but not really. The original versions of our Confession have *au corps* (French) and *na den lichame* (Dutch), both of which mean "bodily, physically."

Particularly in the former case something has been lost because the insertion of this sentence about the hypocrites has a unique background.

Background

In order to learn to see what this background is, we must go back in history.

John Calvin wrote in his *Institutes* about the presence of hypocrites in the Church. He did so over against some of the Anabaptists, whom he reproached because, "Seeing that among those to whom the gospel is preached, the fruit produced is not in accordance with the doctrine, they forthwith conclude that there no church exists" (IV.i.13).

It is from this historical context that our Confession has derived the phrase "the company of the hypocrites." Calvin continues with the following sentence: "Thinking there is no church where there is not complete purity and integrity of conduct, they, through hatred of wickedness, withdraw from a genuine church, while they think they are shunning the company of the ungodly" (IV.i.13).

By way of the French Confession, this element has been incorporated into our own Confession.[209]

Anabaptist thinking

The Anabaptists mentioned above were of the opinion that a real church must be a pure church. Their attention was focused not so much on the organization and activities of the Church (which the French Confession calls "the true order of the Church") as on the life of its members. The crucial point for them was the spiritual quality and the way of life of the believers. This individualistic concept of the Church led to one schism after the other among them. As soon as an imperfection was observed in a certain congregation, those who felt concerned about it withdrew and established another congregation, and this repeated process ultimately led to the existence of a

---

[208] French: *la companie des Hypocrites*; Dutch: *het gezelschap der hypocrieten.*

[209] French Confession, Article 27: "Nevertheless we do not deny that among the faithful there may be hypocrites and reprobates, but their wickedness can not destroy the title of the Church."

large number of splinter groups, which in our Confession are included in the name "sects."

Lesson

This splintering was not a new phenomenon. Many centuries ago the Donatists had developed a similar theory and practice, which resulted in the idea that they were — in contemporary terms — the only true Church in the whole world and that all the other churches were false.[210]

In our own day, a similar individualistic concept of the Church has led to the withdrawal of many members who were bitterly disappointed by the behaviour of other church members or by certain events that had taken place in church life. In its corporate form it leads inevitably to the extreme position: We alone are the true Church!

There is a double lesson in all of this. We must be careful not to give offence to our fellow church members, let alone to become a stumbling-block to them. On the other hand, this concept of the Church can easily be governed by a kind of individualism and subjectivism which is in conflict with the very first words we always use when we speak about the Church: "I believe a holy, catholic Church"!

The point

What it actually says in the sentence under discussion is that it may be true that the membership of the Church is a mixed multitude, but that the presence of hypocrites does not deny it the name of Church.[211]

Proof text

Our Confession states that the hypocrites "are mixed in the Church along with the good." This is an allusion to the well-known parable of the weeds, recorded in Matthew 13:24-30 and 36-43. This parable, however, is not presented as a proof text in the original Dutch version.

The official proof texts are Romans 9:6, "It is not that the Word of God has taken no effect. For they are not all Israel who are of Israel," and 2 Timothy 2:18-20, "[Hymenaeus and Philetus] who have strayed concerning the truth, saying that the resurrection is already past; and they overthrow the faith of

---

[210] A good exposition of the doctrine and practices of the Donatists can be found in Faber, *Lectures* 12-15.

[211] The French Confession says emphatically that their presence "cannot destroy the title of the Church" (Art. 27).

some. Nevertheless the solid foundation of God stands, having this seal: 'The Lord knows those who are His,' and, 'Let everyone who names the name of Christ depart from iniquity.' But in a great house there are not only vessels of gold and silver, but also of wood and clay, some for honour and some for dishonour."

Both texts prove that what is stated in our Confession is indeed true. The Bible shows us clearly that not all the members of the Church are true believers. Membership is a "mixed" matter. The Anabaptists are wrong, and so is everyone who identifies the Church with its members.

"Mixed"

As we have already said, the reference to hypocrites being "mixed in the Church along with the good" is an allusion to the parable of the tares. This, too, is something de Brès had learned from John Calvin. In the same paragraph from which we quoted what Calvin wrote about the hypocrites, he mentions that parable.[212] This allusion to the parable of the tares has also been derived from the French Confession. This confession has Matthew 13:30 among its proof texts for Article 27 where the presence of hypocrites in the Church is mentioned.

Other confessional documents

It is quite remarkable that many confessions and other Reformation documents refer to the parable of the tares and similar parables. Consider the following:

— The First Confession of Basel (1534), Article VII: "Because weeds are mixed with the Church of Christ, Christ has given His Church authority to excommunicate such weeds when they show themselves by intolerable crimes and sins against the commandment of the Lord."

— A document written in the early stages of the English Reformation, *Institution of a Christian Man* (1537). It states that among the members of the congregation there are "as the gospel calleth them very weeds and chaff."

— The Tetrapolitan Confession of 1530, Chapter XV: "The Church of Christ, therefore, which is frequently called the Kingdom of heaven, is the

---

[212] Calvin wrote that the Anabaptists "allege that the Church of God is holy. But that they may at the same time understand that it contains a mixture of good and bad, let them hear from the lips of our Saviour that parable in which he compares the Church to a net in which all kinds of fishes are taken, but not separated until they are brought ashore. Let them hear it compared to a field which, planted with good seed, is by the fraud of an enemy mingled with tares, and is not freed of them until the harvest is brought into the barn. Let them hear, in fine, that it is a threshing-floor in which the collected wheat lies concealed under the chaff, until, cleansed by the fanners and the sieve, it is at length laid up in the granary. If the Lord declares that the Church will labour under the defect of being burdened with a multitude of wicked until the day of judgment, it is in vain to look for a church altogether free from blemish (Matthew xiii.)" (IV.i.13). Calvin derived the sentence in which the Church is compared to a threshing-floor from Augustine.

fellowship of those who have enlisted under Christ and committed themselves entirely to His faith, with whom, nevertheless, until the end of the world, those are mingled who feign faith in Christ, but do not truly have it. This the Lord has taught sufficiently by the parable of the tares. . . ."

— The Scottish Confession of 1560, Chapter XXV: "We acknowledge and confess that many weeds and tares are sown among the corn and grow in great abundance in its midst."

— The Second Helvetic Confession, Chapter XVII: The hypocrites are not of the Church, but they are considered to be in the Church "as the tares or darnel and chaff are found among the wheat . . . and therefore the Church of God is rightly compared to a net which catches fish of all kinds, and to a field, in which both wheat and tares are found (Matthew 13:24ff, 47ff)."

— Zacharias Ursinus, *Commentary on the Heidelberg Catechism*: "Christ says in the parable of the wheat and tares, 'Let both grow together until the harvest' (Matthew 13:30). . . . Christ here speaks of hypocrites, who cannot always be discerned from those who are truly pious. Therefore the meaning is, that hypocrites ought not to be cut off and separated from the Church, when we do not certainly know them to be such; for the angels will do this at the last day" (452).

— The Westminster Confession of Faith, Chapter XXV.2 and 5, which both have Matthew 13:30 and 47 among their proof texts. The Confession was influenced at this point by the Irish archbishop, James Ussher, the man who is said to have written the Irish Articles of 1615. In his *Body of Divinity* he wrote that only those are accounted members of the Church who "are true believers and so inseparably united unto Christ their Head." The others will be removed by Christ on the last day, "as we are taught in the Parable of the Tares, Matthew 13:24 & Matthew 13:47, etc., and of the draw net, and the threshing floor, where lieth both good corn and chaff."

— Antonius Walaeus in *Synopsis Purioris Theologiae* (1625): "Christ compares it (the Church) to a net in which good and bad fish are caught, and to a field and a threshing-floor, on which pure wheat grows and is gathered together with the weeds."[213]

Kingdom parables

A few pages back, we promised to discuss whether the parable of the tares and similar parables can serve as proof texts for the presence of hypocrites in the Church, as in the confessional documents cited above. The question arises: Can the Church and the Kingdom of God be identified? Are they the same? Did Christ identify them?

No. He did not say that the "field" in the parable is the Church. He said, "the field is the world" (Matthew 13:38).

This implies that the tares cannot be identified with Church people. They are outside the Church and must be located in the field of the world, which is indeed the territory of Christ's Kingdom. They are called sons of the evil one and are presented as a very special brand of weed, something that looks very

[213] *Synopsis Purioris Theologiae* (Leiden: Elsevier, 1625) 35.

much like wheat — namely darnel, which is what the original word actually means. All of this is explained by the Lord Jesus in the context of enmity: the darnel was sown by the farmer's enemy. The sons of the evil one can be expected to assume a hostile attitude toward the sons of the Kingdom. They oppose God's Kingdom and deny Christ's royal glory.

Our conclusion must therefore be that the many documents which use the Kingdom parables as proof texts for the presence of hypocrites in the Church should not have followed John Calvin in this respect.[214]

This does not mean that the Confession is wrong when it assures us that we can expect hypocrites to be among the church members, but the effort to base this truth on the Kingdom parables is ineffective at this point when other, better texts could have been produced.[215] We can, however, be happy that Matthew 13 is not among the proof texts but that the Confession only alluded to it.

"WE ARE SPEAKING OF THE BODY AND THE COMMUNION OF THE TRUE CHURCH WHICH MUST BE DISTINGUISHED FROM ALL SECTS THAT CALL THEMSELVES THE CHURCH"

A positive focus

After it has rejected the individualism of the Anabaptists, who strongly emphasized the necessity of holiness among the members of the Church and consequently splintered into a large number of sects, each claiming to be more "pure" than the others, our Confession repeats that our subject is the Church as a body and a communion. This Church must be distinguished from the sects which confuse many people because they "present themselves under the name of church."

By emphasizing that it is speaking about the Church as a body, our Confession introduces what follows: the marks of the true Church and those of the Christians. After all, is not one of its aims — especially in these articles

---

[214] Calvin in turn was following Augustine whose advice he quoted in his *Institutes*: "mercifully to correct what they can, and to bear patiently with what they cannot correct, in love lamenting and mourning until God either reform or correct, or in the harvest root up the tares, and scatter the chaff' " (Augustine, *Against the Letter of Parmenianus* III.ii.15, cited in Calvin, *Institutes* IV.i.16).

[215] W. Huizinga wrote some instructive articles on this issue in *Una Sancta* 37.8, 9 (Feb. and Mar. 1990).

on the Church— to assure the members of the Church that they are at the right address and to help others to find it?

The French Confession

The way in which our Confession does this has been adopted from the French Confession. This confession also commences with some emphasis on the Church as a company. Then it presents a picture of those who belong to that company, before going on to deal briefly in the next article with the marks of the true Church, repeating them from a previous article and, in light of them, condemning the papal assemblies.

So the order in our Confession is the same as that of the French Confession with this exception, that in the latter the marks of the true Church are mentioned first.

To demonstrate this influence we refer to the following lines. The end of Article 25 in the French Confession mentions the following marks: the ministry and preaching of the Word and the sacraments. Article 27 states: "We say, then, according to the Word of God, that it is the company of the faithful who agree to follow his Word, and the pure religion which it teaches; who advance in it all their lives, growing and becoming more confirmed in the fear of God according as they feel the want of growing and pressing onward. Even although they strive continually, they can have no hope save in the remission of their sins." Article 28 then continues with this sentence: "In this belief we declare that, properly speaking, there can be no Church where the Word of God is not received, nor profession made of subjection to it, nor use of the sacraments."

Lesson

It is quite striking that a close connection is established here between the Church as the company of the faithful and the believers themselves. The opening sentence of Article 28 in the French Confession explains this relationship: "The Word of God must be received and one must submit to it." Therefore it is very useful to note that our own Confession is following this example when it lists the marks of Christians.

It is very important, however, to recognize that our Confession — just like the French Confession — strongly emphasizes the necessity of a clear appreciation of the Church as a company — a body and communion, as it calls the Church.

As a side note, we point out that both confessions make it abundantly clear that true believers can not be expected to be perfect or almost perfect, but that they earnestly strive for improvement and growth in faith and therefore need the daily forgiveness of their sins and the indwelling of the Holy Spirit. The Scriptural picture of true believers is a different one from that of the Anabaptists and other perfectionists.

"THE TRUE CHURCH IS TO BE RECOGNIZED BY THE FOLLOWING MARKS"

The true Church is to be recognized by the following marks: It practises the pure preaching of the gospel. It maintains the pure administration of the sacraments as Christ instituted them. It exercises Church discipline for correcting and punishing sins.

"Pure"

As everyone can see, the Confession uses the little word "pure" in connection with the first two marks of the Church. As for the third one, Church discipline, we could silently add the word to the text.

Although it was written after de Brès produced our Confession, it may help us understand the adjective "pure" better if we refer to what I read (with some surprise) in the Representation sent by the Reformed Churches in the Netherlands to the Diet of Augsburg held in 1566. By means of this document, which was accompanied by a formal petition, the Dutch churches tried to convince Emperor Maximilian II that, in accord with the Scriptural duties of a Christian government, he should use his influence and power to have the persecution terminated and grant freedom to establish a church life that is in accordance with the will of God.

In this document, the churches assured the emperor that they acknowledged "the prophetic and apostolic Scriptures," and thus the whole Bible, that they received "the four authentic symbols of the Church" — our three creeds as well as the "Nicaenum" (they called our Nicene Creed the "Chalcedonian" Creed) — and wholeheartedly rejected any heresy. They told him that in their meetings nothing was taught that was not based upon the clear testimony of the Scriptures or that would conflict with what "the fathers of the first and pure Church," in perfect harmony with one another, taught.[216]

"The first and pure Church" — that is what this document calls the ancient Christian Church because it based its teachings and life on the prophetic and

---

[216] Bakhuizen van den Brink, *Protestantse Pleidooien* 2:200. Calvin speaks of "the ancient and purer Church" in his *Institutes* (IV.xii.6), as well as in a petition sent to Emperor Charles V (see Van der Jagt, "Een schema" 39).

apostolic Scriptures — just as the Reformed of the Netherlands were doing as they followed this example some centuries later.

Here we again find the Church's attribute of apostolicity. The marks of the true Church must be seen in the light of its attributes!

Pure — less pure — impure

The Petition also uses the term "true Church."[217] The true Church can also be called the pure Church, not because this Church is perfect but because it teaches nothing but the doctrine of the Scriptures. In other words, the pure-impure distinction can be used as an alternative for the true-false distinction.

That is how Antonius Walaeus in the *Synopsis Purioris Theologiae* used this distinction. To him the true Church is the pure Church, and the false church the impure church.[218] This is fundamentally different from replacing the true-false distinction with the pure-impure one as was done later on. Walaeus was not the first to realize that every church exhibits imperfections, one church even more than another.[219]

This also means that the borderline between the true Church on the one side and the sects together with the false church on the other is not always the same. A church can fall into such decay that it is clear it no longer submits to the Word of God. The evil one is still active! On the other hand, our Lord Jesus Christ is still gathering His Church. His Spirit can work revival and even reformation in an apostate church. Church history produces ample proof of both possibilities.

To every congregation or confederation of churches the apostolic warning is applicable: "Therefore let him who thinks he stands take heed lest he fall" (1 Corinthians 10:12).

---

[217] The Dutch title of this document is "Smeekschrift van de christenen in Nederland, die om de ware religie zijn getroffen" (Petition of the Christians in the Netherlands, who are persecuted because of the true religion).

[218] Samuel Maresius (1599-1673) speaks in the same way in his *Foederatum Belgium*, a commentary on the Belgic Confession (see K. Schilder, *De Reformatie* 16.6 [Nov. 8, 1935], reprinted in *De Kerk* 1:259). J. W. van der Jagt's article "Een Schema" is very instructive on Walaeus.

[219] Several documents from the era of the Reformation emphasize that no church is perfect but that every church shows imperfections (see footnote 24).

Over against this emphasis, people sometimes say that Christ told His apostles to teach the nations everything He had commanded them and that the Heidelberg Catechism, in Lord's Day 7, says that we must believe "all that God has revealed to us in His Word." A little later on, however, the Catechism emphasizes God's promises in particular: "all that is promised us in the gospel." As for what Christ said, we should read these in their proper context, namely that of the "Great Commission," in which He told the apostles to preach the gospel to the nations, making them His disciples and baptizing them into the name of the triune God. Then, since they are His disciples, they must indeed be taught all that He had commanded His apostles. This suggests a long process. Later data in the Scriptures show us that this process nowhere led to a perfect congregation. The same Saviour did not reject those churches which clearly proved that they were not keeping "everything" He had commanded His apostles. In this view, then, we observe a perfectionism which is not in keeping with the Scriptures. John Calvin and others have shown us a better way, and we do well to adopt this wisdom for practical church life.

Despite all of this, it is not advisable to use the pure-impure or pure-less pure distinction. The main reason for this recommendation is that this distinction is no longer used as an alternative for the true-false distinction but is meant to replace it.

We have learned, however, that "pure" means the same as "apostolic." In the pure administration of God's Word, the sacraments, and Church discipline, the apostolic Church manifests itself!

"Recognized"

After what was said in the previous paragraph, namely that the Church must be distinguished from the many sects — which are not to be confused with the hypocrites within the Church — the way lies open now for us to answer the question of how this Church can be recognized. We must emphasize that this can be done only by faith. All that follows in this article is covered by its very first words: "We believe."

That Christ's assurance in Matthew 18:20 that He is in the midst of those gathered in His name, even though their number is minimal, is being fulfilled can be observed by the eye of faith alone. To the worldwide Church of the "Great Commission," which is the fulfilment of God's promise to Abraham (Genesis 22:18), Christ's presence is a strong consolation and encouragement.

Attributes and marks

In our comments on Article 27, we already mentioned the distinction between the attributes of the Church and the marks of the Church. It is of some importance that our Confession first mentions the attributes. It does so in Article 27. Only in Article 29 are the marks of the Church presented.

Of course, this order is in harmony with the line of reasoning followed in Articles 27 through 29. First we confess that there is one Church (Art. 27). Then we confess that, according to the divine Scriptures, the unity of the Church must be maintained, and here the Confession has in mind those who do not do this (Art. 28). And then the location of the Church is indicated by means of the marks (Art. 29).

There is more than this, however. The reason Article 27 sums up the attributes of the Church — its oneness, holiness, catholicity, and apostolicity — is that in so doing it is claiming that the churches of the Reformation are the same as the ancient Christian Church as it was established by Christ and His apostles. The very first line of these articles has an anti-Roman colour. The claim that the Reformed churches were "the legal continuation" of the ancient

Christian Church made it necessary for the Confession to point to the correct address of that Church by elaborating on the way in which the Church which has these attributes can be found. It does so by, as it were, repeating, summarizing, and concretizing these attributes in the marks. The one holy catholic and apostolic Church can be recognized from its activities: the administration of God's Word, the sacraments, and discipline.

This may explain why, in the literature of the ancient Christian era, we do not often read about the Church being recognized by its marks. The attributes of the Church claim most of the attention. Yet the reformers recognized the necessity of drawing attention to its marks because the Church of Rome claimed exclusive possession of the four attributes. That is, the Church of Rome claimed that it alone exhibited oneness, holiness, catholicity, and apostolicity. This claim made it necessary for the reformers to develop a kind of doctrine of the marks of the Church: the attributes show us what the Church is and the marks tell us where the Church can be located.[220]

> Rome reacted by beginning to speak about marks as well. In the days of the Counter-reformation Cardinal Robert Bellarminus produced no fewer than fifteen of them.[221] The *Catechismus Romanus* (1566) returned to the four attributes, calling them marks also. At a later stage, the relationship with the Roman See received more and more emphasis: The oneness of the Church comes from the Pope being the successor to the apostle Peter and thus having authority to guarantee its holiness, catholicity, and apostolicity.[222]

It will be sufficient to deal very briefly with the Anabaptists. For them, the only mark of the true Church is its holiness, which means the absence of sinners.[223]

---

[220] John Calvin also calls the marks "symbols" (*Institutes* IV.i.8, 10).

[221] J. van Genderen, "De kenmerken van de Kerk," *De Kerk* (Kampen: Kok, 1990) 283. I presume that these fifteen marks are the same as those summed up by Rotterdam, *Van Zions Roem* 2:182: (1) the name "catholic church"; (2) its antiquity; (3) its uninterrupted durability; (4) the multitude of its members; (5) the apostolic succession of its bishops; (6) its conformity with the doctrine of the ancient Church; (7) the unity of its members under the Pope; (8) the sanctity of its doctrine; (9) the authority of its doctrine; (10) the holiness of its bishops; (11) the glory of its miracles; (12) the light of the gift of prophecy; (13) the confession of its opponents; (14) the sad end of its enemies; (15) its temporal prosperity.

Some of these marks were mentioned earlier in a negative way in Article 7 of our Confession: "We may not consider . . . custom, or the great multitude, or antiquity, or succession of times and persons, or councils, decrees or statutes, as of equal value with the truth of God."

[222] J. van Genderen, "De kenmerken" 284. In a textbook on the doctrine of the Church of Rome, the question of where we can find the church is answered as follows: "At Christ's command the apostles have established the Church. They have appointed successors to take over their government. These successors are the Pope (successor of Peter) and the bishops (successors of the apostles). Well, wherever these successors (Pope and bishops together) are found, there is the church of the apostles, the Church of Christ. It is the Catholic Church" (N. G. M. van Doornik, *Kleine Triptiek: Handboek van de katholieke leer en het katholieke leven*, 2nd ed. [Utrecht: Het Spectrum, 1954] 48).

[223] The Formula of Concord (1576), the last of the Lutheran confessions, which was compiled to settle some serious controversies among the Lutherans, summarizes the Anabaptist view as follows: "That that is not a true Christian Church in which any sinners are yet found" (Article XII.7). They even go as far as forbidding work of any kind for Lutheran ministers, who "are to be avoided and shunned as perverters of the divine Word" (XII.9) (Schaff, *Creeds* 3:175f).

Two or three?

Our own Confession presents three marks of the true Church. This is the fruit of the development mentioned above. In the earlier stages of the Reformation era some documents had only two marks.

The (Lutheran) Augsburg Confession of 1530 defines the Church and its marks as follows: "The Church is the congregation of saints, in which the gospel is rightly taught and the sacraments rightly administered" (Art. VII).[224]

The Geneva Confession of 1536 says, "We believe that the proper mark by which rightly to discern the Church of Jesus Christ is that His holy gospel be purely and faithfully preached, proclaimed, heard, and kept, that His sacraments be properly administered, even if there be some imperfections and faults, as there always will be among men" (Art. 19).

John Calvin, too, mentions also only two marks in his *Institutes*: "Wherever we see the word of God sincerely preached and heard, wherever we see the sacraments administered according to the institution of Christ, there we cannot have any doubt that the Church of God has some existence, since his promise cannot fail, 'Where two or three are gathered together in my name, there am I in the midst of them' (Matth. xviii.20)" (IV.i.9; cf. IV.i.9-12).

In a letter to the king of France, dated August 1, 1536, intended to accompany a copy of his *Institutes*, Calvin writes, "We . . . maintain, both that the Church may exist without any apparent form, and, moreover, that the form is not ascertained by that external splendour which they foolishly admire, but by a very different mark, namely, by the pure preaching of the word of God, and the due administration of the sacraments."[225] That Calvin speaks of two marks does not mean that he neglected Church discipline. He wrote many pages on this subject in his *Institutes*.[226]

The Confession of Faith used in the English congregation at Geneva and written by John Knox in 1556 already has three marks: "The Word of God contained in the Old and New Testament, given us for instruction, the holy sacraments, and ecclesiastical discipline" (Art. 4).

Together with five others, all named John, John Knox wrote the Scottish Confession of Faith in 1560. Chapter XVIII gives the "notes of the true Kirk." They are "first, the true preaching of the Word of God, in which God has revealed Himself to us, as the writings of the prophets and apostles declare; secondly, the right administration of the sacraments of Christ Jesus, with which must be associated the Word and promise of God to seal and confirm them in our hearts; and lastly, ecclesiastical discipline uprightly ministered, as God's Word describes."

The French Confession does not speak specifically of marks, but it does say that "the Church cannot exist without pastors for instruction" (Art. 25), and in the same article it mentions the ministry and preaching of the Word and the

---

[224] The marks are mentioned again in the next sentence, which reads, "and unto the true unity of the Church, it is sufficient to agree concerning the doctrine of the gospel and the administration of the sacraments."

[225] Calvin, *Institutes* 1:14-15.

[226] *Institutes* IV.xii. It is remarkable that in the Geneva Catechism (1542) Calvin only refers to the marks but does not list them when he says that we can recognize the Church from the marks God has given.

sacraments — again only two marks. Later it speaks in the negative: "In this belief we declare that, properly speaking, there can be no Church where the Word of God is not received, nor profession made of subjection to it, nor use of the sacraments" (Art. 28).

Collectively these documents give us an impression of the development which took place in the era of the Reformation: whereas originally only two marks were mentioned, later on three were listed, as we find in our Confession.[227]

The nature or character of the Church is reflected in these marks. Article 27 describes the Church as "a holy congregation and assembly of the true Christian believers, who expect their entire salvation in Jesus Christ" — which is possible only when the gospel of this entire salvation in Jesus Christ is faithfully preached — and "are washed by His blood, and sanctified and sealed by the Holy Spirit" — which is effected by a faithful administration of the sacraments, accompanied by a Scriptural *disciplina*. In all of this the apostolicity of the Church is manifested.

Once again: attributes and marks

In the marks of the Church its attributes of oneness, holiness, catholicity, and apostolicity come out into the open. Without these attributes the marks cannot be properly understood, let alone applied.

This is no wonder, for the attributes of the Church are at the same time mandates. Their character as mandates is demonstrated in the marks, which serve as instruments for the public identification of the true Church.[228]

The apostolicity of the Church becomes audible to the believing ear and visible to the eye of faith in the pure and undefiled preaching and in the administration of the sacraments as instituted by Christ and maintained by the apostles. The same can be said about church discipline.

On the other hand, wherever these three marks are not found, the attributes of catholicity and apostolicity are missing and the church — or group, or fellowship, or whatever the organization may be called — has broken the oneness of the Church and cannot claim to be holy.

Conversely, we must say that the marks of the Church can be seen and applied only in the light of the attributes. Not all preaching is "pure," for in many churches the catholic Gospel of the apostles is no longer proclaimed. Whether the administration of the sacraments and of church discipline can be called faithful is determined by the same apostolic Gospel.

---

[227] It is often overlooked that the Westminster Confession (1647) mentions the three marks when it deals with the authority of the civil magistrates in Chapter XXIII. In paragraph 3, it says, "The civil magistrate may not assume to himself the administration of the Word and sacraments, or the power of the keys of the Kingdom of heaven." When it deals with the church in XXV.3, it says Christ has given to His Church "the ministry, oracles, and ordinances of God."

[228] Trimp, *The Church* 54.

Pure preaching is not necessarily what we have in mind when we refer to "a nice sermon" or, more to the point, "a good sermon." Faithful administration of the sacraments is not to be identified with the use of the proper formulas and the adopted forms. Faithful administration of Church discipline is not the same as acting according to a set of rules adopted for this purpose. All of these church activities must be in harmony with the apostolicity of the Church and must therefore be based upon what the apostles did and left behind for the generations that followed.

They must also be of such a nature that they are not hindered by restrictive traditions tied to nationality or culture or anything else. The Church is catholic, and therefore a church group on another continent and in a different cultural environment cannot be bound to our western customs and traditions.

Other issues — such as customs and traditions surrounding the celebration of the sacraments, the way in which Church discipline is applied in a number of stages, and other peripheral issues which do not touch either the marks or the attributes — are not essential in this respect. Differences of traditions do not necessarily mean that there is no unity of faith, no common submission to the instructions given from above and passed on in church.

The attribute of holiness is also evident in the marks of the true Church. We can trace the three marks in the proclamation of the covenant of Sinai as documented in Exodus 19. Moses had to declare the terms of the covenant: "Thus you shall say to the house of Jacob, and tell the children of Israel . . ." (the preaching of the Word — verses 3-7). The sealing of the covenant took place when the LORD descended in the majesty of a thick cloud (the administration of the sacraments — verses 9 and 18). The covenant must be received and acknowledged in holiness: the Israelites had to consecrate themselves, and no one was allowed to touch the mountain (the sanction of the covenant or Church discipline — verses 10, 12, 14, 15).[229]

"IT PRACTISES THE PURE PREACHING OF THE GOSPEL"

An activity

A Bible can be found on many pulpits throughout the world.[230] Sometimes it is even a rare or ornately bound copy. After all, is not the Bible the specific symbol of the Church? Yet the presence of "the sacred book" on the pulpit is not sufficient. The Bible must be opened and used; its contents must be

---

[229] Ralph F. Boersema, *Diligent For Unity* (unpublished manuscript, 1992) 25.
[230] In many church buildings, the choir stalls take central position and the pulpit with the Bible is placed to the side. In others, the altar is central.

proclaimed. Therefore the first mark of the true Church — just like the other two marks — is an activity: the preaching of the gospel, and specifically the pure preaching of it.

That our Confession puts some emphasis on that threefold activity in church life will become even clearer when we realize that the original French version has the verb "to use" for each of the three marks, and the Dutch version has it twice. This is an important matter, for the activity of gospel preaching is meant to work faith under the guidance of the Holy Spirit and to strengthen it. Article 24 began with this sentence: "We believe that this true faith, worked in man by the hearing of God's Word and by the operation of the Holy Spirit, regenerates him and makes him a new man."[231]

The proclamation of the gospel is expected to produce fruits. That is why various other documents emphasize that in the true Church the gospel is also heard and professed.[232] That is also why, immediately after it lists the marks of the true Church, the Article continues with the marks of the Christians. Some of the fruits of the pure preaching of the gospel are mentioned! (We shall deal with this important point further when we discuss the marks of Christians.)

Here the adjective "pure" is very important. It is used for the first mark of the true Church and is also applied to the Church itself.[233]

Proof text

There is one proof text, Galatians 1:8: "But even if we, or an angel from heaven, preach any other Gospel to you than what we have preached to you, let him be accursed."

This text seems to place full emphasis on the negative aspect: no false doctrine should creep into church life. But we can appreciate the fact that the apostle Paul aims to make it abundantly clear that the Church, in order to remain the Church, must maintain the faithful preaching of the true gospel as he himself had preached it.

At the same time, it should be clear that in this first mark the apostolicity of the true Church is reflected and manifested. Those who hear the pure gospel preached have found the holy catholic and apostolic Church.[234]

---

[231] Cf. Van der Jagt, *De Kerk* 77.
[232] Geneva Confession, Article 18; Calvin, *Institutes* IV.i.9; and French Confession, Article 28.
[233] Boersema, *Diligent For Unity* 25.
[234] That this mark refers to regular, continuous — not incidental — preaching, is obvious.

Function

The marks of the true Church act as norms and therefore function as questions, as well. Self-examination — with regard to the preaching as well — is beneficial to congregational life. That is why Article 30 declares, "There should be ministers or pastors to preach the Word of God and to administer the sacraments."[235] But it goes on to refer to the office of the elders. They must "see to it that the true doctrine takes its course."

Today some voices are heard asserting their intention to reduce the church offices to two: the offices of the elders and the deacons, with the provision that the minister is considered a full-time elder with the special task of preaching. Others put different forms of Bible-interpretation — for example, an "introduction" at the Bible study club — on the same level as the preached sermon. In agreement with our Confession, we must hold the office of the pastor in honour. At the same time, the office of the eldership must be fully respected and must function: the elders "are also charged with the supervision over the doctrine " of the ministers.[236]

"IT MAINTAINS THE PURE ADMINISTRATION OF THE SACRAMENTS AS CHRIST INSTITUTED THEM"

"Administration"

Again the emphasis here is on an activity in church life: the administration of the sacraments. It is not enough to have a Scriptural doctrine regarding the sacraments, though it is essential. It is a commendable symbol when we see a baptismal font close to the pulpit — and why not a small symbolic table alongside, set with the *instrumentarium* for the Lord's Supper?[237] These things, however, must be used faithfully.

---

[235] We should remember that the French Confession does not set forth the marks of the true Church as clearly as our own Confession does, but places full emphasis on the ministry when it says that "the Church cannot exist without pastors for instruction" (Art. 25).

[236] "Form for the Ordination of Elders," *Book of Praise* 630.

[237] No doubt such a table could remain central and be flanked by extensions during the administration of the Lord's Supper.

"As Christ instituted them"

These words are added, not only over against the doctrine and practice of the Church of Rome and others, but also to remind us of what Christ intended with the sacraments: to portray, as it were, the promise of the washing away of our sins in holy Baptism and the promise of union with Him in the holy Supper — in brief, to strengthen our faith in Him.

Article 33 elaborates on this purpose when it says, "We believe that our gracious God, mindful of our insensitivity and infirmity, has ordained sacraments to seal His promises to us and to be pledges of His good will and grace toward us. He did so to nourish and sustain our faith. He has added these to the Word of the gospel to present the better to our external senses both what He declares to us in His Word and what He does inwardly in our hearts. Thus He confirms to us the salvation which He imparts to us."

As for Baptism, it is not for nothing that the Form warns us against using it "out of custom or superstition." The same warning applies to participating in the Lord's Supper, as the "retention" or "admonition" in the Form shows us. Here again self-examination — not only as individuals, but also as a church — is necessary.

It may be superfluous to refer to the anti-Roman nature of these words. No one has the authority to increase the number of the sacraments — to seven, for example, as the Church of Rome has done.

Proof text

Here the oldest Dutch version of our Confession has the following proof text, 1 Corinthians 11:20: "Therefore when you come together in one place, it is not to eat the Lord's Supper."

It is really significant that this proof text has regard to the Lord's Supper and that there is no proof text dealing with holy Baptism. Nevertheless, the same warning against misuse applies to Baptism. Besides, what the "pure administration" of Baptism means is explained further in Article 34, as the "pure administration" of the Lord's Supper is explained in Article 35, both being among the longest articles in our Confession.

"IT EXERCISES CHURCH DISCIPLINE FOR CORRECTING AND PUNISHING SINS"

Proof texts?

It is remarkable that the oldest Dutch edition has no proof texts for this sentence. We could not find any applicable texts among those presented in the French version of the Confession either. Only the French version of 1580, which Schaff uses, has two texts.[238] The first one is Matthew 18:15-18: "Moreover if your brother sins against you, go and tell him his fault between you and him alone. If he hears you, you have gained your brother. But if he will not hear you, take with you one or two more, that 'by the mouth of two or three witnesses every word may be established.' And if he refuses to hear them, tell it to the church. But if he refuses even to hear the church, let him be to you like a heathen and a tax collector. Assuredly, I say to you, whatever you bind on earth will be bound in heaven, and whatever you loose on earth will be loosed in heaven." The second text is 2 Thessalonians 3:14-15: "And if anyone does not obey our word in this epistle, note that person and do not keep company with him, that he may be ashamed. Yet do not count him as an enemy, but admonish him as a brother."

Once again, these proof texts are not authentic. Was it perhaps de Brès's intention to have the proof texts for the following summary ("In short . . .") act as such for this sentence as well?

Disciplina and Church discipline

The reader may remember what we read about the line in Article 28 that says: "They [the believers] must submit themselves to its instruction and discipline." Here the truly Reformed "twin" slogan *doctrina et disciplina* is used. Christ told His apostles-to-be to make disciples of all nations. These nations must be taught about the great works of the triune God and must learn to observe all that Christ had commanded His followers. Church discipline is a special application of this *disciplina* — which in turn rests upon *doctrina*. Therefore we must never isolate Church discipline from these two. "Correcting and punishing sins" can be carried out — under God's blessing — only when, in Christian love, the person concerned is reminded of what it means to be a disciple of Christ.

---

[238] Schaff, *Creeds* 3:420.

In the regulations and forms adopted by our churches these admonitions take a prominent place. If they are applied as they are meant to be, no valid complaints can be made about "lack of love."

Anti-Roman and anti-Anabaptist overtones

It should be clear that this line has an anti-Rome overtone. This is obvious as soon as we compare it with what is stated further on in this article concerning the false church.

We may even hear a slight anti-Anabaptist tone in these words since, rather than attempting to correct sins, the Anabaptists "punished" them by withdrawing from the sinners and establishing their own "holy" sect.

"IN SHORT, IT GOVERNS ITSELF ACCORDING TO THE PURE WORD OF GOD"

The true Church is to be recognized by the following marks: It practises the pure preaching of the gospel. It maintains the pure administration of the sacraments as Christ instituted them. It exercises Church discipline for correcting and punishing sins. In short, it governs itself according to the pure Word of God, rejecting all things contrary to it and regarding Jesus Christ as the only Head. Hereby the true Church can certainly be known and no one has the right to separate from it.

Reformed

This is a genuinely Reformed sentence. It explains why the Church can be recognized by these three particular marks: the true Church desires to be in full harmony with the pure Word of God in every respect. These marks show the Church's respectful submission to that Word.

The translation ("governs itself") may seem formal and cool. The verb used in the original French and Dutch versions, as well as in Festus Hommius's Latin text, can be paraphrased this way: the Church "regulates itself by God's Word, accommodates or shapes itself to it."[239] The main point is the Church's heartfelt subjection to God's Word. A heartfelt love for the

---

[239] French: *si on se regle selon la parole de Dieu*; original Dutch: *So men hem aenstelt na het suyver woort Gods*; Latin: *si ad normam Verbi divini omnia exigantur*. A more adequate translation is desirable.

Word of God is the comprehensive mark of the Church, and who indeed can deny that the Church of the Reformation has such a love?

Among many people, a Church Order has the reputation of being a book full of formal regulations and therefore being dull and dry. Yet we can be thankful that the really Reformed rule formulated in the sentence under discussion is the basis of our own Church Order. Certainly there are all sorts of man-made rules in it, but we must also realize that its real character is an extension of what we confess in Article 32 of our Confession and is therefore a fruit of the same faith by which we believe the Church. Have we not heard how the French Confession — having listened to John Calvin in this respect also — speaks of the "true order of the Church"? It has in mind the Church of the Lord Jesus Christ in its well-organized and well-ordered form, which is the local congregation. And does not Article 31 of the Church Order clearly prove that our Reformed churches submit themselves respectfully and joyously to God's Word? Is not our Church Order built around the three marks of Article 29?[240]

Proof texts

The original Dutch editions presents the following proof texts.

The first is Ephesians 2:20: "having been built on the foundation of the apostles and prophets, Jesus Christ Himself being the chief cornerstone." The Church is an apostolic Church, submitting itself to the Word of God as it was revealed and proclaimed by the New Testament prophets and apostles.[241]

The second is Colossians 1:23: "if indeed you continue in the faith, grounded and steadfast, and are not moved away from the hope of the gospel, which you heard, which was preached to every creature under heaven, of which I, Paul, became a minister." The apostolic Word is the foundation and norm for church life.

The third is John 8:47: "He who is of God hears God's words. Therefore you do not hear, because you are not of God." The true Church desires to hear what God says — including what He says about church life.

---

[240] In Articles 30-32 the Belgic Confession does not occupy itself with the way in which life in a confederation of churches should be organized. It deals with the local church only. When it was written, the catholicity of the Church determined the relationship between the various churches — Lutheran, Zwinglian, and Calvinist. Common faith, and not life in a confederation of churches, was the decisive factor in acknowledging a church as a true Church of the Lord. Besides, because of the political, national, or "territorial" situation, each group of churches was a kind of "national" church. Even the Dutch churches — which were advised by the Convention of Wesel (1568) to organize themselves into classes, provincial, and national synods — soon found themselves under the guardianship of the (Reformed) government. (Remember the situation around the time of the Synod of Dordrecht, 1618-19). This may explain the mutual tolerance in matters of church order, such as the offices of superintendent (in the Lutheran churches and the London church of Reformed refugees) and bishop (in the Church of England after its reformation). This may be of significance in the relationship between our churches and churches with a structure different from ours, such as Presbyterian churches which originally were "national" churches.

[241] For "apostles and prophets" (in this order), see also Ephesians 3:5.

The fourth is John 17:20: "I do not pray for those alone, but also for those who will believe in Me through their word." Christ Himself prayed for the Church to be established upon the apostolic preaching of the gospel.

The fifth is Acts 17:11: "These (the Bereans) were more fair-minded than those in Thessalonica, in that they received the Word with all readiness, and searched the Scriptures daily to find out whether these things were so." Church life can be grounded properly only on an open Bible.

"REJECTING ALL THINGS CONTRARY TO IT AND REGARDING JESUS CHRIST AS THE ONLY HEAD"

"Rejecting"

We profess our faith in the midst of a sinful world. Consequently, there is a need to declare what we believe, not only in a positive way, but also in a negative way. We must reject certain things. These things can be moral — or rather, immoral — but they can also be doctrinal. That is why the Belgic Confession has already rejected certain false doctrines in earlier articles. At the end of Article 9, a rather long list of false Christians and heretics is presented.

Here in Article 29 we reject all that is contrary to God's Word as far as the regulation of church life is concerned.

Implications

It is obvious that our Confession has in mind the Church of Rome in particular. This is clear when it states that, because the true Church regulates its life according to the Word of God, it regards Jesus Christ as the only Head of the Church.

Following the order of the three marks, we can state that our Confession rejects the Church of Rome's refusal to give the preaching of the gospel the place it deserves in the liturgy. It rejects the *Missa Romana* (Roman mass) because it is, in effect, a sacrifice offered to God as a meritorious good work. It denies the Roman Catholic idea that the administration of holy Baptism washes away sin. It rejects the canon law of the Church of Rome with its view that the Pope is the successor of the apostle Peter as Christ's vicar here on earth. Jesus Christ is the only Head of the Church!

As for the Anabaptists, our Confession rejects their contempt for the offices and the sacraments, together with their misconceptions concerning Church discipline.

Furthermore, this line of the Confession must also be applied to the internal life of the Church. Time and again in the course of Church history there has been reason for reformation. Therefore *Ecclesia reformata semper reformanda est*; the Reformed church must always be open to further reformation. As we are on the alert for the threat of dangers from outside, there must also be continuous vigilant self-examination. Therefore the Church regulates itself according to Jesus Christ, its Head. He is "the only universal Bishop . . . of the Church" (Belgic Confession, Article 31).

Proof texts

For the last part of the sentence ("regarding Jesus Christ as the only Head") there are the following proof texts:

— John 10:4: "And when he brings out his own sheep, he goes before them; and the sheep follow him, for they know his voice."

— John 10:14: "I am the Good Shepherd; and I know My sheep, and am known by My own."

— Matthew 28:20b: "and lo, I am with you always, even to the end of the age."

— John 18:37: "Pilate therefore said to Him, 'Are You a king then?' Jesus answered, 'You say rightly that I am a king. For this cause I was born, and for this cause I have come into the world, that I should bear witness to the truth. Everyone who is of the truth hears My voice.' "

— Ephesians 1:22: "And He put all things under His feet, and gave Him to be Head over all things to the Church."

The last text in particular shows us that our Confession is based on the Scriptures when it calls Christ the only Head of the Church. Church life is a matter of gratefully acknowledging Christ as the Head and carefully and unceasingly listening to His voice. He is present, according to His promise!

The warm relationship between Christ and His people is seen in the sayings which are used as proof texts here and which assure us that He knows His sheep and is known by them. The sheep even know His voice.

In his booklet, *The Lord our Shepherd*, J. Douglas MacMillan — who was himself a shepherd before he became a minister and a professor of Church History in The Free Church of Scotland — tells us that during the days of his study at Edinburgh he missed his sheep, went home, and told his brother, "I'll come down with you and feed the sheep." But when he called them just the way he had always done, not a sheep lifted its head. Then his brother called them. Although his voice was hardly different, every young lamb lifted its head and ran for food. "My voice was just a sound to them, but my brother's voice meant nice warm food on a cold frosty morning, and so they came. They knew the shepherd's voice."[242]

"HEREBY THE TRUE CHURCH CAN CERTAINLY BE KNOWN AND NO ONE HAS THE RIGHT TO SEPARATE FROM IT"

Conclusion

Here the Confession draws its conclusion from all that has been said so far. In Article 27, we confessed the one holy catholic and apostolic Church. The next article showed that in view of the character of this Church every believer has the duty to join it or maintain its unity. In this way, the Confession focused its attention upon those who, for one reason or another, were still outside. The situation is indeed confusing, as the opening sentence of Article 29 indicates. There are so many groups which claim for themselves the name of Church. How can we make the right decision? Where is that Church which we must join? This is why the marks of the true Church are presented. They show us where the Church with those commendable attributes of oneness, holiness, catholicity, and apostolicity can be found. Altogether it is clearly a matter of the Church gratefully submitting to the Word of God, acknowledging Jesus Christ as its Head, and therefore reforming itself whenever needed.

Taking all of this into consideration, no one should feel confused any longer, because everyone has now been confronted with the true Church of the Lord Jesus Christ. He who gathers His Church wants every believer to join it or faithfully remain in it. No one has the right to separate from it.[243]

The Church of which every believer ought to be or become a member can be recognized. This term, "recognized," is used no fewer than three times in Article 29. Our Confession aims to give a firm assurance that those who enjoy the privilege of belonging, together with others, to the fulfilment of the promise given to Abraham are at the right address. It does not condemn those who are hesitant to join but urges them to do so, and it puts this invitation in terms which cannot be misunderstood: "no one has the right to separate from it.[244]

---

[242] J. Douglas MacMillan, *The Lord our Shepherd* (Bryntirion: Evangelical Press of Wales, 1988) 38.

[243] This obligation is well formulated in Craig's Catechism of 1581, the first Scottish Catechism, which is based on Calvin's *Institutes*. It says, "May we leave the particular church where the Word is remained? No, even although many other vices abound there. But the multitude are wicked and profane? Yet there is a true church, where the Word truly remains" (Torrance, *School of Faith* 121).

[244] In this respect, the Heidelberg Catechism runs parallel with the Belgic Confession when, in Lord's Day 21, Q&A 55, it teaches "that believers, all and everyone, as members of Christ, have communion

"THOSE WHO ARE OF THE CHURCH MAY BE RECOGNIZED BY THE MARKS OF CHRISTIANS"

Those who are of the Church may be recognized by the marks of Christians. They believe in Jesus Christ the only Saviour, flee from sin and pursue righteousness, love the true God and their neighbour without turning to the right or left, and crucify their flesh and its works. Although great weakness remains in them, they fight against it by the Spirit all the days of their life. They appeal constantly to the blood, suffering, death, and obedience of Jesus Christ, in whom they have forgiveness of their sins through faith in Him.

Two sets of marks

After our Confession has listed the marks of the true Church, it presents a second set of marks, those of Christians. The word "true" is not used here. However, since it is used for the same people in the first sentence of Article 27 — "the true Christian believers" — it was not necessary to repeat it here.[245]

By presenting two different sets of marks, our Confession differs from others in which the believers' reaction to the gospel is included in what is said about the marks of the Church.

One historical reason why our Confession differs at this point from others may be that — in contrast to the Anabaptist view, in which the church is made up exclusively of holy people — the Confession admits that the membership of the Church is not always very attractive. Nevertheless, this reality does not deny it the name of "true Church," for true believers are well aware of their shortcomings but fight against them and flee to Christ for grace and strength. Christian life is identifiable by the struggle against sin and shortcomings. Christians are desirous of making progress in holiness. A true Christian's spiritual life is never at a standstill but goes on manifesting itself in the power which faith has.

Another reason for the difference could be that — in contrast to the Roman Catholic view, in which the Church really consists of the clergy — the Reformation aimed to emphasize the priesthood of all believers and the great significance of the congregation.

---

with Him and share in all His treasures and gifts" and also "that everyone is duty-bound to use his gifts readily and cheerfully for the benefit and well-being of the other members" — which includes the obligation of church unity between believers.

[245] C. Trimp (*The Church* 7, 53, 56) emphasizes that the little word "true" does not actually add anything to the notion of "Church," but that it is used in the context of falsification and pretence. It was used in a situation in which a choice had to be made. There is a war going on, a war between Christ and Satan, a war between faith and unbelief!

Besides, these "marks of Christians" manifest the reception of and reaction to the marks of the true Church. True Christians want to be disciples of Christ (Matthew 28:19ff.), and therefore they gratefully receive the *doctrina et disciplina* in the administration of God's Word, the sacraments, and supervision.

Misinterpretation

We must be well aware of two possible misinterpretations of our Confession at this point. The first is the idea that the call to join the true Church is not all that urgent because there is an "invisible" unity among all those who show the marks of Christians presented in this sentence. The other misinterpretation draws a wrong conclusion from the connection between the two sets of marks mentioned in this article, namely that there are no believers outside the true Church.

In both cases the Confession would be contradicting itself. In the latter case, there would be no one outside to be urged — as in Article 28 — to join the true Church. And in the former case, the call of Article 28 to join the Church would be of minor importance or of no significance at all.

Relationship

For a good understanding of the relationship between these two sets of marks, the following quotations may be helpful. Some time before the writing of the Belgic Confession, this relationship was described clearly in the Tetrapolitan Confession of 1530, where it says, "Although that whereby it is entitled to be called the Church of Christ — namely, faith in Christ — cannot be seen, yet it can be seen and plainly known from its fruits. Of these fruits the chief are a courageous confession of the truth, a true love tendered to all, and a brave contempt of all things for Christ. These undoubtedly cannot be absent where the gospel and its sacraments are purely administered" (Chap. XV).

The Geneva Confession of 1536 states, "We believe that the proper mark by which rightly to discern the Church of Jesus Christ is that His gospel be purely and faithfully preached, proclaimed, heard and kept" (Art. 18).

In his *Institutes*, John Calvin writes, "Wherever we see the word of God sincerely preached and heard ... there we cannot have any doubt that the Church of God has some existence. ... If they have the ministry of the word, and honour the administration of the sacraments, they are undoubtedly entitled to be ranked with the Church, because it is certain that these things are not without a beneficial result" (IV.i.9). Later, he writes, "We have said that the symbols by which the Church is discerned are the preaching of the word and the observance of the sacraments, for these cannot anywhere exist without producing fruit and prospering by the blessing of God" (IV.i.10).

It is no wonder that the French Confession of 1559 says that the Church is "the company of the faithful who agree to follow His Word, and the pure religion which it teaches; who advance in all their lives, growing and becoming more confirmed in the fear of God according as they feel the want of growing and pressing forward. Even although they strive continually, they can have no hope save in the remission of their sins" (Art. 27). Then comes the sentence on the hypocrites, the presence of which "cannot destroy the title of the Church." Article 28 goes on to state that "there can be no Church where the Word of God is not received, nor profession made of subjection to it."

All these quotations[246] clearly demonstrate that faithful preaching, administration of the sacraments, and Church discipline produces fruits in the lives of the church members. These two sets of marks — those of the Church and those of Christians — belong together and must never be separated.

The second set

We repeat: de Brès must have seen the need to present a separate set of marks, namely those of Christians. Our Confession, then, aims to emphasize the divine power of God's Word as it is administered in preaching, sacrament, and discipline.

We can also say that in our Confession — just as in the Heidelberg Catechism — the emphasis lies on the work of Christ and the Holy Spirit. Christ Himself is the content of the proclamation of the Word of God, which takes the central place in the life of the Church and as a divine work must bear fruits.

This is already apparent in the very first sentence of Article 27: "the true Christian believers . . . are washed by His [Christ's] blood, and are sanctified and sealed by the Holy Spirit." When Article 28 repeats that the Church is the congregation and "assembly of the redeemed," the spotlight is again on Christ's work of redemption. In Article 29 the way along which the believers have come to faith is shown: it is a fruit of the preaching of the gospel. Even after they have come to faith, Christ's work in them continues: faith is strengthened by means of the use of the sacraments, and Church discipline also plays a role in this process.

This is also why, although the topic of Article 29 is the Church and its marks, attention is also focused on true Christians: the preaching of the gospel

---

[246] More quotations could be presented. In Chapter XVII, the Second Helvetic Confession refers to Christ's saying that His sheep hear His voice and follow Him (John 10:27ff.), after which this Confession gives a rather long exposition of the marks of the true Christians. The Westminster Confession of Faith points to the various grades of purity in the "particular [i.e., local] churches . . . according as the doctrine of the gospel is taught and embraced" (XXV.4).

produces fruits. The Confession aims to show us, not only where the true Church can be found, but also who the true members of the true Church are and that they can be recognized. Besides, is not the Church the communion of saints?

John Calvin goes even farther when, in his *Institutes*, he refers to God's eternal counsel regarding our election as the deepest origin. That is why he distinguished between the visible Church and the invisible Church. He writes, "I have observed that the Scriptures speak of the Church in two ways. Sometimes when they speak of the Church they mean the Church as it really is before God — the Church into which none are admitted but those who by the gift of adoption are sons of God, and by the sanctification of the Spirit true members of Christ. . . Often, too, by the name of Church is designated the whole body of mankind scattered throughout the world, who profess to worship one God and Christ, who by baptism are initiated into the faith; by partaking of the Lord's Supper profess unity in true doctrine and charity, agree in holding the word of the Lord, and observe the ministry which Christ has appointed for the preaching of it" (IV.i.7).

Calvin was well aware of the presence of hypocrites within the Church. He even speaks of "a very large mixture of hypocrites" in the Church. This, then, makes it necessary to believe "the invisible Church, which is manifest to the eye of God only" (IV.i.7). He means to say: What is sometimes visible of the Church is not so commendable and could easily confuse us, but let us not forget God's work, His divine plan. The Church is God's work! This pastoral aspect of what Calvin writes about the distinction between visible and invisible is often overlooked, and it was certainly forgotten by those who, at a later stage, used the distinction in a different sense and context to replace the distinction between true and false. Calvin places the invisible church within the visible church while Abraham Kuyper did the opposite.

Application

Some pastoral remarks may be in place. A nominal membership in the Church is not sufficient. Even when, with a clear conscience, we can confess that we belong to the true Church — in other words, that our churches are faithful churches of the Lord Jesus Christ — we must realize that the Church is always a mixture, God's threshing-floor (Augustine).

The marks of Christians are essential for our membership in the Church and even for the true Church itself. We must never isolate the marks of the true Church from the marks of Christians — the latter being, not a kind of fourth mark of the Church, but, as we should now understand, the essential fruit of the three marks and therefore included in them. When the gospel is indeed preached purely, sealed sacramentally, and upheld in Church discipline, the fruits of these activities become manifest.

A true Church is a living Church. The gospel keeps the true Christians' faith alive, as is shown in what follows: "They believe in Jesus Christ the only Saviour, flee from sin and pursue righteousness, love the true God and their neighbour . . . and crucify their flesh and its works." We are expected to be living members of the Church,[247] exhibiting the marks of Christians, and thereby demonstrating our gratitude for being brought to share in the blessing of Abraham's seed for all the nations of the earth.[248]

At the same time this understanding of the marks of Christians keeps us from using the marks of the true Church in a formal, neutral way. It leads us to personal self-examination: Are the fruits of all that happens in Church present in the personal life of the members of the Church? It leads us to collective self-examination: Is our congregational life only "traditional" as a result of sterile preaching? Is the power of the Word of God to bless manifest in our life as a congregation?

Our Confession emphasizes not only the office bearers and the work that they do (which is the Roman Catholic concept of the church), but also the way in which their work is received by the congregation. This is why words such as "assembly" and "congregation" are prominent and even dominant in the definitions of the Church given in Articles 27 through 29!

In other words, a congregation or confederation of churches cannot be called true when a Scriptural Confession alone is maintained and when the office bearers can be called faithful, but when all of this results in the life in the members and in the congregation or churches as a whole. The office bearers' faithful discharge of their duties and the congregation's faithful reception go together. This is how a true Church presents itself!

---

[247] Heidelberg Catechism, Lord's Day 21, Q&A 54.
[248] Genesis 22:18, the first and fundamental proof text of all that we confess, together with the Belgic Confession of Faith, concerning the Church.

"THEY BELIEVE IN JESUS CHRIST THE ONLY SAVIOUR, FLEE FROM SIN AND PURSUE RIGHTEOUSNESS, LOVE THE TRUE GOD AND THEIR NEIGHBOUR WITHOUT TURNING TO THE RIGHT OR LEFT, AND CRUCIFY THEIR FLESH AND ITS WORKS."

Proof text

The proof text for the first line is 1 John 4:2: "By this you know the Spirit of God: Every spirit that confesses that Jesus Christ has come in the flesh is of God."

The word "recognize" in the previous line is really quite significant because it appears no less than three times in our Confession with regard to both the true Church and the Christians. When we see the connection between this proof text and what the Confession says about true believers, we can say that we recognize nothing less than the work of the Holy Spirit — the Spirit of God Himself — in what the believers confess and in their way of life.

True Christians believe that Jesus Christ has come in the flesh. They acknowledge Him as the only Saviour, expecting their entire salvation in Him (Art. 27).

Translation

The translation of the original French and Dutch texts could be improved. The original actually says, "Those who are of the Church may be recognized by the marks of Christians, namely faith, and (from the fact) that, after having received Jesus Christ as the only Saviour, they flee from sin and pursue righteousness, love the true God and their neighbour, do not turn into a side-road either to the right or to the left, and crucify their flesh and its works."

The current translation misses two points. First, the original places full emphasis on faith as the mark of Christians. The current translation refers to the contents of faith, as well, but in the original version the contents follow as a separate entity after the act of faith has been named. Second, the current version suggests that not turning to the right or to the left is part of loving the true God and one's neighbour, but this phrase actually occupies a more independent position: it means that the believers are marching straight ahead in their faith.[249]

Sola fide

The catch-phrase of the Reformation resounds in these words. True Christians are marked by their faith in Christ and not by anything else.

"Flee"

Christians are also marked by the fact that they "flee from sin and pursue righteousness." We learn about this characteristic from the proof text, Romans 6:2, which answers the question, "Shall we continue in sin so that grace may abound?" The answer is "Certainly not! How shall we who died to sin live any longer in it?"

Those who love Christ as their Saviour, and are aware of what He had to suffer for their sins, cannot take any pleasure in what is wrong in God's eyes. They flee from it.

"Justice"

Positively, they pursue righteousness. This should not be confused with the righteousness which they have in Christ and which is confessed in Article 23.

The French and Latin versions can help us understand what this phrase is really saying. They both use the word "justice." The French text may be the clearest of all when it says, "They strive for justice, loving the true God and their neighbours, without turning into a side-road either to the right or to the left" (translation ours).

True Christians know the requirements of God's Law, as Christ has taught them.[250]

---

[249] The French Confession even speaks literally of "marching." It says that the believers want to make progress in the fear of God "according as they feel the want of advancing and always marching forward" (Art. 27).

[250] It is very significant that the Heidelberg Catechism mentions the name of Christ in Lord's Day 2, Q&A 4, though the same two commandments were already known from the Old Testament (Deuteronomy 6:5; Leviticus 19:18). The preaching of the law is the preaching of Christ! See *Our Only Comfort: When, Why, Which, How?* The Reformed Guardian, new series (forthcoming).

Self-crucifixion

It is characteristic of Christians that they crucify their own flesh and its works. The Confession has taken this mark from Galatians 5:24. This proof text says, "And those who are Christ's have crucified the flesh with its passions and desires."

In the French version, this phrase is still part of the sentence which says that true believers strive for justice. In their wish to create or maintain healthy relationships (as far as it depends upon them), they deny themselves. Their own interests no longer prevail, but the honour of God and the well-being of their fellowmen.

Consistency

A true believer desires to grow in faith. That is why the Confession states that true faith embraces consistency: a believer desires to be straightforward, and therefore will not make a detour or turn off into a side-road.

Once again: two sets of marks

All of this is the fruit of the pure preaching of the gospel, the strengthening of faith in the use of the sacraments, and mutual supervision among the believers. Whenever these three spiritual activities are faithfully executed, they result in the marks of Christians. The latter are even included in the former, as we have already seen.

Faith manifests itself in the life of a faithful church. The society for which Christians stand is radically different from today's society which is so strongly influenced toward an egocentric lifestyle.

Kindred spirits

For this reason, those who are outside but who likewise believe in Christ and who are being urged to join the true Church may find "kindred spirits" in that Church, since the gospel preaching in the true Church bears fruit. They can recognize like faith in that of others. This, then, should make them unite with those others and join the true Church. Their own faith must also be nourished by the pure administration of God's Word, the sacraments, and Church discipline. When they join the Church, they can be fully assured that they are at the correct address, for wherever Christ is preached and acknowledged as the only and perfect Saviour, there the Holy Spirit has been at work. God Himself works this faith in people's hearts.

Once again, there is a reason for self-examination here. Can those who are "outside" recognize the same faith in our lives so that they feel attracted to join us? After all, that we belong to the true Church must be demonstrated in our exhibiting "the marks of Christians."

"ALTHOUGH GREAT WEAKNESS REMAINS IN THEM, THEY FIGHT AGAINST IT BY THE SPIRIT ALL THE DAYS OF THEIR LIFE"

Proof text

The Church may be a triumphant Church even in this life, but it is at the same time — and even predominantly — a struggling, militant Church. The believers are also personally involved in a fierce fight against Satan, particularly when they have to struggle against their own weakness. Their strength, however, is the Holy Spirit.

All of this is expressed in the proof text, Galatians 5:17, which reads as follows: "For the flesh lusts against the Spirit, and the Spirit against the flesh; and these are contrary to one another, so that you do not do the things that you wish."[251]

Relevance

Once again, this honest Confession strongly rejects the Anabaptist concept of the Church. As we said earlier, the Anabaptists wanted a Church consisting exclusively of holy people. In their view, there was only one mark of the Church and only one attribute, as well: holiness. Where the holiness of its members is not manifest, there is no church. Our Confession presents a more realistic picture of the believers — and consequently of the Church. Believers exhibit great weakness, although they fight against it.

These Anabaptist ideas are still alive.[252] They are present where strong emphasis is laid on all sorts of other marks the believers should possess, such

---

[251] This text follows another one in the older editions. The French version has Romans 7:7; the later French version used by Schaff (*Creeds* 3:420) has Romans 7:6, 17, etc. Vallensis has Romans 2:5, but suggests that this should be 7:15. In view of this uncertainty we leave it out of consideration.

[252] A modern manifestation of this view is The Church of the Nazarene, as well as the Wesleyan Methodists, who believe absolute perfection to be possible.

as awareness of the exact time and place of one's conversion and other experiences. The concept of the Church in this subjectivistic view is fundamentally the same as that of the Anabaptists. The same is true of the view that, in order to be regarded as a true believer, a person must exhibit all kinds of "signs of the Spirit," such as speaking in tongues, faith-healing, and faith-in-faith healing.

In general, as long as peoples' picture of the Church is determined by the spiritual quality and behaviour of its members and not by Christ's work and its fruits, all that is said against the Anabaptist view here is still relevant. In such views, the starting-point is not faith — "I believe a holy catholic Church" — but experience.

It can be very beneficial to read and study our Confession!

"THEY APPEAL CONSTANTLY TO THE BLOOD, SUFFERING, DEATH, AND OBEDIENCE OF JESUS CHRIST, IN WHOM THEY HAVE FORGIVENESS OF THEIR SINS THROUGH FAITH IN HIM"

By faith alone

Whereas in the previous sentence there was an anti-Anabaptist element, here, we can say, the Confession rejects the Roman Catholic concept of the Christian. The positive aspect of this sentence and its warm tone are more important, however.

"They appeal" is an inadequate translation. The original text actually says, "They take refuge with the blood. . . ." This line is derived from Colossians 1:12, which says, "giving thanks to the Father, who has qualified you to be partakers of the inheritance of the saints in the light."

True believers can always flee to Christ and receive whatever they need in their struggle — and, in particular, grace.

The complete picture

With this sentence, the picture of the marks of Christians is complete. It is a picture that clearly shows us that life in a Church which has the marks of the true Church produces rich fruits: its true members live close to their Head.

All of this should give those who, though they share the same faith in Christ, are still outside the necessary incentive to join the true Church, and it should persuade those who are within the Church to bend their necks to the yoke of Christ.[253]

"THE FALSE CHURCH ASSIGNS MORE AUTHORITY TO ITSELF AND ITS ORDINANCES THAN TO THE WORD OF GOD"

The false church assigns more authority to itself and its ordinances than to the Word of God. It does not want to submit itself to the yoke of Christ. It does not administer the sacraments as Christ commanded in His Word, but adds to them and subtracts from them as it pleases. It bases itself more on men than on Jesus Christ. It persecutes those who live holy lives according to the Word of God and who rebuke the false church for its sins, greed, and idolatries.

The false church

We should remember that Article 29 should not have the unofficial heading found in the *Book of Praise*: "The marks of the true and the false church." The real contrast made in this article is between the true Church and the many sects, those various falsifications of the Church and its doctrine, of which the false church is an extreme example.

If we understand this point, it may explain why, when we read all that is said about the false church, we get the strong impression that de Brès had the Church of Rome in mind. That church is not mentioned, however, and the style of this paragraph is so general that what is stated in it can be applied to other churches as well.[254]

Church?

The question could then be asked: Is it correct to grant the name of "church" to such an institution? Indeed, we have heard other confessions state

---

[253] The conformity between the Belgic Confession and the Heidelberg Catechism is really striking. In this paragraph, we can recognize the Catechism's "three parts" of sin, grace, gratitude — in particular as they recur in Lord's Day 44, Q&A 115.

[254] The *Deed of Secession and Return* of 1834 applied this part of Article 29 to the Nederduitsch Hervormde Kerkgenootschap of that time.

that whenever a certain group does not comply with the conditions set down by the Scriptures, there is no church.[255]

Nevertheless, for practical reasons the name of church is maintained. This name could even underscore the fact that the false church is a falsification — indeed, a forgery! — of the real Church.

The principal mark

Although the word "marks" is not used for the false church, we can state that this is its main mark: it has assumed for itself a false authority. The Confession actually says, "more power and authority."

In church life as in the world, things can be fundamentally the same. First, the hunger for power arises, and then this hunger is cloaked in one theory or another to prove that the person who desires power really has the authority to be in power. In the false church, this hunger for power is cloaked in false humility, as we can learn from Colossians 2:18a, which serves as a proof text here: "Let no one cheat you of your reward, taking delight in false humility and worship of angels."

One of the underlying theories of the Church of Rome is its doctrine of the Pope's position, power, and authority. This is not the place to paint a picture of the way this doctrine was developed in the course of history, but it is well known that the Pope claims to be the successor of the apostle Peter as Christ's vicar here on earth. This may seem to be a very humble claim, since Peter's position was not solicited but given, but it is in fact a very false humility because the Pope has assumed to himself power over the souls of millions of people, whereas originally he would have been just another elder or minister of the local church of Rome.

In different times and situations, a similar false humility can lead to the assumption of power, as was the case in the Netherlands in the first half of the nineteenth century, when it was claimed that the church had gained so much "higher knowledge" from the Enlightenment. The churches of the Secession experienced the implications of this false humility!

The proof text, which urged the Colossians not to let themselves be robbed of the riches of their faith by the false humility of the people who in those days claimed to have gained a "higher knowledge," is still relevant to our own day.

---

[255] E.g. the Geneva Confession of 1536, Article 9.

"IT DOES NOT WANT TO SUBMIT ITSELF TO THE YOKE OF CHRIST"

Continuation

The proof text here is Colossians 2:18b-19, which follows immediately after the previous sentence's proof text: "[Let no one cheat you of your reward, taking delight in false humility and worship of angels] intruding into those things which he has not seen, vainly puffed up by his fleshly mind, and not holding fast to the Head, from Whom all the body, nourished and knit together by joints and ligaments, grows with the increase that is from God."

The apostle's way of reasoning in this chapter is clear. Those who claim a "higher knowledge" (in those days a form of gnosticism[?]) do not show real humility, for they have broken the connection they had with Christ, the Head.

This, then, is exactly what happens in the false church. On false grounds it claims to have been given special authority, and so it no longer submits to Christ, even though it may imagine that it does.

Once again: the yoke of Christ

This verdict is based on another proof text, Psalm 2:3, where we hear the kings of the earth incite one another to rebellion with the words, "Let us break their bonds in pieces and cast away their cords from us." In our Confession these "bonds" and "cords" are once again called "the yoke of Christ."

We encountered this phrase in Article 28 and learned that it refers to what Christ said in Matthew 11:29: "Take My yoke upon you and learn from Me, for I am gentle and lowly in heart, and you will find rest for your souls. For My yoke is easy and My burden is light." We also learned that by His yoke Christ meant His teachings (*doctrina*) and the regulations issued to His disciples (*disciplina*).

Those who claim to have been granted "higher knowledge" no longer submit themselves to the yoke of Christ. Furthermore they put a hard yoke upon the people who entrust themselves to them. Only Christ's yoke is easy and His burden light. That is why our Confession can say, "The false church assigns more authority to itself and its ordinances than to the Word of God." The sentence about the yoke of Christ explains the previous sentence.

"IT DOES NOT ADMINISTER THE SACRAMENTS AS CHRIST COMMANDED IN HIS WORD, BUT ADDS TO THEM AND SUBTRACTS FROM THEM AS IT PLEASES"

The sacraments

Those who leave the paths of the Word of God and want to remain "religious" inevitably end up in one kind of ritualism or another. As for the Church of Rome, this tendency became manifest in the increase of the number of sacraments from two to seven. These sacraments are considered to be either good works (such as the Mass as a sacrifice offered to God) or the carriers of grace — remember the introduction of "emergency baptism," to be administered because a baby which has died before being baptized has not been cleansed from original sin and therefore cannot be saved.

"IT BASES ITSELF MORE ON MEN THAN ON JESUS CHRIST"

The heart of the matter

This sentence reveals the heart of the whole matter: the false church does not build upon what Christ has proclaimed but upon what man has invented. Therefore it is not worthy to bear the name of Church — with a capital C — but it is a false church, an extreme form of the falsification which starts as soon as certain particular theories and opinions begin to dominate life, which is how the sects originate.

We should understand now why John Calvin and others in the days of the Reformation called the Church of Rome a sect: following the ideas of men and not the Word of God is typical of a sect!

Marks

Once more we refer to the unofficial heading of Article 29. It is remarkable that the Confession does not use the word "marks" in connection with the false church. Unlike the paragraph on the true Church, this paragraph on the false church does not explicitly mention the administration of God's Word, the sacraments, and Church discipline in that order.

The administration of the sacraments is indeed mentioned. The falsification of the preaching of God's Word can be seen in the words, "The false church assigns more authority to itself and its ordinances than to the Word of God." Church discipline is replaced by persecution. The false church, however, is characterized by one single mark: "It bases itself more on men than on Jesus Christ." That is why the false church is an extreme example of a sect in the old sense of the word: a group that follows the ideas of its leadership.

The principal mark is thus mentioned in the first as well as the next-to-last sentence of this paragraph: the false church assigns more authority to itself and gives more priority to what men say than to Christ's Word.

"IT PERSECUTES THOSE WHO LIVE HOLY LIVES ACCORDING TO THE WORD OF GOD, AND WHO REBUKE THE FALSE CHURCH FOR ITS SINS, GREED AND IDOLATRIES"

The consequence

What is stated in this last sentence of the paragraph is the consequence of what was said in the previous sentence. As soon as human doctrines and practices are considered to be of divine origin (the Confession calls them idolatries), consistency requires that others be placed under their yoke.

This took place already in New Testament times, as is shown by the first proof text, Revelation 2:9, in which the Lord Jesus tells the congregation at Smyrna: "I know your works, tribulation, and poverty (but you are rich); and I know the blasphemy of those who say they are Jews and are not, but are a synagogue of Satan." This text includes Christ's verdict: the persecutors claim to be a synagogue of genuine people of God's covenant, but this synagogue is dominated by God's great opponent, Satan. Christ's great opponent is behind the decay in church life, which ultimately leads to complete falsification.

Persecution was predicted by the same Lord Jesus who said in John 16:2, "They will put you out of the synagogues; yes, the time is coming when whoever kills you will think that he offers God service."

Here the Confession mentions the extreme misuse of the third mark of the true Church, Church discipline — excommunication for an entirely false reason — and even the ultimate physical violence springing from religious hatred: death.

The history of the Church — and of the century of the Reformation, in particular — also shows us that Christ's Word was accurate: both spiritual and physical persecution actually happened. The false church goes to the extreme! That is what happens when it bases itself more on men than on the Word of God. It is no wonder therefore that the false church is easily recognized and distinguished from the true Church, as the final sentence of Article 29 says.

The reason

The reason for all of this is that the false church cannot accept rebuke "for its sins, greed, and idolatries," and this is indeed one of the characteristics of the false church. It is a reflection of the picture shown in the last proof text, Revelation 17:3, which says: "So he carried me away in the Spirit into the wilderness. And I saw a woman sitting on a scarlet beast which was full of names of blasphemy, having seven heads and ten horns."

With these words, the Confession returns to the first sentence of this paragraph: the false church executes the authority it falsely claims to the extreme. Here is a satanic caricature of Church discipline, that mark of the true Church which safeguards the pure preaching of the gospel and the faithful administration of the sacraments. Here is the beast of Revelation 17, the opponent of God and Christ, who wants to destroy all of the divine work of grace.

"THESE TWO CHURCHES ARE EASILY RECOGNIZED AND DISTINGUISHED FROM EACH OTHER"

Final conclusion

The true Church must be distinguished from all the sects that call themselves the Church. This is not always easy, and therefore the distinction must be made "diligently and prudently."

As for the false church, the distinction is much easier because the false church is an extreme form of falsification, a clear counterfeit. This, then, is the final conclusion drawn from a comparison of the true Church and the false church.

"We believe"

As a matter of course, even this final conclusion can only be drawn by faith. If we do not take our starting-point in the Scriptures, carefully listening to what Christ says as the Head of the Church, who wants to preserve His Church and who therefore also wants to warn against the false church, as He does in the last few proof texts, then we shall join the many who, for example, condemn the true-false distinction as "a black-and-white-scheme." An easier way out of the complex problems created by the existence of so many churches would be to adopt the theory of the pluriformity of the church or denominationalism.

If we do so, however, to formally maintain Articles 27 through 29 as our confession would not be honest. We would even be forgetting that all that is said in these articles is covered by the words "We believe."

This was our starting-point. It is also what we state at the end, after all that we have confessed regarding the Church, in all of which resounds the impressive contents of the first proof text, Genesis 22:18, God's promise of a worldwide Church as the fruit of the blessing for all the nations of the earth which comes in Abraham's Seed, Jesus Christ.

Finally and firmly we confess our faith in Him, and therefore we repeat the simple but so heavily-laden line of our creeds:

"I believe a holy catholic and apostolic Church!"

Part 2

UNITY OF FAITH
AND
CHURCH UNITY
in
Historical Perspective

PREFACE

In 1994, the present writer published a booklet entitled *"True" and "False": How do we read Article 29 of the Belgic Confession of Faith?* It was issued as No. 13 in The Reformed Guardian series.

This booklet was written as a contribution to the discussion on contacts with other churches as it was taking place in the Free Reformed Churches of Australia. But it also made an effort to explain the fundamentals of the answer to the question: When and under which conditions can we and shall we recognize other churches as faithful churches of the Lord Jesus Christ? The "local" flavour of the booklet prevents it from being reprinted, and therefore it has been partly rewritten. It has been combined with material published in a report written for the 1994 Synod of the Australian churches, from which report the title has also been derived.

CHAPTER 1

INTRODUCTION

Application

A commentary such as we have presented in the first section of this book can help us understand what the Church of the Lord Jesus Christ is, which attributes characterize it, and where we can locate it in the multitude of bodies which lay claim to the name "church." It also serves to underline the believers' duty to join the Church in accord with the ordinance of God. We deliberately add these last few words because, as we have seen, one of the aims of our Confession, and in particular of Articles 27 through 29, is to urge and encourage believers who remain outside the Church to join it and so comply with Christ's prayer — a mandate for us! — that believers be one.

There is, however, another aspect as well. Article 28 also emphasizes the obligation of those who are members of the Church to maintain its unity. This duty is expressed in the line that reads, "no one ought to withdraw from it." What our Confession does not mention (because its aim was and is somewhat different) is that there is also a duty to seek unity with believers who have joined together in "another church." To put it differently, we must investigate the possibility of church unity with such churches as, at first acquaintance, appear to be faithful churches of the Lord Jesus Christ.

This, then, is a matter of applying what we confess in the articles of our Confession to a situation in which two or more churches cross paths. In our commentary this application was oblique but certainly not prominent. We shall therefore continue our studies and try to answer some underlying questions such as: When can we say there is unity of faith between believers? On what basis can we achieve responsible church unity? What are the relevant principles?

Church history

It is the application of these confessional articles, therefore, which provides the theme of this section. To apply these articles properly requires us to delve deeply into Church history. Such a study, however, will yield a rich harvest. Already at an early stage, when the first sects and counter-churches began to appear, the matter of Church unity attracted attention. This study of Church history is especially interesting to us since Guido de Brès, the author of our Confession, was thoroughly familiar with the writings of the so-called Apostolic Fathers, Apologists, and others.

We have already observed this familiarity, for example, in the line of Article 28 which says of the Church, "there is no salvation outside of it." Many more confessional phrases and expressions can be traced back to ancient authors or documents from whom and from which de Brès learned so much. In borrowing from these authors he bolstered the claim of the Reformers that the Reformation was chiefly a return to the original direction of the ancient Church.

When we have read many of the relevant parts of the old documents, we shall be in a better position to understand what we confess in Articles 27 through 29 and to apply it to the situation in which we now live.

Patience

We realize that history, let alone Church history, is not everyone's favourite subject. Much patience, therefore, will be required on the reader's part to dig through the material on the following pages. We are convinced, however, that such patience will be rewarded. To accommodate a broad audience this material will be presented at various levels. The main story line will be presented in a larger font, while supplementary material will appear in a smaller font. Footnotes, naturally, are set in a smaller font yet.

Our plan

Since much can be learned from Church history regarding the issue of unity of faith and church unity, we must restrict ourselves to the main points. This is why we shall attempt to present merely the "principles" of certain historical documents. These "principles" were first expressed in the time of the ancient Christian Church.[256] We shall begin our tour of church history, therefore, by browsing through the writings of the Apostolic Fathers, Apologists, and others before providing a summary of some important elements. In a kind of intermezzo, we shall unveil several terms and phrases in the Belgic Confession which have their basis in ancient documents. We shall then turn to the Great Reformation and its confessional documents before reflecting on subsequent church history. Our tour of church history will end with some conclusions regarding the application of the principles we have learned.

---

[256] In some documents the Ancient Church is called "the Primitive Church," with the term "primitive" reflecting its original meaning of "first."

CHAPTER 2

THE APOSTOLIC FATHERS

Preliminary

Because of the multiplicity of ancient documents dealing with the Church and its various aspects, this chapter will be a long one. It will require determination of some readers but not of those genuinely interested in the benefits which a serious study of church history brings to our appreciation, understanding, and application of what we confess regarding the Church.

We must acknowledge, to make another preliminary remark, that the exact date of the historical documents in question is often disputed by the experts. The order in which we deal with these documents, therefore, is not necessarily chronological. This should not affect their contents, though.

Clement of Rome

It was most likely in A.D. 96 that Clement of Rome wrote his *Letter to the Church at Corinth*. Although his name is not mentioned in this letter itself, other historical documents clearly demonstrate Clement's authorship. The letter's introduction reveals that it was sent by the Church of Rome to her sister church.

> Clement's letter was held in high regard by the early Christian Church. It was read in numerous churches besides the Corinthian congregation. We learn from the well-known historian Eusebius that around A.D. 160 bishop Dionysius of Corinth wrote his colleague, Soter of Rome, informing him that Clement's letter was still being read in his church.

This letter from Rome to Corinth was occasioned by the loss of internal peace and unity in the Corinthian congregation which resulted from the deposition of the local office bearers by some younger members in the church. The "generation gap" or "youth movement" was a reality in the ancient Christian Church too! Understanding the ease with which it is disrupted, Clement strongly urges the Corinthians by means of this letter to strive for genuine unity. Some clear parallels between this letter and the canonical letter known as 1 Corinthians surface on this score.

Aside from a brief introduction which states the reason for sending this letter, 1 Clement begins the same way the apostle Paul began many of his epistles — with a *laudatio*, a word of praise and thanksgiving for the faith shown by the congregation.

The letter then urges the Corinthians to restore peace and unity with words reminiscent of 1 Corinthians 12:12-26. We read, "The great cannot exist without the small, nor the small without the great. There is a certain blending in everything, and therein lies the advantage. Let us take our body as an example. The head without the feet is nothing, likewise, the feet without the head are nothing. Even the smallest parts of our body are necessary and useful to the whole body, yet all the members work together and unite in mutual subjection, that the whole body may be saved."[257] The Scriptural image of a body is used here to demonstrate that the Church is a unity.

The following few sentences are significant, and especially the very first words: "So in our case let the whole body be saved in Christ Jesus, and let each man be subject to his neighbour, to the degree determined by his spiritual gift. The strong must not neglect the weak, and the weak must respect the strong. Let the rich support the poor, and let the poor give thanks to God, because He has given him someone through whom his needs may be met."

Throughout the letter we find all sorts of references to the common faith. The unity of the body of the Church lies in Christ Jesus! This, then, is the ground upon which the author makes his appeal for the restoration of peace.

We summarize what we have learned from Clement in this way:
1. The Church is the body of Christ and, as such, is a whole, a unity.
2. Church unity is very important.
3. Church unity is based on unity of faith.
4. Church unity, as the Apostles' Creed would later express it, is "the communion of saints."

The *Didachè*

Secondly, we examine the *Didachè* or *The Teachings of the Twelve Apostles*, sometimes called "the oldest Church Order" of the Christian church.

We know neither its author nor its exact date. It was written either in the second half of the first century, shortly after the last New Testament book, or in the first half of the second century.

In dealing with the Lord's Supper (then called "Eucharist," meaning "thanksgiving") and with the bread in particular, the *Didachè* states, "Just as this broken bread was scattered upon the mountains and then was gathered

---

[257] *Apostolic Fathers* 49.

together and became one, so may Your church be gathered together from the ends of the earth into Your kingdom." In this same prayer, we read, "Remember Your church, Lord, to deliver it from all evil, and to make it perfect in Your love; and gather it, the one that has been sanctified, from the four winds into Your kingdom, which You have prepared for it."

Both passages are followed by similar doxologies which were voiced responsively by the congregation: "For Yours is the glory and the power through Jesus Christ forever," and, "for Yours is the power and the glory forever." Through the *Didachè*, in any case, the congregation was made aware of the Church-gathering work of the Lord Jesus Christ, symbolized and demonstrated in the unity expressed through the joint celebration of the Lord's Supper.

In the next section, the *Didachè* issues warnings to believers to be on guard against false teachers, lest unity be jeopardized. We read, "So, if anyone should come and teach you all these things that have just been mentioned above, welcome him. But if the teacher himself goes astray and teaches a different teaching that undermines all this, do not listen to him." Interestingly, a false apostle or prophet was identified at that time by his desire to stay more than one or two days or by his request for money: "But if he stays three days, he is a false prophet," and "if he asks for money, he is a false prophet."

The ancient Christian church understood that false doctrine destroys the unity of the congregation. For this reason, dissenters were excluded, and as a result the church witnessed, very early on in its history, the rise of counter-churches. Unity of faith and church unity, it was agreed, were to be based on true Scriptural doctrine alone!

The *Didachè*'s concern for true ecumenicity in the church becomes apparent in a long paragraph in which believers are urged to show hospitality to travelling preachers. Unity of faith, according to this ancient document, has worldwide dimensions!

We learn from the *Didachè* that
1. Unity of faith is expressed particularly in the celebration of the Lord's Supper.
2. Unity of faith glorifies God.
3. False teachings disrupt church unity because they destroy unity of faith.
4. The Church has an ecumenical character.

Ignatius of Antioch

Our tour of church history bring us next to Ignatius of Antioch (69-107). We shall focus on a couple of letters Ignatius wrote as a prisoner on his way to Rome, where he would soon stand trial and die as a martyr.

We learn from these letters — addressed to congregations in Ephesus, Magnesia-on-the-Maeander, Tralles, Rome, Philadelphia, Smyrna, and to Polycarp of Smyrna — that there was contact between the churches based on unity of faith. The letters also clearly indicate that in a faithful congregation we meet the universal Church, called here and frequently elsewhere in ancient Christian writings "the catholic [universal, worldwide] Church."

In his letter to Smyrna, we discover that for Ignatius true unity rests on Christ Jesus. We read, "Flee from divisions, as the beginning of evils. You must all follow the bishop, as Jesus Christ followed the Father, and follow the presbytery as you would the apostles." And, "Wherever the bishop appears, there let the congregation be; just as wherever Jesus Christ is, there is the catholic church."

At the same time, Ignatius emphasizes that the congregation should be kept orderly, under the government of office bearers. We find the same emphasis later on in history in Articles 25 and 26 of the French Confession of 1559 which speak of "the order of the Church" or "a true order of the Church," because "the Church cannot exist without pastors for instruction."

> Ignatius strongly emphasizes the need to preserve unity by showing respect for the offices. In his letter to the Trallians he writes, "Similarly, let everyone respect the deacons as Jesus Christ, just as they should respect the bishop, who is a model of the Father, and the presbyters as God's council and as the band of the apostles. Without these no group can be called a church."
>
> Here we find an interesting element. The bishop's position, at least in the churches of Asia Minor, was defined in part as a "Christian" copy of the position of the judge and his assessors in the law-courts of those days: "the bishop occupied a seat on a dais at the centre of a semi-circle of his clergy." In this we have what seems to be a visual representation of the Apostles on their twelve thrones around the Throne of God in which the earthly hierarchy serves as a type of the heavenly.[258] This, incidentally, may be the origin of the tradition in which the elders and deacons sit at both sides of the pulpit as a council, symbolizing and representing the heavenly council.

The concentration of congregational life in the person of the bishop at this time may be explained by the presence of what would later be called "dissenters" or "independents."

Ignatius denies that there is unity of faith with false teachers. In his letter to the church at Magnesia, he writes, "It is right, therefore, that we not just be called Christians, but that we actually be Christians, unlike some who call a man 'bishop' but do everything without regard for him. Such men do not appear to me to act in good conscience, inasmuch as they do not validly meet together in accordance with the commandment."

In his letter to the Trallians, he separates himself from the proponents of Docetism: "Why am I now a prisoner and will I soon have a combat with the

---

[258] Maxwell Staniforth, ed., *Early Christian Writings: The Apostolic Fathers* (Harmondsworth, Middlesex, England: Penguin, 1968) 91.

lions? Why, if Christ's sufferings were not genuine because He suffered only in semblance?" He characterizes them as "people who are not the Father's planting." In contrast to them, he expresses his faith as follows: "Be deaf, therefore, whenever anyone speaks to you apart from Jesus Christ, who was of the family of David, who was the son of Mary; who really was born, who both ate and drank; who really was persecuted under Pontius Pilate, who really was crucified and died while those in heaven and on earth and under the earth looked on; who, moreover, really was raised from the dead when His Father raised Him up, who — His Father, that is — in the same way will likewise also raise us up in Christ Jesus who believe in Him, apart from whom we have no true life."

Here we discover another important element: Church unity finds its basis and strength in the common acceptance of a creed or confession. It is obvious from these letters that the process of expressing faith in fixed forms, as in the Apostles' Creed of later days, was already going on in Ignatius's days. What he wrote has the semblance of a creed. A common confession of faith is helpful to preserve church unity in times when it is endangered by heresies.

> In his efforts to base church unity upon the Scriptures, Ignatius went too far, inviting everyone virtually to participate in God's "oneness." According to him this oneness is revealed in Jesus Christ. In Him God becomes visible. He, as it were, shrouded Himself in the human flesh of His Son, Jesus Christ. The Church — called His body in Scripture — also shares in God's oneness and His divine life. We see from this that Ignatius more or less identified God with all those in a relationship with Him, thereby blurring the distinction between Creator and creature. As far as this idea (and the implication that the existence of two different churches next to each other clashes with God's oneness) influenced his struggle against schismatic trends, we cannot follow Ignatius. We may follow him, however, when he states more than once that Church unity is based on unity of faith in the one Lord Jesus Christ.

For our purposes, Ignatius' letters contain the following elements:

1. Unity is expressed in an well-ordered church life, guided by church officers.

2. Unity is also expressed in a common confession of faith, as in the creeds.

3. Unity is broken by dissenters or dissidents.

4. Unity is broken by heresies.

Polycarp

In the *Martyrium Polycarpi* — the story of the martyrdom of Polycarp, bishop of Smyrna, in 155, compiled by a certain Marcion (not the well-known heretic) on behalf of the Church of Smyrna and sent to the sister church of

Philomelium — we are told that, when arrested, the old bishop asked his captors to "grant him an hour that he may pray freely."

It then says, "Now when at last he finished his prayer, after remembering everyone who had ever come into contact with him, both small and great, known and unknown, and all the catholic church throughout the world, it was time to depart."

> It is quite significant that a man like Polycarp, in the difficult circumstances under which he prayed, had the worldwide character of the Church in mind. To him the Church was "all the catholic Church throughout the world." In this respect he followed the example set by the apostle Paul, who informs us in his epistles about his prayers for the various congregations.

We see once again how the Church is called "catholic," a term which apparently had become a fixed indication of its worldwide character. Even in his last hour this martyr had its unity in mind.

CHAPTER 3

OTHER EARLY CHRISTIAN WRITERS

Development

Some of the Apostolic Fathers were disciples of the apostles. Polycarp, for example, was ordained by the apostle John, according to Irenaeus. Whereas the writings of the Apostolic Fathers were practical and pastoral, the Apologists who succeeded them saw the need in their works to defend the Christian faith against attacks from a hostile heathendom. In turn they were followed by others whose writings show a gradual theological development. Some of our references below will illustrate this.

Justin Martyr

We start with Justin Martyr (100-165), whose *Apologia* emphasizes that the membership of the Christian Church (and its unity) is constituted by a common adherence to the teachings passed down by the apostles and their disciples.

Irenaeus of Lyon

Justin Martyr's conviction was echoed by Irenaeus, bishop of Lyon (approximately 135-202). In a letter written to a certain Florius, we read that Irenaeus' former teacher, Polycarp of Smyrna, and others handed down what the Lord Jesus had taught as they themselves had heard it from eyewitnesses. They called this "the apostolic traditions," which, since they had been transferred orally, were most likely somewhat older than the apostolic writings themselves, though in full agreement with them. This may explain why the so-called canon of the New Testament was not immediately acknowledged and why references to various oral apostolic statements can be found in the early Christian writings.

Another significant element in Irenaeus' writings, found in his *Adversus Haereses* (Against Heresies), is a reference to a baptismal creed, an early version of the Apostles' Creed. One of these versions is introduced by the following sentence: "The Church, though scattered through the whole world to the ends of the earth, has received from the apostles and their disciples the

Faith." In connection with that creed, he adds, "The Church, having received the preaching and this faith, as said before, though scattered throughout the whole world, zealously preserves it as one household."

This shows us that, according to Irenaeus, the contents of the creed had been derived from the teachings of the apostles. It is no wonder, therefore, that in its current version it is known as the Apostles' Creed. Irenaeus emphasizes that unity of faith — and consequently church unity — can be found only where one adheres to what the apostles and their disciples handed down.

A third noteworthy element is what Irenaeus writes about "apostolic succession." It is well known that the Church of Rome and the "high church" section of the Anglican churches are of the opinion that a bishop can fulfil his office legitimately only if he has been ordained by the laying on of hands by another bishop who in turn is one of the many links in a chain of bishops which began with one of the apostles, and preferably the apostle Peter. Irenaeus, however, keeps "apostolic succession" closely connected to the tradition of the apostolic teachings. His teacher Polycarp, for example, always "taught the things which he had learned from the apostles, which the Church hands down, which alone are true."

The Muratorian Canon

The Christian Church at this time was aware of its obligation to busy itself with what the apostles and their helpers had written. This led to the acknowledgment of the canon of the New Testament.

A document originated in those days called the Muratorian Canon. It rejects many writings because they were "forged under Paul's name to further the heresy of Marcion" and therefore "cannot be received into the catholic Church. For it is not fitting for gall to be mixed with honey." On the other hand, "The Epistle of Jude indeed, and two bearing the name of John, are accepted in the catholic Church."

As for the relation between the local churches and the one worldwide Church, it says, "The blessed apostle Paul . . . writes only by name to seven churches in the following order — to the Corinthians a first, to the Ephesians a second, to the Philippians a third, to the Colossians a fourth, to the Galatians a fifth, to the Thessalonians a sixth, to the Romans a seventh; whereas, although for the sake of admonition there is a second to the Corinthians and to the Thessalonians, yet *one* Church is recognized as being spread over the entire world" (emphasis mine).

Here the canonical apostolic writings are honoured as basic to the unity of the Church because, together with the other books of the Bible, they are believed by the whole Church. They create unity of faith.

Tertullian

Tertullian (approximately 160-220) presents a peculiar explanation of what "apostolic succession" means. In his work *De Praescriptione Haereticorum*, another book which defended the Christian Faith against false teachings, he reminds his readers that churches have come into being as a fruit of apostolic preaching. What this preaching consisted of is expressed in terms which are of some importance for our purposes.

Tertullian writes, "The Apostles first bore witness to the faith of Christ Jesus throughout Judaea: they founded churches there, and then went out into the world and preached to the nations the same doctrine of the same faith. They likewise founded churches in every city, from which the other churches hereafter derived the shoot of faith and the seeds of doctrine — yea, and are still deriving them, in order to become churches. It is through this that these churches are themselves apostolic, in that they are the offspring of apostolic churches. Every kind of thing must needs be classed in accordance with its origin." This means that the only faithful churches are those that remain faithful to the apostolic preaching, which was the preaching of "the faith of Christ Jesus."

At the same time Tertullian clearly presents the way in which the apostolic teachings were handed down from place to place, first by the apostles themselves and later by the churches that had come into being. This is "apostolic succession" in the Scriptural sense of the term.

Tertullian then shows us the implications of all of this for the unity of faith and church unity when he says, "And so the churches, many and great as they may be, are really the one Primitive Church issuing from the Apostles, which is their source. So all are primitive and all apostolic, while all are one. And this unity is proved by the peace they share, by their title or brotherhood, by their contract of hospitality; for these privileges have but one ground, the one tradition of the same 'revelation' [*sacramentum*, which in Latin is a revealed mystery]."

In this same work he shows his readers the antithesis: "What is there in common between Athens [the centre of contemporary pagan philosophy] and Jerusalem? What between the Academy and the Church? What between heretics and Christians? . . . Away with all projects for a 'Stoic,' a 'Platonic' or a 'dialectic' Christianity! After Christ Jesus we desire no subtle theory, no acute enquiries after the gospel." It is clear that, although the terms themselves were not used yet, the distinction between "true" and "false" was being developed in connection with the confrontation of heresies which exhibited the strong influence of pagan philosophy.

It is interesting to note that, in his best known work, *Apology*, Tertullian uses the familiar pair of words *coetus et congregatio*. He does so in the following sentence: "We are made a body by common religious feeling, unity of discipline, and the bond of hope. We come together in a meeting and assembly [*coelum et congregationem*], that we, as made by His hand [into a whole, we could add], would offer our prayers to God." Here *coetus* and *congregatio* are used as synonyms and no distinction is made between a human action and a divine one.

When Tertullian elaborates on these meetings and says, "at these meetings we have also exhortations, rebukes, and a divine censorship," we recognize two of the marks of the true Church presented in our Belgic Confession of Faith. (Another of his writings mentions the administration of the sacraments.)

Others

Besides Justin Martyr, Irenaeus, and Tertullian, there were others — such as Hippolytus of Rome (170-253) and Cyprian of Carthage (d. 258) — who had to warn the churches about the danger of false teachings infiltrating church life. They too played a role in the appearance of the "true-false" construct as it emerges in later writings.

That their warnings had implications for the distinction between the true Church and the counter-churches is clear from Hippolytus's statement that a certain Callistus "had the impudence to adopt opinions of this kind, setting up a school against the Church." Callistus, in other words, established a counter-church. The Belgic Confession of Faith would have designated this church one of many "sects," of which the false church is an extreme example.

In Cyprian's work *De Catholicae Ecclesiae Unitate* (On the unity of the catholic Church) we discover an incipient form of the so-called "doctrine of pluriformity," though within the true Church. He writes, "The Church is a unity; yet by her fruitful increase she is extended far and wide to form a plurality; even as the sun has many rays, but one light; and a tree many boughs but one trunk, whose foundation is the deep-seated root; and as when many streams flow down from one source, though a multitude seems to be poured out from the abundance of the copious supply, yet in the source itself unity is preserved." More than sixteen centuries ago, it was readily accepted that the worldwide Church consists of congregations and groups of churches that might vary widely in historical background, culture, and tradition!

Cyprian strongly emphasizes that the unity of the Church is based on unity of faith. This is demonstrated not only in the title of his book but also by a few of his well-known slogans such as, "He cannot have God for his Father who has not the Church as his mother," and "There is one baptism; which of course is in the catholic Church, for the Church is one, and baptism there is none outside the Church."[259] Cyprian's use of the phrase *extra ecclesiam nulla salus*

---

[259] The translation has been taken from Henry Melvill Gwatkin, ed., *Selections from Early Writers* (1893; London: James Clarke, 1958) 153. We plan to write more about this in an issue of The Reformed Guardian, new series, which will deal with the recognition of baptism as administered in other churches.

(outside the Church there is no salvation), which he adopted from Origen, is particularly well known.[260] It is not strange to note, therefore, that Cyprian rather frequently uses the phrase "catholic Church."

It is to be regretted, however, that he put so much emphasis on the office of the bishop and not on the preservation of the apostolic teachings upon which the true unity of faith and church unity rest. Given this misguided emphasis, it should not surprise us that the Church of Rome, in its path of deviation from the apostolic teachings, frequently appealed to Cyprian's writings.

Hilary of Poitiers — a strong opponent of Arianism, who for the sake of his faith was exiled to Asia Minor in 356 — makes a helpful contribution when he states that the unity of believers is not determined by walls and beautiful buildings: "I have more trust in mountains, forests, and lakes, prisons, and deserts. They are more safe, for after having prophesied the prophets hid themselves in them."

Chrysostom of Constantinople (347-407), a famous preacher, in like manner emphasizes that the Church does not consist of walls but of the multitude of God-fearing people. In the confusion caused by the many "churches" established by the heretics of those days, he points to the Scriptures: "They let us know where the true Church can be found. If we look at other things we will not understand what that means: the true Church. Then we will stumble and perish. The deceivers too have their churches. They too read the divine Scriptures, seem to have the same sacraments, honour the apostles and martyrs, just as the Antichrist, although partly, is doing the works of Christ and fulfils all the duties of the Christians, Satan transforming himself into an angel of light." These lines, taken from one of his sermons, are important because he uses the term "true Church" with reference to the main mark of the true Church, adherence to the Scriptures.

We mention, finally, Aurelius Augustine (345-430). Augustine emphasizes the Church's worldwide character when he states that the catholic Church, this "mother," has been spread over the length and breadth of the world. "She did commence with Abel, as Babylon began with Cain." False and true were already present shortly after the Fall. When he speaks of the false church, Augustine must have the Donatists in mind because he denies that they have the Scriptures in common with the faithful believers. We must not seek the Church in our own words but in the words spoken by our Head, Jesus Christ, Who is the truth and Who knows His body.

Certainly the catholic Church is not an entirely pure Church. It is God's threshing-floor. Grain and chaff will be mixed in the Church until the end of the world. The wicked also use the sacraments. This does not mean, however, that we had better withdraw from the Church. It ought to stimulate us to become grain!

---

[260] See our discussion of this phrase above in our treatment of Article 28.

CHAPTER 4

SUMMARY

Conclusions and implications

We may now summarize what we have learned so far. The following aspects can be distinguished:

1. Church unity is very important since the Church is Christ's body.

2. Church unity glorifies God and therefore must be maintained for His sake.

3. Church unity has a view to the worldwide, catholic Church and does not neglect its ecumenical character.

4. Church unity includes the unity of the local congregation as that comes to expression in the celebration of the Lord's Supper.

5. "Apostolic succession," in the sense that the apostolic teachings are continuously imparted from one generation to the next, is essential.

6. The original emphasis on the oral transmission of the apostolic teachings shifted to the apostolic writings now found in our Scriptures as soon as the canon of the New Testament was recognized.

7. Teachings which deviate from the apostolic doctrine disrupt church unity because they sever the unity of faith.

8. The apostolic teachings have been summarized in the ecumenical creeds, among which the Apostles' Creed takes a prominent place.

9. Adherence to the contents of that Creed, in which the works of the triune God are confessed, is crucial for church unity.

10. Faithfulness to and deviation from the contents of this creed determine the distinction between the true Church and the sects, of which the false church is an extreme example.

11. Since the contents of the ecumenical creeds have been attacked — through false interpretations, as well — the Reformed churches saw the need to explain and defend the doctrine of the Apostles' Creed more elaborately. Some confessional documents of the Reformation show the same structure as that creed or amply explain its contents.

12. It is regrettable that the apostolicity of the Church is no longer expressed in one of the questions found in the liturgical forms in the *Book of Praise*. The question "Do you acknowledge the doctrine which is contained in the Old and the New Testament, and in the articles of the Christian faith, and which is taught here in this Christian Church, to be the true and complete doctrine of salvation?" has been replaced by "Do you confess that the doctrine

of the Old and New Testament, summarized in the confessions and taught here in this Christian church, is the true and complete doctrine of salvation?." The phrase "and taught here in this Christian church" was meant to refer to the other creeds and the Three Forms of Unity. The current version contains a double reference to them! The significant function of the Apostles' Creed is no longer clear.

13. Faithfulness to a Reformed confession is crucial for our recognition of "other churches."

14. Unity of faith, though expressed in different Reformed confessions, must be expressed in some form of church unity.

15. Many centuries ago "pluriformity within the true Church" was already acknowledged. Faithful churches of different historical origin, culture, and tradition realized they were one in faith, though no formal relationships were created.

CHAPTER 5

THE REFORMATION

Credal development

In the previous chapter we touched briefly on a development which led ultimately to the compilation and acceptance of the Apostles' Creed. We noted from some of Ignatius's writings that a process of expressing faith in fixed forms and formulas was already in place in his day. We also noted that Irenaeus refers to a baptismal creed, an early version of the *Apostolicum*. That version later matured into what we today call the Apostles' Creed, a title which reflects its contents. What the apostles taught and what their disciples adapted from them for their gospel preaching has been summarized in that creed.

It is no wonder, therefore, that apostolic teaching is frequently mentioned in ancient documents, as we have seen. Since then, the Apostles' Creed, together with the two other creeds received by our Reformed churches (Belgic Confession, Art. 9), has played a prominent role in the act of confessing our faith.

The heart of the matter

Another factor which led to the development of the creeds was a refusal among some to accept what the Scriptures teach concerning God's Self-revelation. Here we have in mind the so-called Christological and Trinitarian struggles which ultimately gave birth to the Nicene Creed and the Athanasian Creed. These were controversies about the Holy Trinity, since the heretics in question could not accept the Bible's teaching regarding the two natures of Christ, and particularly His being the Son of God.

This, then, is something we should not overlook when we ask: With which fellow-believers do we enjoy unity of faith? And even more importantly, with which "other churches" do we enjoy unity of faith? And consequently, with which "other churches" could (and should) we enjoy church unity? The crucial question is: Do they, together with us, acknowledge all that God has revealed about Himself as the triune God?

Of course, we should not oversimplify this, as if mere acceptance of the Apostles' Creed provides sufficient ground for unity of faith and church unity. Permit me to illustrate this assertion. Shortly after the Second World War, a number of church groups in what today is called Indonesia tried to begin anew as one church. In order to avoid the pre-war division it was suggested that the Apostles' Creed be adopted as the only confessional standard. This proposal, however, did not bring about the desired result. Why was this project doomed to fail? Well, first of all, it has to be acknowledged that this creed is a summary of "all that God has revealed to us in His Word."

We should know that the Apostles' Creed originally functioned merely as a public declaration at the occasion of one's baptism. It was a confession baptismal candidates were expected to make following their detailed religious instruction. Already in the early centuries of the Christian Church, such brief confessions of one's faith had to be defended and elucidated, as was done, for example, in the other two ecumenical creeds. It must not be overlooked, moreover, that Article 9 the Belgic Confession of Faith refers not only to the three well-known ecumenical creeds, but also to "that which in accordance with them is agreed upon by the early fathers."[261] After the Reformation, it became increasingly impossible to be satisfied with the text of the Apostles' Creed alone. Our Forms of Unity, whose compilations were required in the course of church history, are perhaps more than a hundred times longer than that Creed.

During those days, all kinds of deviant views regarding God's Self-revelation surfaced. Consider the list Article 9 provides: "Marcion, Mani, Praxeas, Sabellius, Paul of Samosata, Arius, and such like." In subsequent years various heresies were propagated, not only in terms of the *Persons* in the Holy Trinity, but in terms of their *works*. Both our Confession and our Catechism strongly refute what the Church of Rome taught then (and still teaches today) about the atoning work of the Son of God. Our confession also rejects the teachings of the Anabaptists regarding the work of the Holy Spirit. And at the beginning of the seventeenth century, the Reformed Churches of Europe saw the urgent need to condemn the false ideas of the Arminians concerning God's decrees of election and reprobation.

The contents of the creeds, therefore, and in particular that of the Apostles' Creed, had to be further explained and applied to the current situation. Yet we can state that the heart of the matter is the doctrine of the Holy Trinity! That is what our confessional standards seek to defend and explain, with the understanding which Article 9 of our Confession has when it speaks of "the distinct offices and works of these three Persons toward us. The Father is called our Creator by His power; the Son is our Saviour and Redeemer by His blood; the Holy Spirit is our Sanctifier by His dwelling in our hearts."

This is the crucial point of the answer to the question: Under which conditions can we say that there is unity of faith, and when can (and must)

---

[261] It would be interesting if a special study would be undertaken looking into the question as to precisely which decisions of councils and synods and other documents the Confession has in mind. Many ecclesiastical meetings and leading personalities saw the need for the defense of the Scriptural doctrine of the Holy Trinity.

there be church unity? Do others gratefully believe these things together with us?

All about the triune God and His works

In light of our assertions above, we note that the Belgic Confession, following the example of John Calvin's *Institutes of the Christian Religion*, has the same structure as the Apostles' Creed. After an introduction dealing with the source of and basis for all that we believe — the Bible as God's inspired Word — the works of the Father, the Son, and the Holy Spirit are explained and confessed.

What is of even greater significance, however, is that all the articles in the Confession are explained in terms of and are based upon the works of either the Father, or the Son, or the Holy Spirit. This should not surprise us since all of this has been revealed in the Scriptures. The Scriptures are at bottom the Self-revelation of God, of His triune works and the reaction to them, from both man and Satan. Again, this is the pivotal matter in unity of faith and church unity. Unity of faith is present, and church unity should follow, when we and others gratefully acknowledge the works of the triune God as revealed in the Scriptures. The confessions and catechisms of others' may have a different structure and formulation, but only because the Holy Spirit has followed His own sovereign course in their histories. This difference should not hinder the enjoyment of the unity of faith!

Application

If we examine what we confess in Articles 27 through 32 of the Belgic Confession in light of our thesis that adhering to the Trinitarian doctrine of Scripture is crucial for church unity, we discover how frequently all three divine Persons are mentioned. In the first sentence of Article 27, for example, both the Lord Jesus Christ and the Holy Spirit are mentioned. Later in the same article, we read that the Church "is preserved by God." Many more examples could be provided, but we choose to limit ourselves to those lines which clearly indicate how others violate what Scripture teaches us about "the distinct offices and works of these three Persons toward us."

Article 27 begins by defining the Church as "a holy congregation and assembly of the true Christian believers, who expect their entire salvation in Jesus Christ." In the phrase "their entire salvation" we hear an anti-Roman overtone. The Church of Rome, with its doctrine of the meritorious good works and its celebration of the Mass as the ongoing sacrifice of Christ, violates "the distinct office and work" of the Son of God.

We detect a reference to the Anabaptist line of thinking in the last sentence of Article 27 which speaks of how the Church "is joined and united . . . in one and the same Spirit." The Anabaptistic ideal of a perfectly pure and holy Church resulted in one schism after another such that, even though they claimed to be strongly guided by the Holy Spirit, they were divided into numerous sects. Here "the distinct office and work" of God the Holy Spirit is clearly violated.

Article 29 refers to "the sacraments as Christ instituted them." Implicit in these words is a rejection of the Roman church with its "seven sacraments." The Confession here states what it will later restate more concretely when it speaks of how the false church "bases itself more on men than on Jesus Christ." These Romish ideas deny Christ as "the only universal Bishop and Head of the Church," as Article 31 identifies Him.

To apply our thesis to the current situation, we would insist that adherence to the Trinitarian doctrine as confessed in our creeds and confessions is pivotal to the question of whether "other churches" can be acknowledged as faithful churches of the Lord Jesus Christ.

The various voices heard all over the world which reject Christ's death as the once-for-all atoning sacrifice for our sins are in strong conflict with His "distinct office and work" as "our Saviour and Redeemer by His blood."

The same rule in its entirety must be applied contemporarily when God puts other churches in our path. There may be weaknesses in these churches, as there are in ours, but these weaknesses alone are not crucial and decisive. In any case, other factors, such as the sovereign way in which the Holy Spirit has worked in other cultural environments and in the history of other nations, are subservient to this rule and should never be separated from it.

Other confessions

Our Confession is not the only document dating back to the days of the Reformation which presents the doctrine of the Holy Trinity as crucial. We shall examine a number of other Reformation confessions to illustrate our claim.

The Augsburg Confession

First of all, there is the Augsburg Confession of 1530 which begins in this way: "The churches, with common consent among us, do teach that the decree of the Nicene Synod concerning the unity of the divine essence and of the three Persons is true, and without doubt to be believed: to wit, that there is one divine essence which is called and is God, eternal, without body, indivisible, of infinite power, wisdom, goodness, the Creator and Preserver of all things, visible and invisible; and that yet there are three Persons of the same essence and power, Who also are co-eternal, the Father, the Son, and the Holy Spirit." In the second part of Article 1, this confession condemns "all heresies which have sprung up against this article," after which it lists some names similar to those mentioned in Article 9 of our own Confession.

The Church finds its unity in true doctrine, as Article 7 indicates when it states, "And unto the true unity of the Church, it is sufficient to agree concerning the doctrine of the Gospel and the administration of the sacraments. Nor is it necessary that human traditions, rites, or ceremonies, instituted by men should be alike every where, as Paul says (Ephesians 4:5, 6): 'There is one faith, one baptism, one God and Father of all.' "

The Augsburg Confession provides us with evidence that the efforts for true reformation in the church were widespread. It was compiled and read at the Diet of Augsburg, which was convened by Emperor Charles V, who wanted to resolve the controversy between Rome and the Lutherans so that they could be united in war against their common enemies, the Turks.

The Confession itself was penned by Philip Melanchthon at the request of the assembled Lutheran princes, electors, and other authorities. It received Martin Luther's full approval and was subscribed to by John Calvin as a minister of the church at Strasbourg and as a delegate to the conference of Ratisborn (1541), as well as by William Farel, Theodore Beza, elector Frederick III of the Palatinate, and countless others. Its preface reflects the emperor's desire to establish peace in his beleaguered empire. The princes were sure of his wish "that hereafter the one unfeigned and true religion may be embraced and preserved by us, so that, as we are subjects and soldiers of the one Christ, so also, in unity and concord, we may live in the one Christian Church."

Our conclusion from studying the documents of the first centuries of the Christian Church is here repeated and applied to the situation of the sixteenth century. In respectful acknowledgment of God as the triune God, and of "the distinct offices and works of these three Persons toward us," believers and churches of various historical and cultural origin find their unity.

The *Formula Concordiae*

In 1576, the Lutherans adopted the *Formula Concordiae* (Formula of Concord), which was compiled after a number of controversies had arisen between the followers of Martin Luther and Philip Melanchthon. Its opening statement reads, "And inasmuch as immediately after the times of the Apostles, nay, even while they were yet alive, false teachers and heretics arose, against whom in the primitive Church symbols were composed, that is to say, brief and explicit confessions, which contained the unanimous consent of the Catholic Christian faith, and the confession of the orthodox and true Church (such as are the Apostles', the Nicene, and the Athanasian Creeds); we publicly profess that we embrace them, and reject all heresies and all dogmas which have ever been brought into the Church of God contrary to their decision." Even the Lutherans themselves found their unity in a common belief in God as a triune God.

The First Helvetic Confession

The First Helvetic Confession was compiled in 1533 at Basel by a number of Swiss divines, among whom were Martin Bucer from Strasbourg, and Leo Judae and Henry Bullinger from Zurich. It was the fruit of an effort to unite the Lutheran and Swiss (Zwinglian) churches. Upon receiving a copy, Martin Luther stated that he was satisfied with its Christian character and promised to do all he could to promote union and harmony with the Swiss. After some introductory articles on the holy Scriptures as the only source of our knowledge of God, this document also confesses the Holy Trinity when it states: "Concerning God we confess that He is one in essence and triune in Persons" (Art. 6).

The Second Helvetic Confession

Of greater importance is the Second Helvetic Confession, written in 1562 by Henry Bullinger, Zwingli's successor. It was published four years later at the request of elector Frederick III of the Palatinate, who wanted to have a clear exposition of the Reformed faith at his disposal when he had to attend the Diet of Augsburg and defend himself against the charge of apostasy. The Swiss churches in common believed that such a Confession could bind them closer together. Theodore Beza travelled from Geneva to Zurich to take part in the revision of the original manuscript. He later produced a French translation.

The churches at Geneva, Berne, Zurich, and elsewhere — both "Calvinist" and "Zwinglian" churches — expressed their agreement with this confession, as did the Church at Basel soon afterwards. Using this Confession to defend his faith at the Augsburg Diet, Elector Frederick impressed the Lutherans to such an extent that they refused from that point on to brand him a heretic. The Confession enjoyed widespread acceptance throughout the neighbouring countries.

It is remarkable that the text of the Confession itself is preceded by some ancient documents: the Imperial Edict of 380 from the Justinian Code, in which the dividing line between the true doctrine and heresy is drawn — all that departs from the Apostles' Creed and the Nicene Creed is rejected as heretical — and also the so-called Trinitarian Creed, ascribed to Pope Damasus, which was considered at that time a standard of orthodoxy.

The purpose of inserting those ancient documents seems obvious. The Reformed churches of Switzerland wanted to make clear that the Reformed faith is the catholic faith of the ancient Church. "Harmony in the fundamental doctrines of the ancient Church is declared sufficient, and brotherly union consistent with variety in unessentials, such as in fact always had existed in the Christian Church."[262]

As for the unity of the Church, the Confession says, "Furthermore, we teach that it is carefully to be marked wherein especially the truth and unity of the Church consists, lest that we either rashly breed or nourish schisms in the Church. It consists not in outward rites and ceremonies, but rather in the truth and unity of the catholic faith. This catholic faith is not taught us by the ordinances or laws of men, but by the holy Scriptures, a compendious and short sum whereof is the Apostles' Creed. And, therefore, we read in the ancient writers that there were manifold diversities of ceremonies, but that those were always free; neither did any man think that the unity of the Church was thereby broken or dissolved. We say, then, that the unity of the Church does consist in several points of doctrine, in the true and uniform preaching of the gospel, and in such rites as the Lord Himself has expressly set down" (Chap. XVII).

These lines also make clear what the Reformed documents of those days (among them our Belgic Confession of Faith) meant by "the pure preaching of the gospel": it is the proclamation of "the distinct offices and works of these three Persons toward us."

The French Confession of Faith

This Confession begins with this declaration: "We believe and confess that there is one God, Who is one sole and simple essence, spiritual, eternal, invisible, immutable, infinite, incomprehensible, ineffable, omnipotent; Who is all-wise, all-good, all-just, and all-merciful" (Art. 1).

After referring to the Scriptures in which this God has revealed Himself, it says in Article 6, "These Holy Scriptures teach us that in this one sole and simple divine essence, Whom we have confessed, there are three Persons: the Father, the Son, and the Holy Spirit. The Father, first cause, principle, and origin of all things. The Son, His Word and eternal wisdom. The Holy Spirit, His virtue, power, and efficacy." In the last lines of this article, it refers to "the ancient councils" when it says, "And in this we confess that which has been established by the ancient councils, and we detest all sects and heresies which

---

[262] Schaff, *Creeds* 1:395.

were rejected by the holy doctors, such as Hilary, Athanasius, Ambrose, and Cyril."

This Confession was prepared by John Calvin and his pupil, Antoine de la Roche Chandieu, in 1559. During his visit to the church at Poitiers, the brothers asked Chandieu to suggest to the church at Paris that they should prepare a common Confession of Faith. Calvin was consulted and he prepared a draft which was later enlarged and subsequently adopted by the French churches.

From this brief history it is clear that this Confession was intended to function as a "form of unity." Already the letter to King Frances II, which accompanied the copy of this Confession sent to him, shows the difference between true and false when it indicates how "the Roman church, forsaking the use and customs of the primitive Church, has introduced new commandments and a new form of worship of God." The apostolic tradition had been marred and the unity of faith with the ancient Church had been broken.

Here a significant element is brought to the fore. Unity of faith is also to be maintained with the spiritual forefathers in history. For this reason we often read in the documents of both the first few centuries and the Reformation that the apostolic tradition must be maintained. It is really striking that this Confession emphasizes this element so strongly.

The Scottish Confession of Faith

It is also remarkable that emphasis is laid on the common acknowledgment of the triune God as determining factor for unity of faith and church unity in the Scottish Confession of Faith. This Confession was written at the initiative of the Scottish Parliament which convened on August 1, 1560. Six ministers, all named John, composed it and a Book of Discipline in the Magdalene Chapel at Edinburgh. The work took no more than four days, most likely because one of the six ministers, John Knox, had had experience in preparing a Confession. It was ratified on August 17, 1560.

Chapter XVI defines the Church as follows: "As we believe in one God, Father, Son, and Holy Ghost, so we firmly believe that from the beginning there has been, now is, and to the end of the world shall be, one Kirk, that is to say, one company and multitude of men chosen by God, who rightly worship and embrace Him by true faith in Christ Jesus, Who is the only Head of the Kirk, even as it is the body and spouse of Christ Jesus. This Kirk is Catholic, that is, universal, because it contains the chosen of all ages, of all realms, nations, and tongues, be they of the Jews or be they of the Gentiles, who have communion and society with God the Father, and with His Son, Jesus Christ, through the sanctification of His Holy Spirit."

In conclusion

All of these confessional documents confirm what we said was pivotal or crucial. Unity of faith exists and church unity must be established wherever there is a common faith in and communion with the triune God and where "the distinct offices and works" of the three divine Persons are gratefully acknowledged.

More than one of the ancient documents we have studied acknowledges the presence of weaknesses and shortcomings in the life of any church. We realize that it is sometimes difficult to distinguish between weakness and deviation from the Scriptural truth. We wish, however, to abide by the "rule" which we have found consistently in these documents. Unity of faith and church unity rest upon a common adherence to the affirmations of the ancient creeds and, today, to the way these affirmations are explained in the Reformational confessional standards, such as the Three Forms of Unity but also other faithful Confessions and Catechisms.

God's Self-revelation as the triune God in "the distinct offices and works" of the three divine Persons is essential. There would not be a Church if God were not triune. The Church is the fruit of the work of this God, and there is therefore no church wherever God is not acknowledged as such. Acknowledging the one God and at the same time the three divine Persons is fundamental to the existence of the Church and to any faithful Confession. There is even a personal element: The Church is characterized by members who have a personal bond with this triune God and enjoy communion with Him!

This, then, is the crucial point in determining whether there is unity of faith among believers and between churches. It is decisive for the answer to the question whether church unity can — and must — be established between churches.

CHAPTER 6

FROM UNITY OF FAITH
TO CHURCH UNITY?

Efforts

The previous chapter informed us about a number of efforts undertaken to reach church unity on the basis of existing unity of faith. We have seen how a small number of confessional documents were compiled with the intention of functioning as forms of unity. More can be said about such efforts and we shall do that in this chapter.

Martin Luther

We begin with the efforts Martin Luther undertook to restore unity within the church of his day. Luther was no schismatic. He made a serious effort to lead the established church back to a Scriptural basis. After he had published the well-known Ninety-five Theses on October 31, 1517, he debated Cardinal Cajetanus at Augsburg. Since this debate produced nothing positive, he appealed to a general council of the church. Most likely he had been advised to do so by some of his juridically trained friends.

On November 28, 1518, he and some witnesses appeared before a solicitor with an official form for his appeal, the so-called Parisian form. They did so again on November 17, 1520, almost exactly five months after he had received the papal bull. This was a very important move. If the appeal had met with favour, the result would have been a great blessing to the Church of the Lord Jesus Christ. By such an act, the Church would have returned *officially* to the Scriptural moorings of the ancient Church and its great ecumenical councils. Luther, after all, had asked for a free, universal, and Christian council. By "free," Luther meant a meeting which was neither convened nor controlled by the Pope. By "universal," Luther meant a meeting attended by delegates from various countries, as was the case with the great councils of Nicea, Constantinople, Ephesus, and Chalcedon. And by "Christian," Luther meant a meeting whose resolutions and statements were founded upon the Scriptures alone.

Luther tried to lead the Church back into line with the ancient Christian councils, for which he had such great respect. His efforts were in vain, however, for the Pope did not want to lose control and thus strongly opposed any council which might appear superior than himself in matters of faith. More than once, the Pope had issued prohibitions to appeal. Hierarchy won the day and internal church reformation was rendered impossible!

Henry Bullinger

When a council, the Council of Trent, was finally convened, albeit by the Pope and under his control, Ulrich Zwingli's successor, Henry Bullinger, prepared some comments about it in a book published in 1561 during the actual meeting of the Council of Trent. According to Bullinger, such a council could not be expected to bring peace and reformation. On the contrary, serious troubles, revolutions, and wars would inevitably result. Papal councils virtually guaranteed damaging results. Bullinger held forth the great councils of the early Christian era as examples the church should follow and keep in line with.

John Calvin

Both orally and in writing, Calvin frequently advanced the possibility and urgency of Zurich and Geneva coming together. Such prodding on Calvin's part resulted in the acceptance of the *Consensus Tigurinus* in 1549. On several occasions, Calvin contacted Bullinger regarding plans to hold religious talks with the Lutherans and to draw up an inventory of the divergencies and conformities between Lutherans and Reformed.

Calvin frequently published works dealing with the subject of councils for the same reason Bullinger did. The Council of Trent, after all, was in session. You will find his ideas in the *Institutes* (IV.ix: "Of Councils and Their Authority"). In his voluminous correspondence there are several letters devoted to councils and to the efforts of establishing church unity. The frequent use of the term "consensus" is characteristic.

Calvin and Cranmer

Calvin's best-known correspondence was with Thomas Cranmer, archbishop of Canterbury. In a letter to Bullinger, Cranmer, who was of great significance to the Reformation in England, drew up a plan for a synod of "the most learned and eminent men" who should come together in England or elsewhere "in order to talk about the pure doctrine of the Church and in particular about an agreement regarding the controversy on the sacraments."

King Edward VI believed such a synod would be of great use for the sake of the Christian faith.[263]

Cranmer wrote a similar letter to Calvin: "I have often wished, and still continue to do so, that learned and Godly men, who are eminent for erudition and judgment, might meet together in some place of safety, where, by taking counsel together and comparing their respective opinions, they might deal with all the heads of ecclesiastical doctrine and hand down to posterity an authoritative work not only on the articles of the faith themselves but also on their wordings."

Unlike the Council of Trent, such a council could serve to refute Roman heresy, restore pure doctrine, and reach consensus on the Lord's Supper. Cranmer envisioned a commonly accepted Confession of faith which would deal with the Lord's Supper in particular because of the differences between Lutherans, Zwinglians, and Calvinists on this score.

From the response which John Calvin sent to Cranmer we quote the following lines: "Rightly and wisely, illustrious gentleman, you are of the opinion that in the present confusing situation of the church there is no better remedy than for some pious, wise men, who have been well trained in God's school, to come together in order to profess their agreement concerning the doctrine of Godliness."

If only such a dream could be realized that "great and learned men from the principal churches might meet together at a place appointed and, after diligent consideration of each article of the faith, hand down to posterity a definite form of doctrine according to their united opinion." In Calvin's opinion it was "to be reckoned among the greatest evils of our time that the churches are so estranged from one another that human intercourse of society scarcely has a place among us, let alone the holy communion of the members of Christ which all persons profess with their lips, but which few sincerely honour with their actions."

Farther on in his letter, we read a sentence which has become relatively well known: "I would not shrink from crossing ten seas, should that be necessary, for the purpose of attending such a gathering. There would be sufficient reason for me to do so even if I could be helpful to the Kingdom of England alone. But now that a serious Scripturally-founded consensus of learned men is required, for the purpose of which churches that are located far from one another should unite themselves, I am of the opinion that neither energy nor pains should be spared." Regrettably Cranmer had to inform Calvin that this goal could not be achieved. Philip Melanchthon had decided not to respond to the invitation and Bullinger was of the conviction that the timing was inappropriate because of the ongoing war between Germany and France.

---

[263] *Letters of John Calvin* 130-33; Schwarz 2:595.

The *Harmonia Confessionum*

We have just learned that John Calvin dreamed of a Confession which would be accepted by all the churches of the Reformation. Following a long and complicated series of historical events, this plan was once again advanced.

There is evidence that the Reformed did not consider contact with Rome inappropriate, since Theodore Beza, Geneva's replacement for the ailing John Calvin, attended a colloquium held at Poissy in 1561 at the instigation of Catharina de Médici, regent of the young King Charles IX of France. As soon as the papal nuncio arrived and referred to the Council of Trent as the only authorized body to make decisions, however, the meeting was doomed to fail. The Church of Rome appeared to be unwavering. Such inflexibility on Rome's part only encouraged the "Protestants" to forge alliances with one another. Such encouragement resulted in the Convent of Frankfort held in 1577.

The prelude to this Convent coincided with a resolution by Queen Elizabeth I of England to establish a Protestant league in which she herself, the Huguenots in France, and the Dutch Protestants would be protected against Rome. She sent envoys to the Continent, and the plan to compile a common Confession of Faith resurfaced, but without success.

In the meantime, however, a strong controversy had emerged between the Lutherans and the Reformed. Among the Lutherans, the followers of the moderate Philip Melanchthon had lost much of their influence, and the acceptance of a Lutheran Confession which expressed extreme views regarding the Lord's Supper, the *Formula Concordiae*, was imminent.

It was in this context that the Convent of Frankfort was convened. Arrangements were subsequently made for the compilation of a common Confession. Hieronymus Zanchius, who was invited to do the work, wrote a draft and sent it off to Geneva, Zurich, and other places. Geneva, however, would not endorse it. This led to another plan. A *Harmonia Confessionum*, a collection of all Reformed Confessions, would be published, thereby demonstrating the material consensus between the Reformed churches. It was published in 1581. Even the original Lutheran confessional standards were included, to counterbalance the *Formula Concordiae*. Sadly, the effort failed to achieve more than a mere outward expression of material consensus. The unity of faith expressed in this book did not result in church unity.

Lutherans and Reformed

The official, formal introduction and adoption of the *Formula Concordiae* by the Lutheran churches caused the relationship between Reformed and

Lutherans to change radically. The Reformed rejected "the doctrine of ubiquity," which is better known as the theory of "consubstantiation": Christ's body and blood would be present in the Lord's Supper "in, with, and under" the signs of bread and wine. This theory was based on the idea that since Christ's ascension into heaven, He became bodily present everywhere ("ubiquity" comes from the Latin *ubique*, "everywhere").

As a result of the extreme stand the Lutherans took at Frankfort, Petrus Dathenus was forced to cut short his stay there and departed for the London congregation of Reformed refugees. Under the oversight of the Lutheran authorities, the Reformed were prevented from establishing their own independent church life. It is possible to observe in the intolerance of the Frankfortian Lutherans a prelude of what would become more or less common after the introduction of the dogma of Christ's ubiquity. The story would be incomplete, however, if we did not indicate that many Lutherans were genuinely unhappy with this theory.

In The Netherlands some difficulties arose within the church at Woerden, which was pastored by an extremist Lutheran minister. A slander-filled letter he wrote was tabled at the Provincial Synod of Dordrecht in 1574. Arrangements were made to involve Prince William of Orange, who was for the most part a peace-loving person. In addition to this, someone would be sent to Woerden to try to lead this church to reformation.

The Synods of Middelburgh (1581) and The Hague (1586) also had to deal with the situation in Woerden. The latter observed that this congregation had a Confession which differed from that of the other churches in the United Provinces. All of this happened at a time when the *Formula Concordiae* was introduced and the relationship between Reformed and Lutherans worsened. Serious doctrinal differences which clearly concerned "the distinct office and work" of Christ, the Son of God, had emerged out of the Formula.

The same issue presented itself from a different angle. The National Synod of Dordrecht (1578) decided to ask the churches of the Palatinate to send them an authorized copy of the discussions and decisions of the conference at Neustadt, to which delegates from various countries were sent to evaluate, among other things, the relationship between the Reformed and the Lutherans.

At the Synod of Middelburgh (1581) this issue again appeared on the agenda. The congregations at Utrecht and Wesel and in England requested a translation of the Colloquium of Maulbronn. Classis Amsterdam was commissioned to present a translation of a "book written by the theologians of Neustadt *contra formulam concordiae ab ubiquitariis editam*" (over against the *Formula Concordiae*, edited by ubiquitarians).[264]

The relationship between Reformed and Lutherans involved an even wider context as well. The French churches invited the Dutch to send

---

[264] Rutgers, *Acta* 439

delegates to their synod, to be held in the same year, 1581. The latter sent an apology, accompanied by "our prayers that they would promote a Common Confession of all nations."

At the Synod of The Hague (1586), delegates learned that the book written by the Neustadt theologians had not been translated. The story seems to end there, but it is not without merit for us today. The Reformed Churches in The Netherlands were undoubtedly anxious to learn from the discussions and decisions of their colleagues across the border in Germany.

The Synod of The Hague's agenda also included a letter from the church at Amsterdam, recommending that the Rev. Libertus Fraxino of The Hague be sent to them. Fraxino was selected because "he is able to discourage the enemies of the truth as Anabaptists, Libertines, and Martinists." We see here how the Lutherans, called "Martinists" after Luther's Christian name, were now put on a level with Anabaptists and Libertines. The issue at stake was the doctrine of the Church and faithfulness to the teachings of Christ, the apostles, and the Scriptures!

It is no wonder that delegates from churches in various countries — and even from the Church of England with its episcopal system — were invited to the National Synod of Dordrecht (1618-19). The Lutherans, however, were not there, which was expected given the recent history.

This is a sad story! After the adoption of the doctrine of ubiquity there was no longer unity of faith and consequently efforts for church unity had to be dismissed. It was now clear that the Lutherans deviated on one of the fundamentals of the Christian faith as expressed in the Apostles' Creed: "the distinct office and work of Christ, the Son of God." Before such extremism emerged, harmony had existed between Reformed and Lutheran churches in the mutual acknowledgment of each other as faithful churches of the Lord Jesus Christ.

CHAPTER 7

FINALLY

Observations and conclusions

1. Unity of faith is a matter of being one in Christ. Our Catechism is in full harmony with the ancient documents and the confessional writings from the Reformation era when it says that the communion of saints is first of all "that believers, all and everyone, as members of Christ, have communion with Him and share in all His treasures and gifts" (Lord's Day 21, Q&A 55). These treasures and gifts are the fruits of "the distinct offices and works of these three Persons [in the Holy Trinity] toward us" (Belgic Confession, Art. 9).

2. These offices and works are expressed and confessed in the ecumenical creeds, among which the Apostles' Creed enjoys a prominent place.

3. Since new deviations from Scripture took place, the churches of the Reformation saw the need to explain and apply the contents of the Creed in more elaborate confessional writings.

4. It was no longer possible, therefore, to express faith with the help of the Apostles' Creed alone.

5. On the other hand, we regret that in some of our Liturgical Forms, as printed in the latest edition of the *Book of Praise*, the reference to the Apostles' Creed has been omitted and replaced by "summarized in the confessions." This means that there is now a double reference in the Forms to the Three Forms of Unity, because that is also the purpose of the sentence that says "and taught here in this Christian Church." The Form no longer clearly expresses our ties with the Church of previous centuries.

6. There is unity of faith with other churches who have adopted and, in practical church life, maintain other Scriptural Confessions since they also acknowledge the same "office and works" of the three Persons in the Holy Trinity, although they do so in different words.

7. Where unity of faith exists, church unity must be sought.

8. No church is perfect. Every church exhibits weaknesses. Any possible points of concern regarding issues which do not deviate from the apostolic tradition must therefore be discussed on the basis of the recognition of the churches concerned.

9. We must show tolerance in non-essential matters.

Part 3

THE LIBERATION
OF THE FORTIES

INTRODUCTION

The following section was originally published in two parts as No. 14 in The Reformed Guardian series. The first part did not contain all that we had planned to publish. The Rev. K. Bruning took upon himself to write about the significance of the Liberation of the Forties, and he had already made some notes when the Lord took him so suddenly from us on July 6, 1994. That is why the number of pages is much fewer than we intended it to be.

While searching in old volumes of the magazine *Una Sancta*, however, we found an article from his hand, published in the Youth Column of Vol. 21, No. 22 (Aug. 10, 1974). Of course, it was written thirty years after the churches in the Netherlands were liberated, and we commemorated the fiftieth anniversary of the Liberation in 1994. Nevertheless, its contents are still relevant to our present situation. So this is why we have taken the liberty to amend its title and adapt it to include references to the Canadian Reformed Churches. We hereby express our appreciation to Mrs. Bruning and the family for their permission to republish the article in this form.

The second, and larger, part of this section contains my personal recollections of what happened in those days. This part especially addresses those generations of our membership who were not yet born when these events took place. We hope these younger generations can also join in the grateful commemoration of the Liberation of the Forties. After all, our Free Reformed Churches of Australia and the Canadian Reformed Churches owe so much to this act, which we confess was an act of the Head of the Church, the Lord Jesus Christ.

G. Van Rongen

FIFTY YEARS
LIBERATION
1944-1994

by

K. Bruning

The lessons of Church history

It is sometimes expedient to pay particular attention to important events in the history of the Church. We must be mindful, however, that the history of the Church proclaims *the deeds of the Lord*. There would be no sense in spending many words on what *people* have done for the continuance, struggle, and victory of the Church, for the work of human beings is always mingled with sins and shortcomings. The Bible goads God's people to learn the lessons of history. In such cases, the Word of the Lord puts full stress on what God has done for His people. Immediately after the journey through the desert and the entry into Canaan, God commanded His people Israel that the parents must see to it that the children remain aware of the might and loyalty of the Lord. The youth of the Church must be taught the history of the Church and in this way gain a deep respect for the power of the LORD, their Covenant God.

Biblical examples

This principle is also taught in Psalm 78, where we read, "We will not hide them from their children, telling to the generations to come the praises of the LORD, and His strength and His wonderful works that He has done." In Psalm 77 as well, the comfort and the deeds of the LORD are taught: "I will remember the works of the LORD; surely I will remember Your wonders of old. I will also meditate on all Your work, and talk of Your deeds." In this connection we can also mention Psalms 105 and 106 and, from the New Testament, the well-known speech of Stephen before the council of the Jews in Acts 7.

Rich fruits

As the youth of the Church, we can gain rich fruits from a healthy and Scriptural knowledge of the history of the Church. We shall be strengthened in our thankfulness that the Lord has cared so well for His Church in this world *and thus also for us*.

We shall also be encouraged if we perceive that the Lord has preserved and assisted His Church in all these battles and decisive happenings. We shall also understand far better which dangers and attacks are being launched against the Church today. From the history of the Church we can learn that, time and again, the devil uses the same heresies and temptations to ensnare the Church and endanger the work of the Lord. The lessons of church history acutely give us a clearer outlook on the world in which we live and an awareness of the battle which we must wage.

Facts and events

In this section, we wish to list several events from the history of the Church which are related to the Liberation (*Vrijmaking*) of 1944 and which helped form the Free Reformed Churches of Australia and the Canadian Reformed Churches.

It is now more than fifty years since the Reformed Churches in the Netherlands were going through a very serious crisis, the result of which made the Liberation necessary and also made it a reality. Let us first present some facts. On March 23, 1944, Dr. K. Schilder was suspended as professor at the Theological College (now University) and as pastor emeritus of the church at Rotterdam-Delfshaven. This decision was made by the General Synod of the churches in closed session. On August 3, 1944, Professor Schilder was deposed from his offices in the Reformed Churches.

Roots

Of course these events were not unprecedented. The conflict involving Professor Schilder was a matter concerning the whole church; it was a church conflict which had grown for years and which came to a climax in Professor Schilder's removal from office.

The churches had fallen into deformation. The Word of God no longer had the living and inspiring power that it should have had in the midst of the churches. This deformation threatened faith and religious life. Tradition and custom took the place of a living relationship with the Church of the Lord, and fellowship with the Lord was dealt severe and damaging blows. Many did not realize or acknowledge the significance of the Confession and the Church Order, and these beautiful gifts of God often had only a formal value.

Hierarchy

Slowly but surely, hierarchy crept into the church. The synods desired more and more power over the churches, and at the meetings of synods the professors of theology played too dominant a role. The ordinary members of Synod, representing the churches, were being disregarded. The larger portion of the church members had almost no strength or opportunity to oppose these events in a meaningful way. In this way the churches reached a situation in which the synods voiced their dominance over the congregations.

Consequences

This situation had some fatal consequences. In those years the synods of the Reformed Churches, without any fundamental reason and without having been asked to do so by the churches, held lengthy discussions on the meaning of the covenant and of baptism. They did so because, according to Synod, there was uneasiness in the churches about these matters.

This discussion produced dramatic results. After various debates and reports, Synod 1944 decided to issue a number of statements. One of these statements, which concerned baptism and the covenant, greatly upset many people in the churches. The statements made were in conflict with God's Word and in no respect founded on the Confession of the churches. Synod declared this doctrine of baptism and the covenant *binding* on everyone, and therefore no one was allowed to teach anything in the churches that was not in complete agreement with the statement issued by Synod. At that time the doctrine of a *twofold* baptism — a real and a non-real baptism — was introduced into the churches, together with the assertion that there are two types of covenant children: some of the baptized *truly* belong to the covenant while others are only *external* members of the covenant.

All of this had fatal consequences. Many office bearers and other church members could not comply with these unscriptural conclusions, nor could they promise not to teach anything against them. One of the first people to oppose and attack these statements publicly was Professor K. Schilder. This opposition caused Synod to resort to aggressive action. Assuming the role of the general staff of the churches, Synod headquarters suspended and dismissed many office bearers. It also placed entire churches outside the confederation of churches. Synod did so on its own assumed authority and with complete disregard of the local churches!

War time

All of this took place in 1944, the darkest and most dismal year of World War II. The Netherlands suffered terribly under the German occupation, thousands were imprisoned in concentration camps or lived "underground" as hunted refugees, and hunger and hardship brought many to despair. *During this terrible time*, Synod did not hesitate to force the churches into a terrible conflict and crushed their unity. In those dark days many people made appeals to Synod to stop the process and to continue it at a more favourable time, but these appeals were of no avail. People like Professors Berkouwer, Nauta, and J. Ridderbos obstinately persevered. They had but one solution: bend or break!

Liberation

It was a wonder of grace that the Reformed Churches were not obliterated. But it was in those days, which for many of us belonged to the darkest period of our lives, that the Liberation was given to us. Many office bearers and church members liberated themselves from the decisions of the synods and re-instituted the — now free — churches on the old basis of the Scriptures, as summarized in the Confessions and the Church Order. In this manner the Lord preserved His Church and ensured the continuance of the Reformed Churches which could live from His grace. For us too, He has upheld the biblical truth regarding baptism and covenant.

After fifty years

The crisis of the Liberation took place over fifty years ago. In those fifty years many things have transpired. Our churches have passed through new situations of danger and crisis, and our part in the history of the Church has been punctuated with many sins. We remain thankful, however, for the wonderful fact that, not only in the Netherlands and Australia, but also in other countries and on other continents, the Lord has maintained and protected His Church in pure doctrine and life through His Word and Spirit.

The younger generation

We must remain on the alert not to lose what the Lord has granted us. The synodical churches have run into storm after storm since 1944. This has now reached a point where they have lost the Bible as God's trustworthy Word and can no longer counteract the denial of Christ's atoning work as Mediator.

The younger generation in our midst has not experienced the cold and bitter reality of a church deformation caused by the abandonment of the Scriptures and the Confession. The question arises whether this generation realizes sufficiently that the Church can live only by God's grace and Word and that she therefore *must stand unshakably firm on her confession.* The youth of the Church must constantly perceive that — humanly speaking — they are the Church of the future. God's Word will make that possible. For this reason, however, the young members must not let themselves be drawn away from the healthy Word and doctrine of the Lord Jesus Christ (1 Timothy 1:10; 2 Timothy 4:3; Titus 1:9; 2:1; and 2 Timothy 1:13). A Scriptural knowledge of the history of the Church is a positive calling and benefit and must not be lost!

PERSONAL RECOLLECTIONS

by

G. Van Rongen

Fifty years ago

More than fifty years ago an important meeting was held in The Hague, the well-known residence of the Dutch queen. During that meeting, members of the Reformed Churches in the Netherlands (Gereformeerde Kerken in Nederland) who had observed, with deep concern, how their churches were being led in a hierarchical way down a path that drew them away from the Reformed heritage were urged to liberate themselves from the responsibility of this situation. A *Deed of Liberation or Return* was read. In many congregations this Deed was sent to the consistory to urge this body to lead the congregation back to the Reformed paths. In other congregations a different route was taken.

The meeting that took place on August 11, 1944, played a significant role in the Liberation and in reestablishing the Reformed Churches in the Netherlands. Since this is the ecclesiastical background of many of our older church members as well as part of the historical origin of our own churches, it may be useful to tell the story once again.

This time we want to do so in a more personal way by presenting our own recollections.

Prelude

The Second World War was still not over. The Netherlands were occupied territory. They were overrun by a well-equipped enemy, Nazi Germany. The Dutch army had to lay down their weapons on May 15, 1940, after only five days of fighting. Since that day the occupying forces let the people feel that they were there! Slowly they tried to "Nazify" the way of life of the Dutch.

The great majority of the population, however, offered strong resistance to these efforts. They longed for freedom. Many people — and particularly young men — had to go into hiding because the occupying forces wanted to send them to Germany to work in the factories and at the shipyards which supplied their armed forces with new weapons and ammunition. Others had been arrested because of their activities in the "resistance movement" and had been carried away to concentration camps. Most of the Dutch Jews were rounded up and led to the gas-chambers. The rations of food and vital materials were getting smaller and smaller. People talked about "the second front," the imminent invasion of the continent by the Allied Forces. They were encouraged by the BBC's broadcast of "Radio Oranje," to which they listened on their hidden radios. The country was looking forward to its liberation.

Another liberation took place first, however — that of the Reformed Churches. Yes, indeed, there was trouble in church life also. This was perhaps the greatest tragedy that happened during the war!

The church leaders who were responsible for it should have listened to the voice of Professor Dr. K. Schilder — the first man in the country to try courageously, immediately after the capitulation of the Dutch army, to open the nation's eyes, through his weekly *De Reformatie*, to the danger of being Nazified. As a result of his efforts, he was soon arrested, although he was released at the end of 1940 under certain conditions which were imposed upon him. Shortly after the German invasion and the beginning of the German occupation in May 1940, he had warned the church leaders: "Please, bury the whole thing as soon as you can . . . for in days of emergency we need concord and cooperation more than ever before. True concord, however, can be obtained only in the way of truth and justice."[265] But he spoke in vain. Those leaders did not want to listen to him.

How it began

Those troubles in church life date back to 1936. In that year, a small number of members of the General Synod moved — without any authority granted them by any of the churches! — that certain opinions differed from the "current ones" and therefore should be tested against the Scriptures and the Confession, "in order that the unrest in the churches caused by them would cease."

Was there really so much unrest? I do not believe it at all! There was no unrest in the churches themselves. None of them had made a proposal or sent an overture to Synod regarding this matter. Unrest was living in the hearts and minds of those who feared their influence would wane. Indeed, a

---

[265] K. Schilder, *De Reformatie* 20.35 (June 7, 1940), reprinted in *Bezet Bezit* (Goes: Oosterbaan & Le Cointre, 1945) 5.

reformational current was gaining more and more ground in the churches because many people were no longer satisfied with the scholastic and subjectivistic teaching and preaching of many a professor or minister. The most prominent men of this group were Dr. K. Schilder, who was strongly supported by his older colleague, Dr. S. Greijdanus, the school principal A. Janse, and the professors of Philosophy, Dooyeweerd and Vollenhoven, at the Free University in Amsterdam. The latter two, however, made the wrong decision at the decisive moment.

Synod appointed a committee which had to report on the "doctrinal differences" to the next synod. The outcome was that the General Synod issued a number of statements on common grace, the immortality of the soul, "presumptive regeneration" in the infants to be baptized, and other subjects. As we said before, none of the churches had asked for such an examination, let alone for any official statement to be made by the General Synod of 1942.

Here, then, the hierarchical tendency of the church leaders — mostly professors of theology who attended the synods as advisers — came out into the open. At a later stage, this hierarchy became even more impertinent, as we shall see.

It was therefore no wonder that men like K. Schilder and S. Greijdanus protested publicly against this violation of the adopted Church Order which says in Article 30 that major assemblies can deal with only those matters that regard all the churches — such as the training for the ministry — or matters which could not be finished at one of the minor assemblies. Delegates are in no way authorized to add anything to the Synod's agenda!

Preparations

There was much activity in the manse of the church at Waardhuizen in June 1944. Waardhuizen is a tiny village somewhere in the centre of the *Land van Altena*, the most northern part of the province of North Brabant in the south of the Netherlands. Preparations were being made for its new occupants, a young couple that hoped to get married in the near future. They had to face all sorts of problems: How could they obtain furniture for the living room and for the bedroom? For the time being, the study would be all right. That is to say, there was a desk, there were some bookshelves, and there were even some of the most essential reference books. But where could they get floor covering and material for the curtains? The war was not over yet, and these goods were all rationed and very scarce. There had even been the problem of getting the couple's belongings to the manse, but that problem had been solved because they had found a carrier willing to take the risk of having his truck requisitioned for making unauthorized trips. Since there was a severe energy crisis at that time, not even a truck fuelled by charcoal — there was no gasoline — was allowed to ride without the permission of the Germans.

The male half of the new occupants of the manse arrived sitting among his belongings at the back of the old truck, his blood having been nearly churned like butter because the truck's tires were in very poor shape and the roads were in a shocking condition. With the assistance of a student friend, the young couple were very busy furnishing their first home. In a few weeks time they would enjoy their great day, their wedding day!

More preparations

Some more preparations were being made. The minister-to-be had to undergo another exam at the end of June 1944, the so-called peremptory exam, held by Classis Almkerk, the classis to which the congregation he was to serve belonged. This time, there would be more tension than usual in the minds of all the people involved. If the exam would go well — and it did! — an additional question had to be asked, the answer to which would be decisive for the admittance of the candidate to the ministry.

In spite of many protests lodged by the churches or from within the churches, the General Synod made a new rule for admission to the ministry of the Word — another proof of the hierarchical attitude of this body. This rule said, in our own words, that every minister had to agree with the "doctrinal statements" issued by Synod 1942, and if he did not he could make his objections known "in the ecclesiastical way" through Consistory, Classis, Particular (or Provincial) Synod, and finally General Synod. In the meantime, he was not permitted to speak publicly against these statements. But for the candidates to the ministry, the classical assemblies demanded that they had to subscribe to these statements at the end of their examination. Nobody was allowed to teach anything that was not in full accordance with these "doctrinal statements."

The answer

A few weeks later, the candidate did pass his exam. The chairman of the meeting informed him of this result. In accord with the new rule mentioned above, however, the chairman asked him whether he could agree with the "doctrinal statements." His answer was, "Yes, I can, except with the one on presumptive regeneration."

This answer caused some consternation at the meeting. This was the fourth time such a response had been given. The first time was at Classis Gorinchem after the exam of candidate H. J. Schilder, a nephew of Dr. Klaas Schilder, who later became Professor of Old Testament at the Theological University at Kampen. He was not admitted to the ministry of the Word, and consequently the church at Noordeloos, which had extended a call to him, withdrew its call under the pressure put upon it by a synodical committee. Candidate J. H. Hey was the second one to give such an answer, but in spite of the classis' actions the church at Langerak which had called him joined the "liberated" churches and had him ordained. The third candidate was J. C. Janse, the eldest son of A. Janse, whose name we mentioned above. He was not even granted permission to propose for the ministry at his first classical exam, the "preparatory examination"!

A problem "solved"

So at his final classical exam our candidate clearly stated that he could not agree with an essential section of the "binding doctrinal statements" issued by the General Synod. He could not promise "not to teach anything that is not in full accordance with these statements." What about the candidate's position and future? What would happen to him? Would he ever become a minister? Were he and his fiancée making all those preparations in the manse for nothing? All those years of study — had they been in vain? After all, he took the same stand as the other three candidates whose way toward the ministry had been blocked.

As a matter of fact, the chairman of Classis was prepared. He knew perfectly well that this would be the candidate's answer. He knew that the young man belonged to the so-called "concerned." The chairman — one of the older ministers in the classical region — had already heard the answer a few hours earlier. In keeping with an old custom in this region, the candidate, together with the other guests of Classis, had been invited to have lunch at the local hotel (where, later on, he frequently conducted worship services from behind the bar!). These other guests were the deputies of the Particular Synod, appointed to oversee these sort of exams. This time they were the Rev. H. Veltman of Bois-le-Duc ('s Hertogenbosch) — who himself also had strong objections to the "doctrinal statements" and would later belong to the "liberated" churches — and the Rev. J. H. Jonker of Werkendam, who was also a member of Classis and even its chairman and who was acting as deputy-delegate of the Regional Synod for someone else who could not attend.

The meal was delicious. It was wartime, but in this farming district there was plenty of food left at this time. The atmosphere was spoiled somewhat, however, for pressure was put on the candidate to declare that he would accept all the doctrinal statements issued by Synod. He was asked to subscribe to them in acknowledgment that he was still young and did not desire to be wiser than the members of Classis and Synod who were all much older. It should be clear from which side this pressure was put on him: not from that of the Rev. H. Veltman, who strongly supported the young man.

During lunch-time no "solution" was found. The candidate's answer to every suggestion made by Rev. J. H. Jonker was, "Synod requires agreement and subscription. When one is unable to do so, it is simply a matter of being sincere to say, 'I honestly cannot agree with the statement regarding the position of infants.' " So the chairman was well prepared. He knew which answer the candidate would give.

But let's return to the meeting. What happened? Had the chairman found a "solution" to the problem?

This is what happened. After the candidate had given his answer to the crucial question, the chairman asked him another question: "Could the candidate agree with another formula, a 'substitutionary' one, issued by Synod in response to a number of objections made against the original statement?" Again the candidate's answer was in the negative. A third question was asked: "Could the candidate declare his agreement with a formula proposed by the ministers of the church at Amersfoort?" The answer was: "No, I cannot, for Synod has stated that this formula is acceptable only if it is read in the light of the original formula, so it is fundamentally the same." Still there was no "solution" to the problem.

The chairman was a clever man, however. He was himself a strong supporter of the General Synod, although he was not very enthusiastic about the trouble its statements were causing in the life of the churches. He tried to find a way out and in his opinion he did find such a way. He asked the candidate whether he could possibly agree with the contents of a letter sent by the synod to a number of people. In this letter, "two lines" of the doctrine of the covenant were emphasized, God's sovereignty and man's responsibility. Our candidate had read a copy of this letter. At that point he did not have any objection to the contents, although this did not take away his objections to the original statement itself. So he answered, "I do not have anything against that letter."

Then things took place with great haste. The chairman asked the meeting, "I move that we admit the candidate to the ministry on the grounds of this last response. Does everyone agree with that?" Even before anyone could raise his voice to say either yes or no, the chairman signalled with his gavel that the motion had been carried. He added, "Let us sing Psalm 134, stanza 3, for the candidate!"

A truly astonished young man heard Classis sing. He was grateful to be able to commence his work as a minister in a couple of weeks, to continue the preparations in the manse, and to get married. On the other hand, he could not feel fully happy with the course things had taken. It is no wonder that soon afterwards he wrote to his student friend H. J. Schilder about the different ways in which the two of them had been treated. Soon afterwards he began his ministry with the feeling that this was no real solution to the problem; the situation in our churches was still the same.

This present writer knows all about these facts and feelings, since — as our readers may have guessed — he himself was that candidate!

War time

.By the spring of 1945, we no longer were living in the manse at Waardhuizen. Things had taken a dramatic turn.

It may be helpful to tell our readers the circumstances under which the struggle in the churches continued, since, in spite of all the requests made to the General Synod on behalf of approximately the majority of church members to stop these procedures, Synod went on with them.

During the first four years of the Second World War, many inhabitants of the *Land van Altena* had never seen a German soldier. It was therefore no wonder that many young people had gone "underground" in this region. Unlike most other parts of the country, where those who were in hiding had to be careful not to show themselves too often on the public road, the *onderduikers* could move freely here. I clearly remember the evening on which — after we had received the official call from this congregation — we were introduced to its members. Everybody told us his or her name and spoke a few words. But there were also a large number of young men who introduced themselves by their Christian name only: Koen, Kees, Piet, Daan, and so on. We immediately understood the situation and grinned, "Ah, the people with no surnames!" But very soon this quiet time was over.

The trouble started on a Saturday afternoon when a couple of English fighter planes came over and we heard the rat-ta-tat of machine guns. One of the planes dropped its spare tank. It fell on the hydro lines. Of course, the gasoline was soon siphoned into a bucket and the remnants of the tank — priceless metal! — were hidden. Later in the afternoon a group of German soldiers came along the road. This was the first patrol we saw there. On smelling the gasoline, they started to make inquiries. Of course, no one knew anything. . . . They threatened us by saying, "If you do not tell us where the stuff has been hidden, we shall send for the SS and they will comb out your houses!" The SS definitely did not have a good reputation. On the contrary. So this threat made some impression, although not enough to move the new "owners" of the tank and the gasoline to give away their hiding place. I myself got the shock of my life when I was addressed in a very unkind way — to put it mildly — by one of the soldiers, for at that moment I had just given a hint to two *onderduikers* that they should disappear. One of them was a man of Jewish origin.

Another shock came the next morning when we were woken by the sound of footsteps around the manse and soon afterwards we heard a bang, bang! What was happening? We saw some German soldiers on the road and also in our garden. A few of them were knocking hard on the door of our church, which was situated beyond the manse. We first thought that they were of the SS! Fortunately this was not true. These soldiers were the quartermasters of some troops that had been driven out of Belgium — they had just lost the port of Antwerp — and out of the southern part of the province of North-Brabant and were withdrawing beyond the great rivers of the Netherlands. Since that day we know what it means to have soldiers quartered with us!

Evacuation

For several months, the people of our village saw plenty of Germans! During the Christmas period of 1944 we had approximately forty soldiers in the manse. The only room left to us was a bedroom. My study also had to serve as a living room, and we had to share it with an officer and his adjutant. Apart from that, we had to show hospitality to two families of evacuees, so that our house was more than packed to capacity.

Then we heard a rumour that Waardhuizen would be evacuated and we would have to go across the rivers because the region was to be inundated. When we inquired after some official information, this rumour was confirmed. We were given two or three days to prepare, after which we had to assemble at an appointed place to be accompanied by some soldiers and brought to an unknown destination. Of course, before the date set for this we had all disappeared — except for a few families who were given the reassuring message: "You will not be evacuated!"

We ourselves went to a village close by called Uitwijk, where a large number of our congregational members were living. My wife and I were given hospitality in a little house, the property of one of our elders. Five people were already living there, yet a complete room was put at our disposal. It had to be used as a living room for the owners, for ourselves, and for the casual visitors during the evening hours because fuel was scarce and power had been cut off. This room became our dining room, bedroom, study, and even birthing room because our eldest son was born there! My modest library was stored in the attic of a nearby farmhouse. There was not much time for study. Other members of the congregation had been scattered all over the region. Most of the visiting had to be done *per pedes apostolorum*, which means, in the way in which the apostles travelled — on foot, over muddy roads, and during the day because a curfew had been imposed on us. Many old and sick people had to be visited. We even had a few funerals — one of them in between two shellings from the other side of the front.

We had been cut off from the South but also from the North. This also meant that we were not aware of what was going on across the great rivers. We did not even know whether the struggle in the churches was still going on . . .!

Church situation

Later on we received some information by a secret route. Indeed, the struggle was still going on as if there were no war, no danger to human life, no hunger, no evacuation, no bombardments, no executions, no concentration camps. The frontal activities in our surroundings had more or less come to a standstill after the heavy bombardments of Christmas 1944, when a complete division, quartered in the *Land van Altena*, tried to push through to Antwerp at the time of the well-known Battle of the Bulge. After this division was almost annihilated, we had a rather quiet time. We were waiting for the liberation of the rest of the country and for the capitulation of the German troops. This gave us some reprieve so that we could deal with the church affairs again.

A small committee had been established to give the church members in our classical region some information about what was going on. They contacted me, requesting me to write a little pamphlet. After some deliberation I promised them to do so. I planned to present an exposition of both views, that of the synod and its supporters on the one hand and that of the people who objected to its decisions on the other.

During one of the meetings of the consistory, someone raised the point that the congregation needed to be informed about the issues. I then told the other members of the consistory that I had been contacted by the committee. They were all of the opinion that something should be done since, when the war came to an end and the connections with the other parts of the country and the other congregations were restored, we would have to make a decision.

During the ministry of the previous minister, Rev. L. Selles — who later was Professor of New Testament at the Theological College at Hamilton — the consistory had already decided to examine the synodical statements as soon as possible. The consistory based this decision on Article 31 of the Church Order, but this article had apparently escaped the synod's attention. It was a very brave decision, for the opinion and even the policy of Synod and the "synodical" groups was that every church and individual church member — let alone special office bearers — had simply to submit themselves to the decisions made by this major assembly. Unfortunately, the consistory had not followed up on this decision by carrying out the proposed examination. Rev. Selles had left, after accepting a call from the church at Steenwijk, which would later become my last charge (so that I became his successor twice!). We all agreed that this examination had to be undertaken in the near future.

That is why I prepared a paper to be read at the next consistory meeting. During the discussions, no one made any objection to its contents. I also informed the consistory that it was my intention to use this paper at a congregational meeting to be held after the war. In this way the members of the congregation could form an opinion on the matters concerned. At the same time, I told them that I intended to summarize this paper and have it published by the inter-congregational committee mentioned above. I asked them whether it would not be wise to give every family a copy of this pamphlet so that the members could prepare themselves and so that the discussion during the meeting would be useful. They agreed on this. But one elder made a restriction: he was of the opinion that the expenses should not be paid from the church funds; it was the minister's problem!

Pamphlet

It took some time to get the pamphlet printed. I still possess a few copies of it, but they do not look very attractive. Since it was a war product, the paper is very rough. But it has survived half a century! The pamphlet was to be printed and distributed in two parts, the first dealing with the doctrinal aspect, the second with the church political aspect.

One can imagine how astonished I was when, after I was called by the American Reformed Church of Grand Rapids, Michigan, I visited the library of Calvin College for the first time and the librarian of the theological section showed me a copy of the second part of this pamphlet! How it had reached this library is a mystery. Most likely a retired American minister who could still read Dutch had donated his library or part of it to Calvin College. At present this library also possesses the first part of the pamphlet.

This first part was printed soon after the war. It was distributed during the week of August 19 to 25, 1945. A few days later, on the evening of Thursday, August 30, I was suddenly provisionally suspended by the majority of the consistory on the grounds that I was schismatic!

The doctrinal issue

Before we continue our local story, let us see what it was all about. First of all, we shall pay some attention to the doctrinal point that became the subject of the controversy.

Actually we should ask the question, "Which doctrinal issue played the most prominent role?," for there were some other issues as well, such as common grace and the immortality of the soul. The best thing I can do within the context of these personal recollections is to give a kind of translation of the first part of my pamphlet, the doctrinal part.

Here it is: During 1942, the General Synod of the Reformed Churches in the Netherlands issued the following statement on the Covenant of Grace and the position of infants to be baptized:

2. That without any doubt the Lord in the promise of the covenant says He will be the God not only of the believers, but also of their seed (Genesis 17:7); however, He reveals to us no less in His Word that they are not all Israel which are of Israel (Romans 9:6).

3. That consequently — according to what the Synod of Utrecht 1905 (Acts Art. 158) has judged — "the seed of the covenant, according to the promise of God, is to be understood as having been regenerated and sanctified in Christ, until the time of maturity arrives and they prove the contrary by their conduct of life or doctrine." Synod 1905 correctly added, though, that this does not at all mean that each child would be regenerated.

This statement was unanimously adopted by the members of Synod.

Opposition

Why, then, was there so much unrest and opposition soon afterwards? A long story could be told at this stage, a story of all sorts of machinations. Let me tell you briefly what happened.

As we have seen, Synod referred to its predecessor of some forty years ago. In the passage quoted, the teachings of Abraham Kuyper regarding "presumptive regeneration" had been rejected, though in a very soft way. Apparently the rejection was softened because he had just been compelled to retire as prime minister of the Netherlands and the Reformed people did not want to hurt him too much as a theologian as well.

No one voted against this statement at Synod 1942, since its members considered it a kind of repetition of 1905's decision. This statement was meant to function as a pacification formula rather than as a binding statement. Besides, in contrast to what happened during the polemics in the main church magazines, no one had been condemned as a heretic. This was seen as a major advantage after the serious accusations published earlier by the Free University professors H. H. Kuyper and V. Hepp against K. Schilder, A. Janse, and others.

But what happened afterwards? Soon it became known that the followers of the theologian Abraham Kuyper used this part of the declaration of 1905 as a sort of belated rehabilitation of Kuyper's doctrine of "presumptive regeneration" and the covenant of grace. They saw their way clear to let their own opinion dominate church life. This became apparent when Synod presented a semiofficial interpretation called "Elucidation" (*Toelichting*). Later a formal and official explanation was issued under the name of "Pre-advice." From this document it became clear as crystal that any views which differed from this explanation were condemned and illegitimate and should be treated as such. At a later stage, these two documents were dropped, but it was never stated that their contents — their doctrine — were retracted. This gesture was merely a matter of bad "church politics"!

Reasoning

How, then, did Synod reason? After all, it was indeed a matter of reasoning, not of simple Bible reading! Certainly, the commandment tells us that we have to serve the Lord "with our whole mind" also, which includes our intellect, our brains. But on the other hand, we must also realize that our mind has been affected by sin and by nature is corrupt. The consequence of this belief based upon God's Word is that we should be very careful in our logic and our reasoning. The church must especially be on guard against this danger when issuing statements made by its major assemblies. It is so easy for her to put the believers under a yoke that is definitely not Christ's. This danger may become clear even to simple believers as soon as they see that no Scriptural proof is offered to support the statements issued.

This was exactly the case with the statements and other documents issued by the Dutch synods of the 1940s. It is therefore no wonder that there is hardly anyone left today who really believes the theory of those days. In the meantime, however, it caused much harm.

Once again: reasoning

We can approach the doctrinal issue from various angles. But let us do it in the same way as it was done in the "Elucidation" mentioned above. The "Elucidation" states that sacraments are signs and seals. They were given to strengthen us in our faith. But this implies that faith must be present, since otherwise there is nothing to be strengthened. This sounds perfectly logical. But let us listen to the way in which it is applied to holy Baptism.

The "Elucidation" reasons as follows: As a sacrament Baptism is supposed to do something, to confirm faith. Otherwise it would be null and void, an idle ceremony. Someone even dared to say, "Every now and then Baptism is nothing but a spilling of water, namely when the baptismal candidates show later on that they are unbelievers." The reasoning continues by stating that holy Baptism must seal something present in the heart of the candidate, namely faith or regeneration or the remission of sins already received, "as gifts that have been granted to the person to be baptized." But it is true that we do not know whether or not our infants have already been regenerated, whether or not they are believers. Therefore — and this is the conclusion of this long line of reasoning — we should "consider them to be regenerated and sanctified in Christ, " that is to say, "until, as soon as they grow up, they prove the contrary by their conduct or doctrine."

Who are the participants in the promises of the covenant of grace? Following the way of reasoning in the "Elucidation," the conclusion is unavoidable: only the elect, only God's chosen people! Of course, all our infants have been baptized, all the little children of the believers. But what, then, is the position of the non-elect among those who are baptized, of those who later on prove to be unbelievers? The answer is that they received an external sign only; they belong to the covenant in a strictly external way.

To the question of whether all the children of believers are entitled to baptism, the answer given is that we must make a distinction between "full baptism" and "baptism-not-in-the-full-sense-of-the-word." Referring to Acts 2:39, which says, "For to you is the promise and to your children," the supporters of the synodical doctrine answered that there is a "general offer of grace" to all who hear the gospel, but that there is also an unconditional promise of salvation for the chosen ones only. In other words, the promise is exclusively for the chosen ones; one should insert the word "elect" in Peter's statement on the day of Pentecost. We must understand him to be saying, "For the promise is to you and to your elect children."

Questions

Now all sorts of questions must be asked if one wants to learn whether or not a certain theory or doctrine is based on the Bible. For example, "Where in the Scriptures does it say that only the elect belong to God's covenant of grace?"

Then there is a second question: "Does the Bible not clearly speak of God's covenant wrath? What is left of this covenant wrath if it is true that only the chosen ones belong to the covenant?"

The next question is, "Where in the Bible does it state that there is a twofold baptism, one which is baptism in the full sense of the word and one which is not?"

Then there is also the question, "Does Acts 2:39 indeed speak about the elect children only? Would the people who were listening to the apostle Peter on the day of Pentecost have silently added the word 'elect' to what they heard?"

At the invitation of a local consistory, a "synodical" professor delivered a lecture during one of its meetings. One of the elders present was Dr. R. J. Dam, rector of the local Reformed grammar school and lecturer at the Theological College at Kampen. This learned man asked the professor a very simple question: "In your opinion, what can I say to my little children? Can I tell them that the Lord Jesus loves them? Or can I no longer say this to them?" The answer was, "No, strictly speaking you cannot say that, for you do not really know whether they belong to the covenant, to the chosen ones of God, even though we may presume this." I think this little incident makes it perfectly clear that the reasoning here was entirely wrong. It was a clear illustration of a bad kind of theology. If this were true, the parents would be robbed of the security of the covenant and the children of its riches. No one could be sure that the Lord had promised anything to his children.

Is not the "proclamation of the covenant" as we read it in Exodus 19:3-6 very clear in this respect when it says, "If you will obey My voice indeed and keep My covenant . . ."? Does this not mean that the whole nation of Israel, the children included, belonged to the covenant? Did they belong to an "external covenant" or did they really belong to the covenant? Is not this "proclamation" repeated by the apostle Peter in his first epistle (1 Peter 2:9-10)? Is today's situation not the same as far as this is concerned?

These last few questions were answered by making a distinction — a sort of contrast even — between the Old and the New Covenants, as if the New Covenant was not a renewed covenant, a renewed covenant in a changed situation. We need to maintain the unity of the Old and the New Testament, the Old and the New Covenant!

No wonder

This "doctrine" then had to be accepted and taught by every minister and office bearer. Even ordinary church members had to believe it. It was no wonder that many people objected strongly to this unbiblical theory and the ungodly binding force given to it. It was no wonder that a complete flood of petitions covered the tables of Synod and other church assemblies. It was no wonder even that some candidates to the ministry of the Word — although they were very eager to enter into the ministry — as honest men, had to state after their exams, "I cannot believe this, let alone teach it!" It was no wonder that many a father and mother told the local consistory, "This is not how I understand the questions in the Baptismal Form; if I must answer them in line with the 'synodical' interpretation, I cannot answer them in the affirmative." Consequently, some of them were denied baptism for their children.

Hierarchy

In spite of all of this, Synod decided "that nothing shall be taught that is not in full accordance with the doctrinal declarations concerned." Hierarchy never gives in! There seems to be no point of return for hierarchical persons or bodies. A hierarchical synod and its successors took the risk of tearing the churches apart. The Liberation was a real liberation indeed. We felt free again! We could breathe in the fresh air of the liberty of the free children of God!

Church government

This hierarchy was not unopposed. We can even say that there were two widely differing opinions with respect to the matter of Church polity or Church government.

One of them was the traditional Reformed view, the other that of the great majority of delegates to the General Synods who apparently could not evaluate their own position properly. This stand was taken, in particular, by many of the professors of theology who attended almost every session as advisers. It actually started in the 1920s, but we cannot elaborate on that now. One hint may be sufficient. The procedure concerning Dr. Geelkerken may be well known. In contrast to the "synodical" churches which, some years later, withdrew the decisions of 1926-1927 which led to his being deposed as a Reformed minister, we are of the strong conviction that this man taught dangerous things with regard to the first chapters of the book of Genesis. These "synodical" churches, however, still maintain that the synod concerned was fully entitled to depose a minister of a local congregation, even if the deposition was against the will of that particular church. In their opinion, a Classis is already a higher authority in the confederation of churches, a Particular or Regional Synod is higher still, and the General Synod is the highest of all and has a say in any matter, including the issues in the local churches. This stance has now been made legitimate in the "New Church Order" adopted by the synodical churches after World War II. Men like Professor Dr. S. Greijdanus protested, not against the rejection of Geelkerken's false teachings — a rejection with which he fully agreed — but against the fact that Synod itself assumed the authority to deal with an office bearer of a local church. Dr. Greijdanus strongly warned against the danger of hierarchy!

More serious

The situation became more serious when in 1942 the General Synod (which had begun in 1939!) prolonged itself, and the date for the convening of the next synod was postponed to 1943. This move was clearly in conflict with the agreement and rule adopted in the Church Order.

Dr. K. Schilder wrote a letter to the consistory of the church at Kampen, of which he was a member, referring to the Church Order which had been neglected and violated. The church of Amersfoort published a resolution that said they could no longer acknowledge the assembly as a lawful General Synod as of August 1942 when the delegates should have gone home. The strong pressure applied upon this church compelled the consistory to withdraw its resolution. Professors Schilder and Greijdanus — the latter had also made his objections known — were required to answer with a categorical yes or no the question whether they were prepared to help execute the decisions of Synod which had been made after the date on which the proposal to prolong this synod was accepted. One of these decisions was the appointment of Professor Greijdanus' successor, Dr. Herman N. Ridderbos. Although this appointment was unlawful, the two older professors declared they would cooperate fully with their newly appointed colleague.

Unwanted delegations

Hierarchy is not typically Dutch. Some twenty years ago, we read that a synod of the Christian Reformed Church in North America decided to send a delegation to the First Christian Reformed Church of Toronto. These delegates had to explain a letter which they had to give to the consistory. In this letter the consistory was admonished because it had given notice to Synod that it would not keep as settled and binding several decisions Synod had made.

Similar delegations were sent in the Netherlands during 1942. The consistories of the churches at Kampen and Giessendam-Nederhardinxveld were of the opinion that they could not accept the binding force of the famous doctrinal statements of 1942 or apply it to others. They were compelled to receive some delegates sent to them by Synod, who told them that their negative attitude was schismatic and had to be rectified — and these consistories gave in under protest, for the time being, because of the threatening attitude of Synod in its hierarchical actions.

We have been told that at Bunschoten-Spakenburg things took a different course. Without the knowledge, let alone the consent, of the consistory, the local minister invited a few synodical delegates to give "information" and "instruction" to the members of the consistory. This happened on a Friday evening when the fishermen had just returned to their home-base. But the chairman of the consistory, the minister concerned, as well as a small number of elders and the invited delegates of Synod — a professor and a prominent minister — waited and waited. At last, the minister went outside to have a look to see where the other consistory members were. They were all standing there. He invited them to come inside because it was time to commence the meeting. They flatly refused. One of them asked the minister whether the delegates of Synod had been invited by the consistory and when the decision regarding this had been made. The minister could only answer, "I did it personally, on my own initiative." Then the men told him that he would first have to send those delegates away; otherwise they would not come inside. They wanted to discuss things in full freedom, including even the question of whether or not they would receive the synodical delegates. This is indeed what happened then. The delegates had to leave the room and wait for the decision. It was decided not to grant them permission to attend the meeting and speak. The brothers were of the opinion that they had no need of this unwanted and unrequested help. They did not like to be put under pressure. This is the way in which to deal with hierarchy!

Verdicts

Since he was of the opinion that the new Synod of 1943 had been closed, Professor K. Schilder sent all consistories a copy of a letter he had sent to Synod. He did this in January 1944. In his letter, he replied to the well-known "Pre-advice" mentioned above. He had been unable to attend Synod because he was hiding from the Germans who were after him again. Later on we heard that he had stayed with doctor P. Jasperse in Leyden, who had arranged for him to borrow a great number of books from the Leyden University. The floor of his temporary study had been littered with books. His reply to the "Pre-advice" was very thorough. It was ripped to pieces!

This letter was intended as a simple way of informing the consistories about the opinion of their Professor of Dogmatics and as a preparation for the next synod. Some people became angry. A number of ministers from The Hague sent letters and a telegram to Synod, requesting this body to take measures against this "revolutionary" activity of Professor Schilder, as they called it.

After several closed (!) sessions and without hearing the defendant, Synod declared on February 25, 1944, that Professor Schilder was guilty. He was a schismatic! He was given two weeks time in which to answer five questions categorically and express regret for his actions. The answer had to be received by 11 P.M.! Professor Schilder could not feel any regret and answered all the questions in the negative. This resulted in his suspension on March 23, for the duration of three months, as Professor at the Theological Seminary at Kampen and as minister-emeritus of the church at Rotterdam-Delfshaven. This suspension was later prolonged for another month and was then followed by his deposition.

Great was the indignation of many people because the consistory of the church at Rotterdam-Delfshaven had never been consulted about this matter. Great was the indignation also because the grounds for this disciplinary action were absolutely insufficient. They were based on the hierarchical ideas of Synod. Is a synod entitled to administer church discipline? Can such a body suspend and depose a local office bearer?

Later on, the Church Order was altered and in this way the measure Synod had taken was "legitimized" in retrospect. Even among unbelievers such a thing is branded as immoral.

Prayer letter

Synod went even farther. It sent a letter to all the consistories which was intended to be read publicly from the pulpit just before the "Long Prayer" in the next worship service. This letter was not a kind invitation to a consistory to consider its contents. It was based upon the supposition that a consistory simply had to do whatever a synod *required*. The church members were urged to pray for the repentance of Professor Schilder.

At that time I was an assistant pastor somewhere in the province of Utrecht. On the Sunday the letter was to be read, I had to fill in for a minister who was ill. The clerk of the consistory gave me the letter. I supposed that there had not been a special meeting of the consistory to deal with it so that some of the other brothers may not have seen it at all. I kindly asked the consistory to grant me permission to leave the letter unread since I could not pray for the professor's repentance with a clear conscience. From my "boss" at Breukelen, Rev. O. W. Bouwsma, I had heard about the letter and its contents. The consistory was wise not to insist and decided to discuss the matter as soon as their own minister had recovered.

I remember that his refusal to read this letter became one of the grounds on which Rev. B. Telder of Breda was suspended. Synod was lording it over men's consciences, although it knew perfectly well that several ministers could not read this letter to their congregation and pray with a clear conscience for the repentance of Professor Schilder. What else is this but hierarchy?

More verdicts

General Synod also suspended old Professor Greijdanus in 1944 because he continued to demonstrate that the doctrinal statement on the position of infants, issued by Synod 1939-1943, was unscriptural. In the opinion of the Synod of 1943-45, he was guilty of the sin of schism.

The consistory of the church at Kampen declared that it could not admonish Professor Schilder on the alleged sin of schism. It stated that his suspension by Synod was in conflict with God's Word. This resulted in the suspension of the majority of the consistory members. Only those who had voted against the consistory's decision were "maintained" in their office. As if a synod, as a kind of super-consistory, would have any authority in this respect!

One of the members of General Synod, delegated by the Regional Synod of Groningen, was the Rev. D. van Dijk. He strongly opposed the doctrinal as well as the "canonical" decisions. When he continued to offer opposition to them he was sent home — not by the body that delegated him, the Regional Synod, but by the General Synod. This voice had to be silenced!

The church at Bergschenhoek also had strong objections to the rule that candidates to the ministry had to declare their agreement with the doctrinal statements of 1942. They were also against the self-continuation of Synod and the suspension of Professor Schilder. This church received word from Synod that as of September 1, 1944, it was no longer considered a Reformed church within the confederation of churches. This happened after a long process. The assistant pastor of this church was candidate H. J. Schilder. On the advice of General Synod his "license" to be a candidate for the ministry had been withdrawn by Classis The Hague. Since this was also part of the hierarchical actions of Synod, the consistory decided to let the candidate conduct a worship service. Not acknowledging Professor K. Schilder's suspension, the consistory invited the professor to preach. This was now possible because the German occupying forces had let K. Schilder's brother Arnold know they no longer intended to arrest him because they did not wish to be branded as persecutors of the church or of church members.[266] All of this led to the expulsion of the church at Bergschenhoek.

Liberation

This was the beginning of the liberation of the churches from a hierarchical yoke, the beginning of a return to the Scriptural way of living together in a confederation of churches.

The Liberation was also strongly stimulated by a meeting held on August 11, 1944, in the Lutheran Church at The Hague. There a *Deed of Liberation or Return* was read, in which the consistories were urged to throw off the yoke of the hierarchical Synod, return to the Scriptural freedom within the church of the Lord Jesus Christ, and consequently go back to maintaining the adopted Church Order, which does not allow major assemblies to act as if they were "higher assemblies."

At many places this *Deed of Liberation or Return* was indeed used. In other places, people freed themselves from the responsibility of the un-Reformed actions of Synod in a different way. In whatever way they did it, people felt free, really free, again!

The oppression from the side of the occupational forces during the years 1940 to 1945 was a very unpleasant thing to say the least. But, as Professor B. Holwerda later wrote in our guest book when he had stayed with us in our manse, "the ruins on church territory are the worst of all."

---

[266] See Rudolf Van Reest, *Schilder's Struggle for the Unity of the Church* (Neerlandia: Inheritance, 1990) 318-321.

Article 31 of the Church Order

Our readers may remember that we mentioned a decision made by the consistory of Waardhuizen during the ministry of the Rev. L. Selles: they would examine the statements issued by Synod in keeping with Article 31 of the Church Order. This could not be done immediately. When Rev. Selles left Waardhuizen for Steenwijk, this examination had not yet taken place. In 1945, we as a consistory — unanimously even! — decided to do this as soon as the war was over and the other half of the congregation had returned from the places to which they had been evacuated.

As soon as the first steps had been taken — according to the plan explained before — I would write a pamphlet explaining in a simple way the views of both the synod and the "concerned." All of a sudden, however, I was provisionally suspended by the majority of the consistory (some members had been replaced by others by this point).

The story of this suspension will be told below. What I want to relate first is that at the beginning of the first worship service held after the official liberation of the local church, the following statement was read: "Brothers and sisters, here we stand in the holy presence of the Lord, before Jesus Christ, the Head of the church, as the Reformed Church at Waardhuizen and the surrounding area, liberated according to Article 31 of the Church Order of Dordrecht. This is happening from sheer need only. In deep sorrow everyone may borrow the words spoken by Martin Luther, who said, 'Here I stand, I cannot do otherwise. God help me. Amen.' " Reference was again made to Article 31, not as part of a new name for the church — it was and remained the same church — but as an indication that, by God's goodness, the church had now been liberated in accordance with Article 31 of the Church Order.

Its text

What, then, does this Article say? In the text of the Church Order of our Australian churches, it reads as follows: "If anyone complains that he has been wronged by the decision of the minor assembly he shall have the right of appeal to the major assembly; and whatever may be agreed upon by a majority vote shall be considered settled and binding, unless it is proved to be in conflict with the Word of God or with the Church Order."

As everyone can see, this Article consists of two sections. The first section includes the agreement of the churches and church members that the decisions of major assemblies "shall be considered settled and binding." If we did not agree upon this, there would be no possibility that we could live together in a confederation of churches. Chaos would reign in the confederation.

Regretfully we must say that the relaxing of this agreement has played a role in the history of our Dutch sister churches. Some years ago a classis had to state that a consistory should admonish its minister because he no longer agreed with the doctrinal standards of the churches. This minister no longer maintained what he had promised in the Form he once signed, which stated that if he could no longer agree with any part of the adopted doctrine he would not publish his view but inform his consistory and go "the ecclesiastical way." But what happened? The consistory did nothing at all! They just took the classical statement for granted. As a matter of course, this is impossible. It is not in accord with what the churches have agreed upon. This behaviour leads to chaos within the confederation and fundamentally means the destruction of the confederation by "independentism."

The second section of Article 31, however, makes room for considering a certain decision or resolution not to be settled and binding. Room is given when one is of the opinion — and also tries to prove, of course! — that the decision concerned contradicts the Word of God or the Church Order (which is less important, though important enough).

This section, then, includes one of the most significant principles of our Church Order and of the life of our Reformed Churches. This principle is that only the Word of God shall reign in the churches. Jesus Christ is the Head of the Church, and His Word is the only authority!

A new interpretation

The trouble, however, was that the hierarchical synods and their supporters introduced a new and wrong interpretation of this Article. They said that a certain decision or resolution may be considered not to be settled and binding only as soon as the person who is objecting against it has convinced the major assembly (that is, the next classis or synod) that the decision was indeed in contradiction with the Word of God or the Church Order. In the meantime he must respect and *accept* it and give his support to its execution.

If this interpretation were true, Article 31 would contain nonsense! After all, as soon as such an assembly is convinced, it reverses or revokes the decision or resolution concerned. And, on the other hand, you would be appealing a decision which you have accepted. Consequently a situation in which a decision is not binding would never exist! If this interpretation were correct, the whole section of Article 31 would be superfluous.

Nevertheless, this interpretation was introduced to defend the hierarchical claims made by these Synods. There is every reason to thank the Lord that our churches are free from this kind of hierarchy. Jesus Christ is their only and universal Bishop and Head and that God's Word reigns in them. These are our riches and at the same time our great commission!

Prelude

We repeat that there was a twofold situation which caused the Liberation of our sister churches in the Netherlands during the 1940s. There was the doctrinal aspect, which concerned the position of the children of believers and the value of God's promise sealed to them in holy Baptism, and there was a concern in the field of Church polity and Church Order, in which the main point was the interpretation of Article 31. Taking these two things together, we can say that the Confession of the churches was at stake. The fundamentals were being undermined. Would the churches remain truly Reformed or not?

Some people stood for their wrong principles and opinions in a very fanatical way. Sometimes we ourselves — and in particular our brothers and sisters in the Netherlands — are branded as extremists and fanatics, but the following story may make it clear where the real *extremists* and *fanatics* were to be sought. It is the story of the prelude to the Liberation of the local church of which I was minister at the time.

But first I must report something about a visitor.

A visitor

Our readers will remember that a committee had requested me to write and publish a little pamphlet on the differences in the churches. I had also made an agreement with the consistory that this pamphlet would be distributed among the congregation to enable its members to prepare themselves for a congregational meeting, during which the situation in our churches would be discussed. This brought a visitor to the manse at Waardhuizen.

This visitor was the same person who presided over the classis when I had to undergo my last ecclesiastical exam. He told me that he needed to ask me a question. He had received some information that I intended to publish a pamphlet on current church affairs. Was this true? He strongly urged me not to execute my plans, for this would cause unrest and take away the peace that had been within the classis until then.

Now it was a matter of fact that the whole country was flooded with all sorts of pamphlets from both sides of the issue. This happened even though paper was very, very scarce and printing had to be done in secret because the Germans did not grant permission to print anything that was not approved by them — that is, Nazi propaganda. Even after the liberation of the country, it was very hard to lay one's hands on printing paper. Many people still possess a large number of these pamphlets and little booklets that were distributed in those days.

I remember exactly what I answered my older colleague. I pointed out that Synod continued to bind the churches to its wrong decisions and that as long as that happened there would be no real peace. Furthermore, I referred him to our consistory's policy of examining the synodical decisions and actions and informing the church members about what was going on. I told him it was my intention honestly and fairly to present a summary of the beliefs of *both sides* of the issue so that the people would be able to form their own opinions and make up their own minds. I felt very sorry for him, especially because I supposed he had the best intentions, but I could not give in to this sort of pressure.

A letter

Soon afterwards I realized that these intentions were not as good as I had supposed. I received a letter from him in which he asked me: "Did you attend the worship services of the 'separated' group in Schiedam on a Sunday in the month of May? Did you do the same a couple of months later? Is it true what I heard about this? And have you chosen in that way to favour the *schismatic* Rev. C. Vonk and his followers?"

After reading this letter it was easy to draw the conclusion that no one was "safe." Gossip was doing its job. Someone must have told him. I answered that I had indeed attended the services in this congregation. The first time I had done so was when my father-in-law had passed away and was going to buried the next day — he was one of the suspended and deposed elders of the church at Schiedam. The second time, however, my choice was much clearer. I told my correspondent that the consistory of Schiedam had decided to call a fourth minister, but only on the condition that this man agreed with the decisions made by Synod. A minister who had reservations or objections regarding these decisions would not be eligible for call. In my opinion, this was a very serious decision — a schismatic one — since at that stage no one had yet been *condemned.* As for me as a "concerned" person, let alone as a minister, there was no room in this church anymore. I never heard an answer to this reply. But it was clear that "they" were watching me!

It was no surprise that on the evening of August 30, 1945, I was suspended by the majority of the consistory members. These brothers had to admit that there had been some influence from outside the congregation. They had consulted that older minister, my visitor and correspondent!

August 30, 1945

Early in the morning, I was riding my bike toward a neighbouring village to buy some bread from baker Van der Mooren. On my way I met one of the elders. He stopped me and asked if it would suit me to have a brief consistory meeting that evening, after the counting of the collections. The counting of the collections was a monthly ceremony in which all the elders and deacons took part. It gave them an opportunity to discuss certain things in an unconstrained way.

I was so surprised that I forgot to ask him, "What is it for, brother?" Soon afterwards it became clear to me. When I returned home, my wife told me that the young girl who helped her in her household duties had told her that the same elder was visiting certain members of the congregation to discover what people thought of their minister and of the pamphlet he had written. He had arranged a sort of opinion poll. To his surprise, some of the people had answered that they fully agreed with the "concerned." They believed what they had been taught at catechism class and thought that what Synod taught was something new and could not be correct!

Later on that day, I went to visit the elder to ask him what the meeting would be about. He answered that it was about my pamphlet. I replied, "You knew everything about it and even agreed with the plan to write and distribute it." He could not deny this but claimed that, instead of a pamphlet, it was supposed to have been only a brief letter. Later on, the members of consistory who had just retired confirmed that it was certainly not supposed to be just a brief letter but a pamphlet containing exactly the same things which I had read during a consistory meeting. I still possess the manuscript of that speech.

Evening

The atmosphere was strained that evening as the collections of the last few Sundays were counted. Even the minister took part in the ceremony this time!

Immediately after this, the consistory meeting was opened. There was no electricity yet, since the whole network had been destroyed during the last winter of the war, so we did not use our small and dark consistory room but sat in the front section of our church building. As long as it lasted we sat there in the dimming daylight. As soon as it was dark we lighted an oil-lamp, which made some ghostly effects.

My first question was, of course, for what special purpose the meeting had been arranged. Then the elder I had met in the early morning of the same day cleared his throat and said, "Is it your intention to cause a split in the congregation? Is this what you had in mind with the publishing of your pamphlet?" I replied with a counter-question, "Do you ask this for yourself only or on behalf of any others also?" The answer was, "I ask this on behalf of the four of us," these four being one more elder and the two deacons.

Later on it became clear that these four had held a secret meeting from which the third elder and, of course, the minister had been excluded. The third elder was supposed to be opposed to Synod. The questions being asked had obviously been formulated during that secret meeting.

A long discussion followed, in which this third elder took a firm stand and tried to convince the others that they had not acted in true Christian love. To the original question about my intentions, I answered, "I have not the slightest intention to cause a split in the congregation. I only acted in a way to which the consistory agreed." I also added, "You know that I have never acted without the foreknowledge or consent of the consistory," trying in that way to show the brothers that what they had done was in strong contrast with what could be expected of them.

Then it was my turn to ask a question. It was this: "Were there any influences from outside the congregation?" The spokesman of the four had to admit that he had visited the minister of Werkendam, the man who had visited me and later on wrote the letter mentioned above. He had asked this minister how he could call a meeting of the consistory together. I replied, "Well, could you not have asked me? I would have told you immediately that whenever you want to arrange a meeting for something important you can always do so." It was a bit naive to suggest that he had taken his bike and made the trip of approximately 25 kilometres and back for this little formal point only. Honesty was clearly absent!

More questions

Then the four asked the second question they had prepared: "Will you inform the congregation next Sunday that you retract your pamphlet?" As a sequel to the answer to the previous one, this was an illogical question. No wonder I had to answer it in the negative. However, I also added, "You have always known where I stand. You fully realized that you called a candidate who was known not to agree with the synodical decisions. Yet you called me, just over a year ago. Afterwards I have told the consistory more than once that in my ministry I would have to come into conflict with these synodical statements. Besides, this Sunday I have to deliver a sermon on Lord's Day 25 of the Catechism dealing with the sacraments. Even in this sermon I have to disagree with the synodical doctrine concerning the sacraments."

For the third time the elder spokesman, following the prepared lines, spoke, "Then we must decide that the minister is not permitted to preach this coming Sunday."

I asked him, "Does that mean that I am suspended?"

He answered, "Yes indeed."

Then my fellow elder delivered an address full of emotion. The old man was really shocked by this sort of fanaticism. He seriously warned the others that they should be well aware of what they were going to do by suspending the minister: they would split up the congregation. They themselves were the schismatics and not the minister!

It was to no avail. My own efforts to make clear to them what they were actually doing were not successful either. They charged me with something that was considered so serious that if it had been committed by an "ordinary" church member he or she would be deemed worthy of excommunication — as it says in Article 79 of the Church Order. I therefore asked them whether this meant that I was also denied access to the Table of the Lord. The answer was, "Yes, you are!"

When I asked them further, "Do you really mean that this is the way that you have to suspend me?" one of the elders even dared to say, "Yes, for God's sake!" It sounded like a curse.

Suspended

So, after a ministry of just over a year, it was solemnly stated that I was provisionally suspended as a public schismatic on the ground of Article 80 of the Church Order. Article 79, which says that a neighbouring church has to give its opinion too, was completely overlooked. I immediately informed the consistory that this verdict was unacceptable and that I would not acknowledge my suspension because it was in clear contradiction with the will of the Lord Jesus. It was my strong conviction that He had not suspended me!

And now?

What now? What was to be done after this? Nothing was very clear yet because we had never expected things to go this way. We could be sure that a small number of church members would never accept this evil decision of the majority of the consistory. But would they be able to support a minister financially? Many of them had suffered substantial losses during the last year of the war and, even apart from that, most of them were not well off but rather poor. No other congregation in the classical region was expected to "liberate" itself from the synodical yoke, although a few ministers were known to be "concerned." What was going to happen? My wife and I were afraid that we would have to leave. But this appeared to be a matter of little faith! The Head of the church was there too!

August 31, 1945

This day was the first birthday of Queen Wilhelmina to be celebrated after the liberation of the country. It was expected to be a day of joy and thanksgiving. In our village, however, people had decided not to celebrate it but to do their normal daily work. The reason for this was that one of the inhabitants had been fatally wounded by a shell splinter during the last stages of the war. The members of our congregation did not do much work on this remarkable day, however.

In the early morning, word was already spreading: "Our minister has been suspended!" Apart from the members of the consistory, no one knew the reason, and so several people called at the manse to get first-hand information. There was a farmer, for instance, who had promised a few days before to bring us some potatoes, which at that time were very scarce. There he came, pushing his wheelbarrow. He greeted us as usual and asked where he could drop the potatoes. When I showed him the proper place, another person arrived on his bike. Stepping off, he went straight to the heart of the matter by asking me, "*Dominee*, is it true that you have been suspended?" Before I could confirm the bad news, the other interrupted and said, "Yes, that is actually what I came for too, but I did not dare to ask you!" When they heard the reason they were perplexed.

They were the first of a great number of brothers and sisters who came to see and encourage us. This was really heartwarming and comforting. After they heard the grounds for my suspension, they all agreed that it was completely wrong and that something should be done about it. They urged my fellow elder — who had arrived in the meantime — and me to convene a congregational meeting, to which the other four members of the consistory would also be urgently invited. This meeting was then arranged.

September 1, 1945

And so, on September 1, 1945, we had our meeting. It was attended by at least two of "the four" — I am not completely sure about this figure. I informed the congregation amply about what had happened and about the background. Then an open discussion followed.

All sorts of suggestions were made. The "two" were urged to cooperate in arranging another meeting of the consistory to be held that very night. It was suggested that, if necessary, they had to continue through the night, for the suspension had to be revoked. They flatly refused to do so, however. From our own side, we stressed the point that regardless of what had to be done to restore peace within the congregation, we would never be able to accept the synod's decisions and actions, for we were not allowed to compromise.

Then one of the members of the congregation rose and said, "*Dominee*, I cannot accept the binding decisions of Synod either. Nor can I put myself and my family any longer under the supervision of a consistory that is doing these awful things. I can only accept the supervision of a consistory that is free from this evil." After these words the great majority of members spontaneously rose, stating in this way that they fully agreed with him.

This is how the church of the Lord Jesus Christ at Waardhuizen was liberated from a yoke, a strange and unchristian yoke, and released again into the freedom of the Word of God.

Afterwards

It would be quite easy for me to fill more pages with the story of the aftermath. After some time, the "synodical people" — who had expected that only a few people would support my fellow elder and me and who were therefore deeply disappointed and angry — denied us the right to use our church building. They even wanted to put us out of the manse. Our own congregation took a fair stand: "Together we have built this as an undivided church, so both of us will use the church building." But "the other party" wanted to possess everything. So they took us to court.

At first they were not successful. The court complied with our request for common use. When they appealed this decision, they won the case, even though it must have been a load on their consciences: they had fed their lawyer a pack of lies which I could not contradict since I could not attend the court session because of sickness. For many years now, however, our congregation has possessed a nice new building and manse.

Blessing

No more about this unpleasant aspect of the events. Of greater importance is the fact that the liberation of the church had some heartwarming fruits. They were closely related to the doctrinal issue: the sure promises of our Covenant God as sealed in holy Baptism. Until then, there had been some "mysticism" in this congregation and its surroundings. Many people asked themselves, "Is God's Word really for me, too? For do I belong to the elect? And how can I know that?"

The preaching of the sure promises of God and the significance of the sacraments, which some previous ministers had already proclaimed, was slowly becoming clear to the congregation and resulted in a real reformation indeed. Faith began to flourish again. Even very old people, who never had had the courage to take part in the Lord's Supper, came forward. A sister of over eighty years of age made public profession of faith.

More could be said, but these few lines may be sufficient to prove that there is every reason to be grateful to the Head of the Church for what He did in the Liberation of the 1940s. Please, let no one say that the Liberation of our Dutch sister churches was not a genuine reformation. In this respect I am happy to be able to point to my first congregation, where the King of the church, our Lord Jesus Christ, has done wondrous things!

We may all learn something from it. Here in Australia, too, we owe much to what a gracious God did for His church some fifty years ago. It is part of our origin, part of our heritage.

Lest we forget! That is why these pages were written and published.

EPILOGUE

Personal

Any job that a person performs may be his last. That is especially the case when one is getting along in years. For that reason, a somewhat personal note may be in place at the back of this book.

When I attempt to survey my life as an author, I can compare it to my sporting activities in the years during which I attended grammar school. I loved to play soccer — too much, some of my teachers said. My position in the school team was outside left forward — and here the word "left" has no political, let alone church-political, overtones.

According to the soccer rules of some sixty years ago, an outside left forward is not expected to score many goals. His role is rather to supply crosses which those playing in the middle could pick up and "put away." This is the way in which I prefer to view my limited capacities in the field of theology and church life, and consequently my contributions to the religious scene as well.

Three occasions

On three occasions, I saw the necessity of taking an initiative, for the simple reason that no one else — not even persons who were more skilled — was taking action.

The first time this happened was approximately a decade after the Liberation of the 1940s. When those first ten hectic years had ended, the churches in the Netherlands were able to enjoy a period of rest and thus were able to pay attention to other things. Among these was the liturgy — still my favourite subject. It was in that situation that I compiled my first more elaborate work.

When, after no fewer than forty years, a person is informed that the first book he published — now accompanied by more recent work — is still being used for the purpose of training ministers in a distant federation of sister churches, he can only be grateful that the "cross" appears to have been useful.

The second subject I dealt with was the covenant of grace. This is not surprising, since this question still cannot be ignored It was one of the prominent issues which led to the Liberation of the 1940s and consequently to the establishing of our churches here in Australia and in other countries.

My office as a minister serving an immigrant congregation brought me into contact with literature on this subject published in the English-speaking world. New research and intense study resulted in the discovery that the biblical covenants have much in common with — and, at the same time, far surpass the meaning of — the vassal treaties of ancient times and cultures. I attempted to pass this discovery on to our Reformed community. No one within that community, despite their better faculties, had taken up the challenge of writing on this important subject and thereby giving more depth and colour to what we had learned about the doctrine of the covenant during the past decades.

It was somewhat disappointing, however, to find that the "cross" this book provided was used by no more than a few learned authors.

The situation described in the Prologue called for a third "cross." It became necessary for me, as well as for others, to pay special attention to the doctrine of the Church and to the way we confess this part of God's revelation in our Belgic Confession of Faith.

I provided this "cross" in the booklet *"True" and "False"* mentioned in the Preface to the second section of this book. It is to be regretted that here in Australia the publication of this booklet did not result in a quiet and thorough discussion of the topic. I have the impression that the misreading of its contents resulted from fear of the implications the catholicity of the Church. The catholicity of the Church and how we apply this doctrine in our situation is a crucial matter indeed. In our contact with other churches it raises questions, but these questions require thorough study and a good discussion. Avoiding them can only damage the life of our churches and the life in our churches.

Hope

This is why I express the hope that this extended third "cross" — perhaps my very last one — may be taken up in a brotherly way by the "middle players" who are expected to "score goals."

If this is the method we are going to follow, we cannot disregard the middle field players and those in the back — the non-deputies and non-delegates. Even the non-players in the stands, the supporters, are also there to contribute. In our church life, we try to avoid synodocracy, ministeriocracy, and even consistoriocracy. All of our church members are involved in the issues that require our attention, and that is why I express the hope that all who have reached the years of responsibility would join me in contemplating what we actually believe regarding the Church.

Let us not forget that it is the Church of our beloved Saviour!

Scripture Index

General Index

The Liberation of the Forties was originally written as No. 14 in The Reformed Guardian series. Other issues which are still available are:

No. 4: *The Catholic Character of the Churches of the Reformation* by K. Bruning

No. 6: *The Charismatic Church* by W. Huizinga

No. 8: *"That They May Be One . . ."* by G. Van Rongen

No. 9: *The New Age Movement* by G. Van Rongen

No. 10: *Dr. K. Schilder Commemorated* by K. Bruning and G. Van Rongen

No. 11: *"I Do"* — Part 1: On the Vow Taken at Our Public Profession of Faith by K. Bruning

No. 12: *Serve the Lord with Gladness — The Church on Her Way to the Year 2000* by K. Bruning

No. 15: *"I Do"* — Part 2: On the Vow Taken on the Wedding Day by K. Bruning

New Series

No. 1: *"Thy Kingdom Come" — The Lord's Prayer as a Kingdom Prayer* by G. Van Rongen

No. 2: *The Church as we confess it in Articles 27-29 of the Belgic Confession of Faith* by C. Trimp